Praise for *Sexuality and Holy Longing*

"Eureka! We've finally found the book our students keep asking for. Lisa McMinn's thoughtful insights on body-soul connection (Incarnation theology) is just what the Christian community desperately needs. She is one of the few authors who dares write about sexuality with human compassion and strong conviction."

—Judith K. Balswick, Ed.D., and Jack O. Balswick, Ph.D., professors, School of Psychology, Fuller Theological Seminary, Pasadena, California

"*Sexuality and Holy Longing* provides an invaluable service to the church that finds itself surrounded by a culture obsessed with sex and not understanding the fullness and richness of sexuality as God intended. Dr. McMinn challenges the church to embrace the beauty and sacredness of beings created in the Image of God rather than attempting to shield our children from their sexuality."

—Trevecca Okholm, minister of children's ministries, St. Andrew's Presbyterian Church, Newport Beach, California

"This book reads like the work of a friend who has brought warmth, wisdom, knowledge, balance, and candor to an aspect of our lives in which many of us feel the need for healing and hope."

—Richard Sartwell, director, Friends Center, George Fox Evangelical Seminary, Portland, Oregon

"Sexuality is so broken in our society, and we the Church can make a difference. This book will help us think deeply, beyond commands to creation and beliefs and principles and choices."

—John P. Casey, senior pastor, Blanchard Road Alliance Church, Wheaton, Illinois

"This book provides a very useful and faith-based perspective to the public discourse on sexuality. Communities of faith seeking to help those struggling with sexual brokenness will find a healthy framework for understanding these issues."

—Skip Trudeau, president, Association for Christians in Student Development

"In my seventeen years as a pastor and now as a seminary president, I have looked for a book like this one. Dr. McMinn has dealt with human sexuality directly but sensitively, theologically and practically, candidly but tastefully. Even after finishing sections of the book in which I was still unconvinced of one of Dr. McMinn's perspectives, I nonetheless was stretched to reconsider my own viewpoints and to rethink long-held positions. One of her gifts is that of dealing with complex and controversial issues clearly and, while doing so, (to use her words) 'staying vulnerable to the arguments of other positions.' I will recommend this book highly to all pastors, Christian leaders in training—in fact, to all who want to understand sexuality in the context of human identity and God's grace."
—Greg Waybright, president, Trinity Evangelical
Divinity School, Deerfield, Illinois

"This book is a timely and needed reminder that sexuality is a gift from God to be celebrated and shared."
—Michelle R. Loyd-Paige, professor of sociology, Calvin College

SEXUALITY AND HOLY LONGING

Embracing Intimacy in a Broken World

Lisa Graham McMinn

o

Foreword by
Stanley J. Grenz

JOSSEY-BASS
A Wiley Imprint
www.josseybass.com

Published by Jossey-Bass
A Wiley Imprint
989 Market Street, San Francisco, CA 94103-1741   www.josseybass.com

Jossey-Bass books and products are available through most bookstores. To contact Jossey-
Bass directly call our Customer Care Department within the U.S. at 800-956-7739, outside the U.S. at 317-572-3986 or fax 317-572-4002.

Jossey-Bass also publishes its books in a variety of electronic formats. Some content that
appears in print may not be available in electronic books.

Scripture taken from the New Living Translation. New Living Translation is a registered
trademark of Tyndale House Publishers, Inc.

Excerpt from "No Easy Victory" used by permission, *Christianity Today,* 2002.

Library of Congress Cataloging-in-Publication Data
McMinn, Lisa Graham, date.
  Sexuality and holy longing : embracing intimacy in a broken world / Lisa Graham
McMinn.
     p. cm.
Includes bibliographical references and index.
  ISBN 0-7879-6818-8 (alk. paper)
  1. Sex—Religious aspects—Christianity I. Title.
  BT708.M43 2004
  241'.66—dc22

                                                                      2003018750

Printed in the United States of America
FIRST EDITION
HB Printing   10 9 8 7 6 5 4 3 2 1

CONTENTS

To Mark

insights she has gained through her work on the sociology of sexuality. She is surely correct when she presents sexuality as deeper than genital sex. She rightly reiterates the biblical view that sexuality is not simply about physical attraction, but that it arises out of and is intended to facilitate the universal human quest for wholesome relationships—indeed, above all, relationship with God. But most importantly, McMinn insightfully points out that the contemporary acknowledgment of the sociological embeddedness of our conceptions of sexuality offers an unprecedented opportunity for Christian communities of faith to take seriously their rightful, God-intended role in the task of forming persons who live out the biblical vision of sexuality, which elevates this all-pervasive dimension of our humanness as God's good gift intended for our human well-being. In short, McMinn offers a profound call to us to be a people who know firsthand the divine grace that comes to us through the holy longing we call "sexuality," so that we can truly embrace this aspect of our being despite the brokenness of the world in which we are called to live and minister.

STANLEY J. GRENZ
Pioneer McDonald Professor,
Carey Theological College, Vancouver, British Columbia;
Author of *Sexual Ethics: An Evangelical Perspective*

ACKNOWLEDGMENTS

WHEATON COLLEGE GRANTED MY HUSBAND, Mark, and me sabbaticals in the same semester to write. Reading each other's writing over a cup of coffee at nearby coffee shops became a rich part of our Sabbath day rest. Mark read and re-read chapters, giving me an honest critique and wonderful affirmation and inviting me to think deep and wide. Thank you, Mark, for partnering with me in this book. And thank you, Wheaton, for a sabbatical that allowed me time to study, read, ruminate, and write.

Students in my Sociology of Sexuality and Gender Roles classes granted me permission to share pieces of their journals, and men and women I interviewed let me walk loudly into some of the quiet places they reside in as single men and women. Thank you for your willingness to let your thoughts be known. You have enriched this book tremendously by allowing your stories to be told.

I am also indebted to writers and readers who critiqued all or pieces of this manuscript. The people at Jossey-Bass, particularly my editor, Mark Kerr, embraced this book from the beginning and kept pushing me to connect the dots, stay connected with readers, and see this book as one with potential for serving the Church. Sheryl Fullerton marvelously picked up where Mark left off. Mary O'Briant is a gifted copyeditor; she refined and smoothed many rough edges. They and others at Jossey-Bass (including the three anonymous reviewers who made insightful comments) have made me a better writer and this a better book. My writing group—Cindy Crosby and Camerin Courtney—kept me from being too much of an academic (and from using too many parentheses). Pamela Nelson, a registered nurse who works at Wheaton College, fed me several studies on adolescent sexuality. The following people all read and responded to various chapters: Pamela Augustine, Allison Belt, Christina Bieber, John Casey, Lynn Cohick, Brian Howell, Dennis Hiebert, Jana Sundene, and Dan Trier. Thank you for taking the time to read and respond to these ideas.

My daughters, Danielle Rae, Sarah, and Megan, redefine and further shape me through motherhood and bless me with friendship now as women. To each of you, thank you. You have shaped me and blessed me with your lives.

Winfield, Illinois   Lisa Graham McMinn
2004

SEXUALITY AND HOLY LONGING

INTRODUCTION

Our hearts are restless until they find their rest in you.

—St. Augustine

ON OUR WAY BACK FROM CARIBOU COFFEE, I got into a conversation about kissing with my two older daughters, Rae and Sarah, both in their twenties and home for their sister Megan's high school graduation. I grew up watching Westerns starring John Wayne (my Dad's favorite), *Star Trek,* and *Love Boat* (which Dad would have forbidden if he had ever watched it, given its disregard of traditional Christian morals). In all cases, couples kissed by mashing their lips together.

With the passing of years, couples mashed said lips for longer periods and with greater intensity, but it was still just the magical meeting of lips. I thought it very romantic and sensual, and my expectations for kisses reflected what I observed. But my daughters grew up in a peer culture that watched *Friends, Dawson's Creek* (both of which we discouraged for reasons not unlike my Dad's disapproval of *Love Boat*), and open-mouthed, tantalizing tongue kisses in the movies, which over time came to include the increasing exposure of Other Things also thought to titillate and draw in young and old audiences alike at $9.00 or so a ticket. They found such kissing romantic and sensual, and their expectations of kisses also reflected what they observed, read about, and heard among their peers.

My daughters and I grew up with somewhat different notions and expectations regarding kissing, specifically, and our sexuality more generally. But the kissing evoked similar emotions in our adolescence: a longing to belong, to be loved. God created humans so that we would yearn for human companionship, and our sexuality keeps us restless and striving for meaningful connection. "It is not good for the man to be alone," God said before creating Eve as Adam's companion. When God

1

presented Eve to Adam, Adam's first words were, "At last!" (Genesis 2:18, 23). Companions ease the existential loneliness of being created sexual—a reminder that we are not quite complete, not so self-sufficient as we sometimes imagine. Sexuality is central to the human experience; it is embodied in our maleness and femaleness. We will all experience longing, even as our culture's tolerance and ways of expressing sexuality (for example, the mashing of lips versus tantalizing tongue kissing) changes over time.

Ways of expressing sexuality and tolerance for different behaviors change because ideas about sexuality change. Ideas about sexuality are embedded in cultural beliefs about bodies, sex, and sexuality. We learn about these beliefs at home, through peers, at school, through the media, as well as in church, Sunday School, and youth group. Humans are social creatures by nature, so when we are unsure what is expected of us, when gaps are discovered in our knowledge, we look around to pick up cues. Movies, music, magazines, billboards, and TV fill in any discernable gaps—so completely, in fact, that not much is taboo anymore.

The long-running TV show *Seinfeld* broke through norms of privacy by introducing masturbation as a topic for public consumption and everyday conversation. We learned that all men do it (which we suspected already), that women do it, too (which we were less sure about), and that a contest to see how long one can go without doing it demonstrates how much we need to be able to do it. We can tune into a variety of talk shows and listen while guests describe their sexual indiscretions, unusual sexual preferences, and sordid sexual experiences. From soft-porn billboards on the freeway to invitations to pornographic sites popping onto our computer screen, images, attitudes, and values about sex make their way into our lives.

I teach at Wheaton College—a Christian liberal arts school in the Midwest. One of the most challenging and rewarding classes I teach is Sociology of Sexuality. My goal for that class and for this book is to help students and readers understand and embrace their sexuality in ways that honor God and acknowledge the longing for consummation and completion that God has imprinted on our bodies and souls. I tell my students the story of a Jewish rabbi who carried a satchel of dust in one pocket and a satchel of gold in the other. It reminded him that he was precious yet ordinary, made in the image of God, yet also broken. So it is with our sexuality; it is precious, yet fallen.

The Church is a community of sojourners making their way toward God through the dust and ashes of a broken world. There is much beauty along the way, as God has long been about the business of exchanging ashes for beauty and mourning for joy (Isaiah 61:1–3). We know about ashes. We see them in priests who molest children, pastors who are caught red-handed in pornography addictions, sexually transmitted diseases, teen pregnancies, the high divorce rate. Some ashes are subtle—so subtle that taken-for-granted assumptions about life are not recognized as distortions of sexuality. When girls and women hate their bodies, disdain their periods, fear childbirth, feel competitive with other women, or are crippled by fears of abandonment, these too are ashes—distortions of sexuality. When boys or men want to (or think they are supposed to want to) sleep with every girl or woman they encounter or want to be independent, silent loners like the Marlboro Man, or if they feel that inadequacy in any perceived area can be compensated for by asserting sexuality in some way, these are distortions of sexuality. Because we take distortions for granted ("boys are subject to their raging testosterone"; "menstruation really *is* horrible"), we fail to recognize how our sexuality is misunderstood, stifled, reduced to sexual interactions.

Communities of faith sift through ashes for beauty. Culture powerfully shapes our ideas about sexuality, but so can the Church. The Church resides within culture, always influenced by culture, but it is a unique institution that reminds us there is more to our existence than what we can see, feel, smell, and hear. Living with a longing for heaven has the potential to change the way we see and live our lives as sexual people. When Christians examine their taken-for-granted assumptions about life, then myth and distortion can be recognized, maybe dispelled; perhaps ashes can be exchanged for beauty. A student in the Sociology of Sexuality course wrote the following about his out-of-class discussion group:

> My small discussion group was illuminating when it comes to the differences in the sexuality of men and women. It was there that I was able to more clearly understand that a woman's period is an important part of her sexuality, that women also want to enjoy sex, that they may not feel free to do so, and that pornography among men is a big deal to women. This was good for me to learn because before I did not consider a woman's period to have anything to do with sex, I thought that women would find sex gross, I never worried about whether I as a man would enjoy sex, and I considered pornography a relatively small detail in my personal history.

In the sifting, examining, and challenging of assumptions, this student began to experience the grace and power of God to redeem broken ideas and patterns regarding sexuality.

Sexuality: Embedded and Embodied

Human sexuality is both *embedded in culture* and *embodied in physical, biological bodies*. Adam and Eve's experience in the Garden of Eden might have been the only human experience largely unencumbered by cultural traditions and norms. With subsequent generations, norms about sexuality emerged, multiplying quickly in the biblical record. The account of the Jewish people shows a culture with numerous laws and practices regarding sexuality. Male circumcision, laws about intercourse, and rituals of cleanliness that surrounded menstruation and emissions of semen were spelled out and meticulously followed as taken-for-granted practices in Hebrew culture. Beliefs about sexuality are embedded in culture and cannot be separated from how a culture understands, legitimizes, and practices sexual behaviors.[1]

Sexuality is also *embodied* in that being human is to exist in a body that is generally either male or female.[2] To be male or female is to see, relate to, interpret, and experience the world through bodies that are male or female. Everything we experience, we experience as females or males; we cannot compartmentalize ourselves from our sex. We note, consciously or unconsciously, whether the teacher of a course we've signed up for is female or male. We notice the sex of the person who cuts our hair. We note whether our doctor, pastor, boss, or child's coach is male or female; their sex affects how we experience them and how we relate to them. The simplicity of a cold glass of water we enjoy on a hot summer day may be relished in the same way, no matter which sex we are; nevertheless, we experience drinking the water through bodies that are male or female. Words whispered or shouted come to us through bodies that are female or male. We are moved by a rocket taking off in space or by the sight of Michelangelo's David through bodies that are male or female. We inhale ocean air or each other's bodily odors through bodies that are female or male. We caress, push away, hold, release. All this we experience and interpret as sexual creatures because we are embodied, either female or male.

Ideas about how we are to define and experience our sexuality and how we are to relate to others according to our sex emerge from our biology (the embodied dimension), our interactions with others, our religious beliefs, and our particular time and place in history (the embedded dimension). That five-year-old Jason thinks five-year-old Jacqueline has cooties is related to his time and place in history. It comes from his culture. If thirteen-year-old Jason has wet dreams, and thirteen-year-old Jacqueline is menstruating, this is a result of biology and would generally occur for any male and female, at any point in history. That Jason and Jacqueline believe sex should be saved for marriage comes from their culture, likely their religious upbringing. If sixteen-year-old Jason walks around in a perpetual state of sexual arousal that causes him a certain amount of anxiety, and Jacqueline (who finds Jason interesting and a bit frightening) walks around in perpetual state of anxiety regarding her looks, it is an interaction between biology and culture. Jason and Jacqueline have learned to assign particular social meaning to physical and emotional feelings and have adopted cultural patterns that reinforce assumptions they have about males and females. Thus our ideas about sexuality filter up to us through our embodied biology (chromosomes, genes, and hormones) and down to us from our embedded social environment (parents, peers, and pastors). The interaction of our embodied and embedded realities is taken for granted. We learn cultural scripts that give meaning to and interpret experiences in our physical bodies and relationships, telling us how to negotiate being girls and boys, women and men.

Of course, some argue that the essence of sexuality is only what can be reduced to physical or biological dimensions and that meaning and values given to sex are arbitrary and can be accepted or rejected without consequence. True independence and freedom, then, is to regard sex only as a physical, biological act not meaningfully connected to relationships or cultural values. In *The Sexual Life of Catherine M.*, published in 2002, French author Catherine Millet's quest for the meaning of sexuality takes her through a promiscuous lifestyle. She participated in her first orgy shortly after her eighteenth birthday and writes about her participation in group orgies, gang-bang sex, and serial sexual experiences. In defense of her memoir, Millet says, "I couldn't care less if people think I'm a nymphomaniac or not. I don't think I am. For me sexuality is a way of life."[3]

Indeed, sexuality is a way of life for all of us. But how we envision sexuality, understand it, and live with it is shaped by our time, beliefs, and place in history as they interact with our social relationships and our physical biology. Millet's sexuality is as much embedded in a culture as the sexuality of a fundamentalist Muslim woman who wears the *jihab*—a garment that covers her from head to toe—and who cannot leave her house without a chaperone. Religious and secular ideas alike give meaning to sexuality. All perspectives of sexuality are thus embedded in a cultural context.

Because our ideas about sexuality come from a variety of sources, communities of faith can be powerful agents of change and redemption for broken ideas about sexuality. As a community of faith, we can hold assumptions to the light of theological truth and exchange unhealthy ideas about body and sexuality for a spiritual reality that recognizes the significance of our embodied lives. Our sexuality is fundamental to being human, but sexuality is not fundamentally about sex. Sexuality is much broader, deeper, and more inclusive of human experience than just sex.

The Role of Relationship in Sexuality

Simply stated, two theological truths fundamental to our sexuality are that (1) we are made for relationship but are incapable of satisfying our longings in relationships, and that (2) living in grace bridges the chasm between our longings and our inability to satisfy those longings.

Longing for Relationship

We are made for relationship, drawn into relationship with others. In the movie *Castaway,* Federal Express employee Chuck Noland, played by Tom Hanks, is the lone survivor of a plane crash in the Pacific Ocean. He spends four years living on a small island in isolation. Noland is so desperate to escape his aloneness that he turns a Wilson brand volleyball that was boxed up in a FedEx package that washed on shore with him into a companion he aptly names Wilson. Noland talks to Wilson, seemingly listens to Wilson's replies, argues, kicks him around (literally at times), makes up, and then grieves profoundly when he loses Wilson at sea. We are desperate for relationship.

Fundamentally, our longing is for God, though we may not recognize it. Augustine acknowledged this in *The Confessions* when he said of God, "Our hearts are restless until they find their rest in you." The Heidelberg Catechism asks, "What is your only comfort in life and in death?" It answers, "That I am not my own, but belong—body and soul, in life and in death—to my faithful Savior Jesus Christ."[4] Our primary longing is to rest in the arms of God, recognizing that we belong to God.

We also long to be loved and known by others and to love and to know others. In their introduction to *Sexuality and the Sacred,* Nelson and Longfellow say this:

> Sexuality is intended by God to be neither incidental to nor detrimental to our spirituality, but rather a fully integrated and basic dimension of that spirituality . . . human sexuality . . . is most fundamentally the divine invitation to find our destinies not in loneliness but in deep connection . . . we experience our sexuality as the basic eros of our humanness that urges, invites, and lures us out of our loneliness into intimate communication and communion with God and the world.[5]

In our maleness and femaleness, in our embodied aloneness, we are drawn toward others for completion. Theologian Stanley Grenz argues that God is the foundation for human sexual bonding, forging the bridge between the Creator and the created.[6] We are made to be in relationship, to be social, to live in community. The author of Hebrews encourages us to persevere in living the good life, to continue to meet together with other believers, encouraging and instructing each other, bearing witness to the life of faith. The concluding chapter of Hebrews reminds readers to love each other with true Christian love that shows hospitality to strangers and care for people in prison, honors marriage, remembers leaders, and submits to the authority of spiritual leaders. We are made for relationship, called to live vibrant, active lives in community.

We are also drawn to the other sex—a longing that echoes throughout history in art, poetry, and stories, resonating with our own hopes and yearnings. Most of this book is about that particular longing for another with whom we can share an intimate sexual relationship.

To be human is to be drawn to others. We cannot exist in the world apart from relationships that define and shape us. By our very nature we can all say, as Catherine Millet does, that sexuality is our way of life. Sexuality is good; its very foundation emanates from God, whose image we bear. Our sexuality allows us to experience the world as embodied creatures fundamentally drawn to relationship with others. This theological truth that we are made for relationship bestows hope and blessing on our sexual nature that draws us into relationship.

Of course, perfect fellowship, perfect communion with others—either a community of others or one particular other—will not be realized this side of heaven. As Catholic priest and theologian Ronald Rolheiser says, all symphonies are incomplete this side of heaven. We are Grand Canyons without a bottom, longing for completion, for perfect communion with another that we will not experience this side of heaven.[7] But we are made in the image of God. In our fundamental longing for unity, communion, and consummation, we simultaneously reflect *imago Dei* and, whether or not we know it, we are yearning ultimately for the One who can satisfy our deepest longing to be known and loved.

Because our ability to perfectly reflect the image of God was utterly broken by sin in the Garden of Eden, our sexuality has been utterly broken as well. Cornelius Plantinga's book *Not the Way It's Supposed to Be: A Breviary of Sin* reminds us that all of life is affected by sin.[8] The world in which we live is not supposed to work this way. Romans 3:23 tells us, "All have sinned; all fall short of God's glorious standard." Spouses are not supposed to have affairs; children should not be sexually abused; men and women should not become trapped in sexual addictions. Our sexuality is not the way it's supposed to be; it falls short of God's glorious standard. We long for relationship—a perfect communion—and in an effort to satisfy unmet yearnings, we fill our lives with whatever we think will satisfy, often compromising the very relationships that hold the most promise for fulfillment. Psychiatrist Gerald May describes addictions as attachments to things that do not satisfy our deepest desires and longings. To escape the pain of unfulfilled longings, we experiment with behaviors that give us momentary pleasure or relief but soon enslave us in a cycle of unfulfilled hopes and expectations that multiply our suffering.[9]

Living in Grace

The second theological truth brings hope to the first: *living in grace bridges the chasm between our longings and our inability to satisfy those longings.* We have a yearning that ultimately only God can satisfy, yet God extended grace to humanity by creating us with a desire for relationship that extends to others. While we wait for completion in eternity, we love and learn and find easement from our loneliness in relationships with others. When we acknowledge that our yearnings will never be fully satisfied, we can welcome God into our disappointment and then turn toward the abundance yet available through the temporal blessings of relationships, knowing they were never intended to completely satisfy our longings.

Sometimes God's redemption of our broken sexuality manifests itself in a satisfying marriage and healthy sexual expression with a lifelong partner. Sometimes it is in richly satisfying friendships and belonging to a community that eases the ache of our longings.

Redeeming broken sexuality also manifests itself in the ongoing work of recognizing our inability to love selflessly and unconditionally and to be loved selflessly and unconditionally. Grace accepts the imperfections of others and those in ourselves while striving toward greater virtue and better love.

Other times, God's redemption of our broken sexuality calls us to comfort the pain experienced by others. Henri Nouwen speaks of compassion as being the ability to sit with those who suffer.[10] We do not much care to sit with suffering but would rather escape it, using Advil to escape physical pain and TV, movies, daydreams, shopping, and a variety of addictions to escape emotional pain. To extend grace is to be willing to sit with brokenness rather than escape or fix it—to look at and own our failure. God redeems and restores that which is broken and calls us to be hands and feet of mercy, easing the suffering of others. We learn something of our human condition and our need for God when we sit with our suffering and with those who suffer.

God's redemption of our broken sexuality is a lifelong journey toward wholeness that never achieves the measure of wholeness we hope for. Henri Nouwen's biographer, Michael Ford, says Nouwen struggled with a homosexual orientation throughout his life and never experienced the wholeness he sought. Some struggle to overcome the pain of a sexually abusive father, an unfaithful wife, paralyzing insecurity, infertility, the inability to accept one's body, or the body's betrayal through sexual dysfunction or disease.

Mary Jo Valenziano, my Franciscan spiritual director, once confronted my impatience for achieving the wholeness and holiness I longed for by reminding me that the woman whose hemorrhaging Jesus healed had spent twelve years seeking help. Part of her journey toward healing was to crawl toward Jesus in the midst of a throng of people where she hoped to touch the hem of his robe. Some of us will be crawling still until we reach heaven, where all symphonies are completed, all wounds are healed, all tears dried. Sometimes we need to receive a grace that allows us to endure and embrace suffering from which we may never be healed in ways we hope. Sometimes, we need to extend grace to others who will never be healed in ways we, and they, look for. When we accept suffering and embrace our incompleteness, we experience more fully the grace of a God who invites us, woos us, lures us into communion with God and others.

Contents of This Book

My hope is that this book will be a step toward helping the Church develop a theology of grace that embraces our sexuality in a broken world. Culture shapes our views of relationships and sexuality. Historically, so has the Church, and it continues to do so in this present day. We need help understanding our yearnings and stretching toward God and the abundance of love found in authentic relationships and communities, knowing neither will fully satisfy the longing of our hearts.

Books are informed by conversations we engage in, classes we take (or teach), churches we attend, and the words of others we read and ponder. This book is a compilation of the words of such informants—conversations, written reflections, and interviews with mothers, fathers, high school and college students, single men and women, colleagues, pastors, and theologians. They graciously opened their hearts and told me their stories and beliefs; they raised questions and sometimes named fears. To protect their privacy, their names and, in some cases, identifying characteristics have been changed, but the words are always their own.

Many authors have also shaped the thoughts reflected in the following pages—social scientists inside and outside the field of sociology and perhaps, most notably, theologians such as Stanley Grenz, Ronald Rolheiser, Neal Plantinga, and Henri Nouwen. I am grateful to them all.

I tell students to stay "vulnerable to the argument" of positions they initially distrust or disagree with. I want them to be willing to bracket their own ideas long enough to absorb the argument of another position. They do not have to agree with the other position ultimately, but I want to see that they have grappled to understand it. Understanding helps them recognize blind spots in their own thinking, distorted ways of seeing. A metaphor that sociologist Peter Berger used to help people begin this process is to imagine stepping off the stage and sitting in the audience to examine the various actors, props, scripts, and mechanisms that shape the unfolding human drama surrounding a particular issue. At times throughout the following chapters, you may be best served if you can step off the stage and join me in the audience for a while.

In Chapter One, "Rites of Passage: The Quest for Manhood and Womanhood," I consider ways bodies change over the life cycle, altering our views of ourselves, our longings, our relationships to others, and our rights and obligations. Historically, societies provided rites of passage to help individuals negotiate change. In the absence of formal rites of passage, boys and girls create their own rituals (often detrimental) that validate who they are becoming as men and women and how they relate to each other. Those of us in Christian communities can channel the desire for the validation of maturity and the clarification of rights and responsibilities in relationships by constructing rites that draw all toward healthy relationships and commitment to community.

Chapter Two, "Adolescence: Awakenings and Choices," explores the longing for intimate connection and sexual awakenings that begin a lifelong journey of yearning. Teen sexuality is embedded in a culture that expects and assumes teens will act out sexually; subsequently, the culture is notorious for its dangers, most notably sexually transmitted diseases (STDs) and pregnancy. Although it is necessary to present accurate information on the consequences of premarital sex, that is not sufficient. Teens begin to desire intimacy with peers and affirmation that they are loved and lovable by their peers. Christian communities can strengthen youth when they offer an inviting alternative to joining the fray in exploring sexuality by sexually acting out with peers that still recognizes and validates their longings.

Chapter Three, "Sleeping Alone: Sexuality and Singleness," acknowledges that not everyone marries, even though everyone longs for relationship in one form or another. Embracing sexuality for Christian singles includes identifying with God in their singleness. Unmarried people uniquely reflect God's inclusive, expansive, open love of others. Even so, singleness comes with a diverse array of challenges, reflecting different life experiences, hopes, and disappointments. Christian communities that understand the multifaceted experiences and challenges of singles will better integrate, serve, utilize, bless, and be blessed by singles in their faith communities.

Chapter Four, "Birthing Babies: The Essence of Early Motherhood (and Fatherhood)," takes the most evident biological outcome of intercourse and explores its embodied and embedded dimensions. To embrace the physical aspect of birth experiences is to welcome the whole embodied experience of birth and parenthood that profoundly affects mothers and fathers. Embracing birth experiences means understanding how laboring bodies do the work of birthing babies and how women can support other women, actively participating in the process of growing community. Our tendency has been to turn control over to medical practitioners, and in the process women have become alienated from their bodies. Authentic, whole sexuality integrates body and soul, not only in sexual intercourse but in the birthing and caring of babies in ways that draw and connect us to others.

Chapter Five, "Mysteries of Marriage: Bone of My Bone, Flesh of My Flesh," recognizes that we long for completion in marriage, and a lingering fragrance of Eden keeps individuals pursuing relationship, even given unhappy stories and high divorce rates. We are presumptuous to assume that full fulfillment can come from marriage, yet we can live with a hope that marriage still provides abundant love. Communities of faith attempting to support and uphold marriages explore damaging myths and contemporary challenges associated with sex and marriage in the twenty-first century. Myths can be countered with a vision of marriage as a temporary home—one that will never satisfy completely our deepest longings for home but, nevertheless, a place for sexual expression and celebration, a place for forgiveness and grace, a place to belong and to be loved.

Chapter Six, "Sexuality and Culture: Bodies and Scripts," explores the essence of female and male sexuality. We journey through life, always aware that we make our way in bodies that are male or female. We come to understand what it means to be male or female, according to cultural scripts that tell us how to play the roles associated with our particular biological reality. At the core, our maleness and femaleness is relational, but our expressions are sometimes grossly distorted and broken. Redeeming sexuality includes understanding where our ideas about maleness and femaleness come from and realigning our perceptions with a Christian understanding of humans made for relationship and created in God's image.

The Epilogue, "Beauty from Ashes," reminds us that God offers comfort for the broken-hearted and joy instead of mourning. Our sexuality is infused with beauty, but also reduced to ashes in the wounds and distortions of sin. God is always working to heal, to comfort, and to exchange ashes for beauty in ways that draw us toward each other and toward the God from whom our ultimate fulfillment comes.

My prayer is that this book offers a redemptive picture of sexuality in a broken world; we are dust but also gold. I hope it begins conversation among couples, friends, and communities of faith that will enable us to respond more thoughtfully and honestly to the challenges of living well and embracing our sexuality as broken people in a broken world.

Newberg Friends Church introduced me to the Quaker concept and use of queries—questions that do not have simple answers or even necessarily correct ones but that prod introspective reflection and examination. To facilitate conversations about sexuality, I have adapted the Quaker use of queries at the end of each chapter. These are thought-provoking questions that can move our conversations forward and deeper.

RITES OF PASSAGE

THE QUEST FOR MANHOOD AND WOMANHOOD

---

*Ritual knowledge is nothing if not sensual. A rite is
an activity that engages the hand and pricks the ear;
it catches the eye and lifts the heart.*

—Ronald Grimes[1]

I SPENT MY ADOLESCENCE IN OREGON, where the state issued me a
driver's permit at fifteen years of age and a license at sixteen. At eighteen,
I entered a voter's booth for the first time, casting my ballot in the presidential race between Jimmy Carter and Ronald Reagan. At twenty-one, I
could legally go to a bar and order a drink.

Modern societies tend to grant privileges according to years lived rather
than rites of passage per se—ritual ceremonies that determine one is
responsible, tied into a larger community, and ready for the rights and
responsibilities of adulthood. With the exception of obtaining a driver's
license, the rights, privileges, and responsibilities of adulthood are usually
achieved by reaching certain birthdays rather than by successfully making one's way through a series of training, preparing, and testing rituals.

Historically, societies have provided rites of passage to ensure that people negotiate social and relational changes associated with growing up
and aging. Arriving at puberty, parenthood, and menopause alters our
view of ourselves, our longings, our relationships to others, and our rights
and responsibilities. In the absence of tribal rites of passage, we have relied

on the institutions of our culture—education, religion, civic life—to pass on the proper skills, values, and beliefs to manage sexuality, adulthood, and aging.

In the absence of recognized rites of passage, boys and girls (and to a lesser degree men and women) create their own rituals to validate who they are becoming as men and women and how they are to relate to each other. Those of us in Christian communities can channel the desire for the validation of maturity and for a clarification of identity and place in a community by constructing rites that draw everyone toward healthy relationships and commitment to community.

French anthropologist Arnold van Gennep described and classified various rituals that traditional cultures (those unaffected by the Industrial Revolution) used to mark significant transition points throughout life. Among the most important were initiation rites conducted around the time of puberty. Van Gennep's work was translated into English in 1960, about the time the angst of adolescence was taking Europe and America by storm. In the last couple of decades, others have built on van Gennep's work to resurrect ritual and re-create rites of passage in the hopes of bringing children through the confusion of adolescence to adulthood.

Rites of passage depend on markers that identify physical changes requiring a shift in roles, rights, and responsibilities. Transitions related to one's status as a sexual person are particularly significant. Children do not suddenly become sexual in adolescence, though their sexual status changes. Boys and girls have powerful longings for attachment from birth that are directed toward their primary caregivers. They also experience sexual feeling very early in life, generally discovering the pleasant sensation that comes from stimulating their genitals by the time they enter preschool. Most children then enter a phase of sexual hibernation about the time they head for first grade; they stop stimulating themselves (and forget they ever did), and their sexuality is put on hold until puberty. At puberty, everything changes for girls and boys, including their sexual status. Longings for attachment begin to shift toward peers—a desire to belong, to be counted worthy, to be accepted, loved. Although the underlying longing is universal, its expression and experience in embodied (physical changes) and embedded (cultural expectations) aspects of being male or female is different.

Physical Markers of Womanhood

Puberty marks the beginning of a girl's reproductive life. Her sexuality is embodied in changes that move her into puberty, through a long time of potential fertility, followed by menopause. Traditional cultures marked these transitions with an assortment of menstrual rites, prewedding rituals, birth rituals, and menopausal rituals. A girl's self-concept is defined and shaped through her interactions with others—parents, siblings, relatives, those in authority, and peers. How females and males understand and embrace their physical bodies, as well as the subsequent roles they adopt, is shaped through their interactions with others.

When traditional cultures celebrated the beginning of menstruation, other women surrounded young pubescent girls, instructing them in the skills and knowledge of womanhood, nurturing them, and initiating them into the circle of women. "Menstrual sanctuaries," which were the tents, cabins, or special places set apart for menstruating women, gave women the opportunity to deepen connections and ties with other females, thus becoming part of their larger community.[2] Affirming traditions was a way to celebrate being female, and rites of passage connected women meaningfully to other women, transferring the blessing of being women from one generation to the next.

Redeeming Menstruation

The absence of affirming menstruation rituals today is evident in women's disdain for their periods. Early on, girls learn to be embarrassed by menstruation, to use products that help hide it from the boys around them, from each other, and, as much as possible, from themselves. Nineteen-year-old Nicole said, "I hated it when I started my period. No one should have to start in fifth grade. I felt like I was looking into a future that was going to be horrible, like, wow, my life is over. Now I try to ignore my period. I don't think about it. If you put a tampon in, you don't have to think much about it."

Nicole's perspective is common among the women I've talked with. The possibility that menstruation is something positive was sometimes acknowledged but only in the context of being the process that allows women to make babies. The possibility that this monthly cycle—one that in some cases would never produce a child and, on average, in industrialized countries would only do so twice—could offer something potentially enriching and enhancing for women seemed remote.

Cultures that treated menstruation as important demonstrated the significance of it with menstruation taboos and rituals. In some cases, the rituals emerged out of fear, and taboos kept menstruating women secluded to protect people who could be damaged by her menstrual power. In other cases, the rituals emerged out of respect for the sacred, and seclusion was intended to bring renewal and blessing.[3]

In her best-selling novel *The Red Tent,* Anita Diamant imagines how early Jewish women might have experienced life and the monthly ritual of menstruation. Only menstruating women entered the red tent, and as their cycles were synchronized with each other[4] they spent three days together inside the tent every month. They rested from the tasks of daily living, retold their stories, and reflected about life. Older women passed on traditions and wisdom to younger women.

Since the summer after sixth grade when my own journey into womanhood began, I have been alternately fascinated and annoyed by this thing female bodies do every month. My friends and I experienced menstruation as a nuisance at best and a dreaded nightmare at worst during years when our cramps were so painful they kept us home from school or work. Yet I also knew something amazing happened every month, reminding me that my body could create and sustain new life. That it happened regularly suggested a rhythm to life, a pattern of marking my days not unlike the seasons of the year.

In the last few years, I have begun attending more carefully to the rhythm of my cycle and reading and listening to other women's attempts to reconnect something of who they are to the menstruating bodies they inhabit. In accepting this thing as good, I have come to embrace the amazing gift God gave women by making us God's partner in creating and sustaining human life. Apart from producing children, my menstrual cycle connects me to a rhythm of life that is a grounding of sorts—a point of reflection on where I have been and where I am headed. When there is pain, it prepares and reminds me that I can endure the pain I will experience as a member of a broken and suffering world.

The collective shame and hate of menstruation that women share has emerged partly out of a long-running history of considering femaleness inferior to maleness. Many cultures considered female sexuality not only as being dangerous but as causing women to be frail, irrational, and illogical. By the time humanity reached the Victorian era, Western women had long accepted femaleness as a curse to be borne but not celebrated. They saw themselves as fragile and weak. Middle-class women of the time took on the "half-life of the parlor women,"[5] who lounged on couches all day, too frail (and constrained by corsets that made it difficult to breathe and exert oneself at the same time) to do much else. Women of means gave the task of breast-feeding over to wet nurses and that of childrearing to nannies.

Hysterectomies became the solution to hysteria in women and a host of other female ailments. At the turn of the twentieth century, some medical journals suggested that hysterectomies were the cure-all for female problems. Because the uterus caused women an assortment of illnesses like nervousness, irritability, moodiness, and depression, once she emptied her womb of the babies she intended to have, it was better for everyone if she had the now unnecessary organ removed. Being in therapy would help, too. She would be more pleasant to live with and could thus better fulfill her role as nurturer and keeper of the peace. Ultimately, a woman was doomed for what she did not have (a penis) and damned for what she did (a uterus).

As the mid-twentieth-century women's movement gained momentum, equality became the goal, ensuring that women had the same opportunities as men and received the same pay for the same work. Inequality had been justified on the basis of differences between men and women, so some argued that, except for a few reproductive organs, women were just like men. If women were just like men except that they were taught to feel inferior and weak, then a woman could be resocialized to do anything a man could do.

Shulamith Firestone, a radical feminist of the sixties and seventies, supported the development of technology that would allow women to be free of the task of baby-making. She thought a woman's inferior status was linked to her reproductive system and called for a revolution that would free women from the constraints of that system. Women would not have equal status with men and be truly free until they were released from the chore of making babies.[6]

Most people rejected Firestone's ideas and continued to have babies, but the curse of femaleness was so deeply embedded in culture that many women disdained the reproductive process. The uterus was deemed necessary for producing babies but bad in every other way; the number of hysterectomies hit an all-time high in the 1970s. Physicians counseled women to have their uteruses removed for a variety of reasons, including eliminating the discomfort of menstruation or the possibility of uterine cancer *at some point later in life*.[7] Hysterectomies were the fourth most commonly performed operation among fifteen- to forty-four-year-old women in the 1970s, following abortions, diagnostic dilation and curettage (D&Cs), and tubal sterilizations.[8]

Although women have learned that it is detrimental to so lightly regard their uterus, and they no longer remove them at the alarming rates they did thirty-five years ago, at the dawn of the twenty-first century the medical community is still trying to mitigate the curse of menstruation. Some medical researchers argue that "incessant menstruation" comes as a liability, along with benefits of modernity that allowed women to live (and thus menstruate) longer and yet give birth to fewer children. They claim the benefits of helping women to menstruate less outweigh the potential risks of messing with their menstrual cycles.[9] Late in 2003, the drug Seasonale will become available—a birth control pill prescribed so that it manipulates a woman's menstrual cycle, enabling her to suppress her periods so that she only has them once every three months.

Our culture stretches toward solutions that allow women to do away with the mess of menstruation without doing away with the uterus. Soon women will be able to take another step toward becoming more like men; they will no longer be required to bear the monthly curse of menstruation.

I don't know how Eve experienced menstruation prior to the introduction of sin in the fall. Probably it was pain- and trouble-free. But sin has now permeated everything. When I experience menstrual cramping and bloating, I consider it evidence of the fall, but I cringe when I hear women name their femaleness as a curse and work hard to escape an experience that is fundamental to being female. Instead of accepting menstruation as a curse, women can try to understand how having bodies that menstruate and are able to bear and nourish children can affect how they see themselves and how they live in relation to God, to others, and to the world. They can see the reproductive process as a significant part of sexuality. Women-affirming voices reject definitions that have emerged from cultures in which females and all things female were regarded inferior and cursed and were held in suspicion. We are embodied souls.

A menstruation ritual imparts blessings to girls and opens the possibility of thinking redemptively about all aspects of being female. Every month a girl is reminded of her uniqueness as a woman. She can attend to this rhythmic cycle that allows her to mark her days. She can look for ways to honor her menstruating body, such as allowing herself to pull inward a couple of days every month to review where she has been and to think intentionally about where she is headed. Some women notice that dreams intensify prior to, during, or immediately following menstruation. Others recognize a desire to be in a calm and quiet place during the heavier part of their bleeding. Some experience menstruation as a time of increased awareness and creativity, or sensitivity and insight.

My daughter Sarah recognizes a heightened sensitivity a few days before her period. She is more keenly aware of and troubled by the brokenness and suffering she sees around her and is easily moved to tears. We have discussed this as a gift that could be embraced rather than a nuisance and a pain of menstruation. In her heightened sensitivity, she can weep with God and share in God's suffering over a world that is not as it should be. During these days, she is awakened to her longing for heaven. Every month, she has the potential to connect with God in this way.

A twenty-nine-year-old married woman named Grant expressed something similar. She said, "I feel increased sensitivity and heightened emotions which are sometimes helpful. I'm forced to confront emotions I ignore the rest of the month. So I pray a lot, meditate, and am drawn to God through the emotional discomfort. I'm thankful for that."

Annie, a twenty-two-year-old artist, said, "Menstruation mirrors the creative process for me. It is a time of gathering, incubating, releasing, and then creating. Its rhythm is a metaphor, if not more, of the creative process. At the midway point in my cycle, I seem more articulate and have clearer thinking. During my period, I dream more intensely and create my best art."

A few women are reconsidering the ancient patterns of separating menstruating women from others. Although we have long assumed that the separation was perceived as necessary for the sake of sanitation, for some cultures it appears to have been a time for women to draw away alone or with other menstruating women in a silent or near-silent retreat to reflect on the wisdom of life, the passage of time, and what was to come. One student responded to the bonding possibilities of women supporting each other in menstruation by telling this story:

> I really appreciated the ideas in the text on the "menstrual sanctuaries" and how in some cultures menstruation is treated as a time for rest and retreat and to be with other women. I had just finished reading that part and decided to go to the store to get my shopping done for the day. On my way home from the store, I was suddenly overcome by the most excruciating cramps I have ever experienced. I literally had to roll out of my car and stumble through the door of my apartment and collapse on my bed, groaning and sobbing at the amount of pain I was in. My roommates immediately jumped into action, one going for the hot water bottle, another one making me some tea and fetching the Advil, and the other one taking off my shoes, covering me in a blanket, and giving me her stuffed elephant to squeeze. I was whimpering and grimacing at the pain I was in, and I looked up to see my roommates' sad, concerned faces but also looks of knowing all too well what I was going through. When I was finally able to move again a few hours later, we all laughed together and shared the "worst time ever" stories. It was a very bonding time, and we connected in a way that is so special, a way to connect with women through the one thing that makes us uniquely women. . . . Being women themselves my roommates knew exactly what I needed, and the whole incident became a way for them to care for me as a woman. I think I underestimate the power of having other women around to share these experiences that are a part of being women. Women everywhere are bonded by this dreaded "curse," which actually turns out to be a blessing when it becomes a way to connect with other women.

Suffering and grace reside together. Allowing other women to be familiar with our menstrual cycle invites women to receive blessing and to bestow blessing on each other.

Women who believe menstruation is good give themselves an opportunity for growth and blessing. Women bleed for some time before they bear children and long after they are done bearing children and whether or not they *ever* bear children. One postmenopausal woman who had never married or had children said, "I used to laugh and say, 'I had all those periods for nothing.' I think menstruation was about more than having babies. We don't understand the mystery of our bodies very well."

Women inhabit physical bodies that menstruate every month, and their personhood cannot be separated from their bodies. Attending to a cycle that is fundamental to women's physical nature opens the door for potential insight and unexpected blessing.

Redeeming Menopause

In many industrialized cultures, not only is the onset of menstruation perceived as a curse, so is the cessation of menstruation. Girls are cursed when menstruation comes, cursed as the ones to go through the pain and suffering of childbearing, and cursed with the irrelevance of old age when they stop menstruating. In 1969, psychiatrist David Reuben wrote:

> As estrogen is shut off, a woman comes as close as she can to being a man. Increased facial hair, deepened voice, obesity, and decline of breasts and female genitalia all contribute to a masculine appearance. Not really a man but no longer a functional woman, these individuals live in a world of *intersex*. Having outlived their ovaries, they have outlived their usefulness as human being.[10]

The results of these changes, according to psychoanalytic theories, were increased problems coping with life after menopause. Women were in a crisis of loss and identity; they were no longer able to bear children—the essential marker of female identity. Menopause came to be accepted as an illness needing medical and psychological intervention.

Researchers questioning the assumptions of this model of female reproduction have been exploring the connection between mental and physical health and menopause. In a five-year study of 541 women, researchers from the University of Pittsburgh concluded that menopause did not lead to detectable changes in women's well-being. It did not make them more anxious, angry, depressed, self-conscious, stressed, or nervous and did not make it more difficult to sleep or increase the number of neck- and headaches. In fact, the only reliable effect of menopause was that women who did not use hormone replacement felt less self-consciousness and reported more often that they experienced hot flashes.[11]

Theories that menopause makes women physically and psychologically ill and unstable have been proven false over the last ten to fifteen years,[12] but the fear and curse of aging lingers, negatively affecting women's self-perceptions. In many traditional cultures, women gained social status as they aged. As their responsibility for children lessened, they became the administrators of households and clans, as well as leaders in politics, religion, and medicine. A woman was now worthy of the respect she had given older women in her younger years.[13]

Today, much of a woman's felt worth is in her physical appearance, and aging represents declining social value. Our culture markets to this fear, selling products or procedures promising to stay the horrors of aging and help women maintain a youthful appearance. This culture of youthful beauty has created a general perception that to look postmenopausal is to be unattractive, nonsexual, and undesirable. But consider this alternative view of aging by Naomi Wolf:

> You could see the signs of female aging as diseased, especially if you had a vested interest in making women too, see them your way. Or you could see that if a woman is healthy she lives to grow old. As she thrives, she reacts and speaks and shows emotion, and grows into her face. Lines trace her thought and radiate from the corners of her eyes after decades of laughter, closing together like fans as she smiles. You could call the lines a network of "serious lesions," or you could see that in a precise calligraphy, thought has etched marks of concentration between her brows, and drawn across her forehead the horizontal creases of surprise, delight, compassion and good talk. A lifetime of kissing, of speaking and weeping shows expressively around a mouth scored like a leaf in motion. The skin loosens on her face and throat, giving her features a setting of sensual dignity, her features grow stronger as she does. She has looked around in her life, and it shows when gray and white reflect in her hair, you could call it a dirty secret or you could call it silver or moonlight. Her body fills into itself, taking on gravity like a bather breasting water, growing generous with the rest of her. The darkening under her eyes, the weight of her lids, their minute cross hatching reveal that what she has been part of has left in her its complexity and richness. She is darker, stronger, looser, tougher, sexier. The maturing of a woman who has continued to grow is a beautiful thing to behold.[14]

We age, and aging represents bodies that are breaking down and wearing out. But aging also represents a life lived. We can choose to see how living long yields great potential for inner wisdom and knowledge; only with aging can wisdom fully develop. The role of an old woman or grandmother in some cultures is still highly valued because she is granted the status of sage, or wise one. Her work changes from that of directly nurturing the young to one of teaching, mentoring, healing, and tending other men and women less far along in the journey. Her contribution changes as she transitions through life; it does not diminish in importance or magnitude. We grant honor to aging women when we refuse to allow women's social worth to be determined by a youthful appearance. Communities of faith that invite older women to teach, mentor, arbitrate, discern, and lead validate God's work in those who have gained wisdom through a lifetime of living—observing, learning, absorbing, and growing ever older.

Rites of passage can become powerful means by which women identify positively with the physical changes of their bodies. Rather than feel cursed by female bodies that menstruate or betrayed by female bodies that age, they find richness and a centering calmness in their embodied state as women. Women comfortable in their bodies are less encumbered by resentment and doubts about being female; they live and work with greater confidence, validated and celebrated for who they are and are becoming as women transitioning through life.

Male Markers of Manhood

With the exception of puberty, boys' and men's lives are not marked as clearly by reproductive changes that occur throughout their lives. At puberty, boys develop more muscle and deeper voices, as well as pubic and facial hair. But deeper voices, bigger muscles, and more hair do not turn a boy into a man. Boys prove manhood by showing they are skilled and competent like their fathers. As they develop skills and muscle, boys desire to test their competency and strength. They want to be capable, assured that they can make it in the world that awaits them. In the absence of clear rituals or markers that prepare and test them for manhood, many create their own initiation rites. Some of these occur in the context of life-affirming friendships through recreational and organized sports, outdoor adventures, theater, music, student council, and social activism. Boys test their strength, courage, intellect, and skill against themselves and other boys as they move through adolescence.

My extended family gets together every few years for a reunion. Wrestling is and has been a big sport in my mother's family. Uncle Art wrestled, as did my brother Dan, as do some of the nephews. One summer, Dan and one of our nephews decided to have an exhibition match. Everyone watched sixteen-year-old Zach take on his thirty-four-year-old uncle. Uncle Art officiated. The intensity of the match equaled those I'd watched at other meets. Neither wanted to lose. Zach was proving he had acquired the strength of a man; Dan was proving he could still hold his own. Dan and Zach were stretched to the max, testing their strength and skill against each other. I don't remember who won, but that's not the point. The match, held in the yard of the farm where my mother was born, with an audience of fifty-some family members from four generations, was an initiation rite of sorts, a testing of strength and skill, a welcoming of Zach into the family as a man.

There comes a point in every boy's life where he stands up to and challenges his father, proving his manhood.[15] Some of these are positive efforts to prove strength and skill, like Zach's wrestling match with Dan. The desire for boys to be competent and affirm their manhood through the testing of skills is life-affirming. But in the absence of strong male role models or effective rites of passage that guide how boys think about themselves and the communities to which they belong, boys turn elsewhere for guidance. In their desire to belong and be accepted, it is often their peers they turn to for guidance.

Sometimes this skill-testing takes a detrimental turn and involves taking risks to cheat the system and rebel against parents, school, or legal authority. This may mean striking back at a father who hits his adolescent son. Or it may be an indirect attack on authority: stealing cigarettes from the neighborhood convenience store, bashing in mail boxes in the next suburb over, driving recklessly, skipping school, or binge drinking. These risk-taking behaviors prove a boy's manhood to himself and his peers. In their power to affirm manhood, they become valuable initiation rites.

Having sex also makes a man out of a boy, as described in numerous coming-of-age classics such as *The Summer of 1942* and *The Graduate*. So deeply ingrained is the idea that boys must have sex to become men that to be twenty, male, and still a virgin means one needs therapy to explore the problem. In the movie *Antwone Fisher*, we discover that the reason Antwone had not yet had sex, even though he was a virile, attractive man enlisted in the navy, was because an older woman had molested him as a boy.

Yet adolescent boys receive conflicting, simultaneous messages: girls and women deserve respect, but things feminine are undesirable; girls should be treated well, but females are inferior; to have sex with a girl only for personal gratification is to exploit her; but prematurely committing to monogamy is both old-fashioned and unreasonable.

Psychologist and researcher William Pollack has interviewed, studied, and written about boys over the last two decades. He talks about the double message boys get regarding their sexuality: "Here again is the double standard of masculinity that pushes boys to feel they need to 'prove themselves' sexually and then castigates them when they do so."[16] Boys are not encouraged to talk about their questions, anxieties, and fears as they move from boyhood to manhood. They long for meaningful relationships, but the longing is considered effeminate, a sign of weakness. Pollack sees boys who are often depressed, lonely, and confused internally, though they learn to put on a tough, hard exterior.

Skill training and instruction in how to think about being male has existed in clubs sponsored by various communities, most notably the Boy Scouts. These clubs foster a sense of belonging, solidarity, and obligation. The Boy Scout movement emerged in response to an increasing anxiety during the years between 1880 and World War I that boys were not being adequately socialized in becoming men. Changes in fathers' occupation meant mothers were spending more time with their sons, and promoters of Boy Scouts feared boys would not become masculine without adequate time and training led by other men. The 1914 Boy Scout manual read, in part:

> The wilderness is gone, the Buckskin Man is gone, the painted Indian has hit the trail over the Great Divide, the hardships and privations of pioneer life which did so much to develop sterling manhood are now but a legend in history, and we must depend upon the Boy Scout Movement to produce the men of the future.[17]

The training, awards, and rituals were well defined, prescribing what it meant to be male. Boys were taught the skills needed to be men and instructed in the responsibilities of manhood. The description of the 1912 Boy Scout shows the founders' fear that boys were becoming soft:

> The REAL Boy Scout is not a "sissy." There is nothing "milk and water" about him; he is not afraid of the dark. Instead of being a puny, dull, or bookish lad, who dreams and does nothing, he is full of life, energy, enthusiasm, bubbling over with fun, full of ideas as to what he wants to do and knows how he wants to do it. He is not hitched to his mother's apron strings. While he adores his mother, and would do anything to save her from suffering or discomfort, he is self-reliant, sturdy and full of vim.[18]

Balance is hard to achieve in a fallen world, but, in fact, men do not now have to choose between the sensitive New Man and Iron John. They can be emotionally vulnerable, desire intimacy, admit weakness, and also strive to acquire skill and competence and be "sturdy and full of vim." The difficulty that creates so much confusion for boys is the lack of consensus about what ought to define manhood. This lack of consensus also means that the rituals that were effective in shaping boys in the past do not carry the same power they once did. In some places, belonging to the Boy Scouts is a sissy thing to do.

For boys headed to a college or university, fraternities become a place to find identity and belonging. Unfortunately, the initiation rituals for some fraternities require that pledges prove their manhood by drinking vast quantities of alcohol. A string of alcohol-related deaths from 1997 through 1999 (many of them tied to fraternity initiations) brought this ritual into the limelight of national news. One freshman pledge described his experience on the television show *20/20,* a segment of ABC News titled "A Sea of Alcohol."[19] Pledges were taken to a bar where five plastic-lined garbage cans were clustered in the center of the room. The purpose of the night, he said, was to get all the pledges drunk and sick. "Be a man," they were told. "If you want to belong to this fraternity, you've got to do this. You wouldn't want to get kicked out now." Even after vomiting blood along with alcohol, he was pressured to keep drinking. When asked why he would do that to himself, he said, "I just wanted to fit in; that's all I ever wanted. I just wanted to fit in and meet people and stuff."

Incoming freshmen often face the uncertainty of a new environment. Their identity, roles, rights, and obligations are shifting. In their longing to belong, many are willing to endure hazing ordeals that humiliate, are sometimes violent, and in a few cases have led to death. "They had to do it, so they were going to make us do it. . . . It's kinda like a ritual to them 'cause they do it the same way every year."

Boys find another kind of community and brotherhood in street gangs. In the absence of strong relationships in family or community, boys will seek relationship elsewhere. Once they pass through initiation rites that can include violence and illegal activities, they are welcomed into the gang as brothers, becoming loyal members of a family they love passionately and would die to protect. Sometimes gang membership is more about survival than replacing family connections, but it is always about belonging. The longing to belong is fundamental to human nature—a good longing that corresponds to being made for relationship. The desire to be competent and capable and to test one's skills against another is also good. In a broken, sinful world, good desires sometimes turn to destructive ends.

Men mark other transitions with rituals as well. Because they are one-time events and not connected to training and preparation, they have less impact than gangs, fraternities, and Boy Scouts. Nevertheless, they are statements of what it means to transition through life as a male. Men sometimes have a stag party before they get married; such a party can be a meaningful gathering of male friends or one last fling with the boys. In either case, the party is not intended to prepare men for marriage. Neither are retirement parties intended to prepare men for the transition at hand; they are to celebrate the ending of work and the beginning of a long vacation. In general, men are not encouraged to reflect on what it means to transition from one phase of life to another, whether it be the end of boyhood, of living as a single man, of fatherhood, or of work.

But men still gather, encourage one another, and support each other. They find community and affirmation on the football field and in the locker room, watching a basketball game and coaching their children in little league. Churches host Men's Retreats and Men's Breakfasts, encouraging men to come together to support, learn from, and bless each other. Men gather for informal rituals, too, like the one my brother Dan prepared for his son Taylor, before sending him across the country to college. Dan invited men who knew Taylor to come together one evening, bringing an appropriate verse, thought, or a few words of advice. They shared these with Taylor, gave him their words on a CD, and gathered around him to pray.

The desire for relationship emerges out of our embodied aloneness, drawing men into relationship with other men, with women, and with God. We witness grace in the midst of brokenness in our longing for connection, even if that connection sometimes leads down detrimental paths. Even though boys will craft and seek out their own rituals and rites, whether we want them to or not, a better way is for communities of faith to create ritual that takes the desire for validation and clarity of identity and helps males be reflective during the transitions of life. Rites of passage can connect changing identity, sexuality, longings, and the passage of time in ways that strengthen relationship with others, with community, and with God.

Crafting Rites of Passage

With the onset of puberty comes the desire to loosen the strong ties children feel toward their parents and to expand and create new bonds between peers in intimate and sometimes sexual ways. The longing reflects an appropriate shift in desire, as the possibility for sexual intimacy awakens.

Traditional cultures did not assume children would exchange their connection with parents (and the corresponding norms of behavior) for other appropriate connections and norms of behavior without assistance. Rites of passage offered training that passed on core values, beliefs, and skills. The rituals solidified the new identity, helping individuals figure out how to function and fit into the community as adults. They also evoked a sense of awe and created a lasting and powerful image.

A modern version of an effective ritual is the one Sarah Kilmer experienced. Sarah was a young foreigner living in Switzerland when she started her period. She felt awkward, terrified, and very much alone except for her mother and her mother's friends. These women prepared her for the onset of menstruation and arranged for her to go on a vision quest. On the day of her first period, she eagerly went home after school to tell her mother. They gave her a chocolate party first, celebrating and congratulating her as the new woman in the group. In preparation for her quest, Sarah fasted for four days. On the fourth day, they left her on the porch of a deserted cottage where she spent the night. It was winter, and snow covered the surrounding area. She wrote:

> My company that night were the trees and the stars. I was even told to take off my watch and to tell time by the stars. Alone and wide-eyed, I scoped out my terrain and watched the stars appear, one by one. The crisp night air and the clarity of my sharpened mind added to my feeling of alertness. This, plus the slight edge of fear, made it impossible for me to sleep, impossible to do anything but stay awake and wonder. Why am I doing this? What do they expect me to discover about myself? It was all a mystery, but I was completely in the element of my solitude. Many, many nights hence have I longed to be whisked away, back in to that element, back on that mountain. . . .
>
> My life was transformed that night. . . . I consider myself very fortunate for having the opportunity to experience that night of my vision quest. I was holding a vigil and making a truce with myself. I decided to be reborn as a more dignified woman, and that is exactly what happened.[20]

Sarah's experience gave her a sense of awe and left a lasting impression on her.

Van Gennep identifies three elements of rites of passage that were present in Sarah's ritual: (1) separation, (2) transition rites, and (3) rites of incorporation.[21] Many modern-day rituals have been modeled after these three elements.

Avoiding Mistakes

People can err by responding in one of two ways to traditional practices. We can embrace them unquestionably and idealize them or reject them out of hand and consider them barbaric. Both are mistakes. We need to avoid the noble savage syndrome by not romanticizing and idealizing traditional rituals. To embrace them unquestioningly is to forget that sin permeates everything, including rituals that belonged to African or Indian tribal people or medieval knights. Some rituals reinforced the consequences of the fall—legitimizing aggression and oppression, teaching boys that winning mattered most, that winners could name and claim their prize, even if it exploited or oppressed others. Some rituals taught boys to suppress and deny emotion, pain, and fear. Some rituals taught girls that menstruation was a curse, that they were unclean, that they needed to have their clitoris cut off so their passions would not control them. Some rituals reinforced and reproduced gender roles for boys and girls that reflected a broken culture rather than godly community. We want rituals that ensure a transition into adulthood that connects children to others with a strong sense of belonging, identity, and obligation for others.

We also err if we reject traditional rituals out of hand. We can, in fact, look reflectively at the underlying values of particular elements of rituals that may have something to say to us. For example, traditional rituals were held in the context of community; children were initiated together by the community. In contrast, contemporary rituals are focused on the individual and have very little connection to a broader community. Traditional rituals took time and involved training, preparing, and taking a test or facing a challenge. Contemporary rituals are often one-time events that take place over the course of a day, an evening, or an hour. Traditional rituals involved real tasks to be mastered and a quest to complete. Contemporary quests are "virtual journeys," that is, mythical or imagined connections to a knight or warrior or priestess or adventurer.

Effective rites of passage evoke awe and leave a lasting impression. Those most likely to do so happen within the context of a supporting community; they incorporate training, preparation, and real challenge or testing, and include a clear vision for adulthood that outlines rights and responsibilities.

A final caution is about the pursuit of a spiritual, personal experience. Spirituality is a popular pursuit, and so is personal growth; rites of passage promise both, as they are deeply spiritual and personal events. Contemporary rites of passage tend to focus on individual growth and reflection, seldom on obligation or connection to a larger community.

David Oldfield, director of the Center for Creative Imagination in Washington, D.C., developed "The Journey," a program for adolescent boys and girls.[22] The Journey takes adolescents on a five-stage imaginative adventure to help them overcome crises of adolescence. Spiritual quest is combined with personal reflection and symbolic storytelling. Participants craft a story, relying on the power of imagination to transform, shape, and change them as they reflect on what it means to come into adulthood. Participants discover themselves and figure out their own path, direction, and way.

The Journey has been helpful for many of its participants, yet it deviates from traditional rituals in a number of significant ways. Most important, The Journey focuses on the individual, without emphasizing or strengthening the bond that adolescents have to their parents and grandparents, aunts and uncles—to some community outside themselves and their peer group with whom they share a heritage.

Most white, middle-class North Americans are not, in fact, looking for an initiation ritual that requires them to connect with their heritage or a community of people, nor are they looking to increase their obligation and social responsibility. However, connecting with community has always been important for people of color in North America, providing positive models of manhood and womanhood that are culturally sensitive and self-affirming—models not typically available through media or other social institutions. One African American woman said she asked her daughter where she gets information about how to be a woman, and all her examples were of black women and black institutions.

For most white, middle-class North Americans, rites of passage lead to personal growth and self-enhancement; they promise adult identity and spiritual competence. Yet connecting to a larger community and recognizing increased obligation and social responsibility were also central components of traditional initiation rites, giving them staying power and effectiveness.

Individualism, however, encourages the pursuit of self-fulfillment. If community obligation becomes onerous, we are told that our psychological health depends on our ability to disregard that community and pursue our dreams. Rites of passage can become narcissistic efforts to find oneself, to assert and legitimate one's chosen path. In contrast, the wisdom of traditional rites of passage bonded children to the community, creating a strong sense of belonging and a place where longings could be sanctioned and satisfied. God made us for relationship, for community; God made us to serve and be served. In finding a place in community rather than pursuing a life of self-fulfillment, loneliness and alienation are assuaged.

The Ritual-Crafting Process

What then, is necessary for ritual rites of passage to effectively provide boys and girls a transition through the physical, sexual, spiritual, and psychological confusion of adolescence? Ronald Grimes, a professor who researches rituals, suggests that rituals should be rooted in language, region, time, and culture, not adaptations of bygone eras that are irrelevant to today's culture.[23] Much of the stuff of rites of passage is ordinary—things we already do that are so embedded in our culture we don't think of them as ritual. When Rae and Sarah wanted to learn how to knit, teaching them passed something of my heritage along. Mark taught Megan some basketball skills and has gone with several offspring to buy their first car, instructing them in negotiation and discernment. When parents and churches teach children the value of loyalty and respect for authority, and when they encourage the development of friendship and introduce them to the God who pursues them, they are strengthening connections children have to others. Teaching children to take responsibility for their education and to become involved in civil and religious communities reinforces the importance of functioning in community.

To recognize these ordinary aspects of parenting as "training" and to become intentional about what we are teaching our children are *a priori* steps toward developing a rite of passage. Using times when transitions occur to punctuate the training allows children to demonstrate their acquisition of new skills and their ability to incorporate physical changes into their identity. Rather than setting an age as the criterion for moving to some new status, Robert Eckert, a holistic therapist, says parents must set evidence of appropriate emotional maturity, ethical behavior choices, and problem-solving skills as standards.[24] Ceremonies marking transitions then rise above the ordinary to set it off as significant. In rising above the ordinary, the ceremony should connect the individual to some larger history, community, and obligation. For Christians, the community of faith is a natural choice.

Contemporary Rites of Passage for Females

Parents create rituals for their daughters, though we may not recognize them as such. Rites of passage do not have to be exotic to be real. When we told our daughters they could pierce their ears at age eleven, we marked their growing up with a ritual of sorts. At sixteen, they could double the number of holes in their head. At eighteen, they were on their own—our acknowledgment that with greater responsibility came more rights. (During the height of the piercing craze, Mark tallied the hole count among his three daughters and wife and came up with a total of twenty-nine. I think he was exaggerating. At any rate, we're back down to something more reasonable now.)

We also gave each of our daughters a ring on their thirteenth birthday, symbolizing a shifting of their primary focus from our relationship with them to their relationship with God and peers. With it, we recognized their ability to develop solid and healthy friendships, and they expressed an ongoing desire to make God-honoring decisions in relationships and life choices. We are not without ritual in our culture, but our focus, intentions, and goals are sometimes fuzzy as we find ourselves making up rituals linked neither to heritage nor a larger community.

A woman at our church, Gina LaRusso, wanted to offer her daughter something poignant that would also connect her to a larger community. For Adrianna's thirteenth birthday, Gina wrote a letter to twenty women who had known Adrianna and asked them to write letters that celebrated her as a young Christian woman and encouraged her to continue to pursue God and to develop her gifts. She encouraged them to share from their own experiences and to include their memories of Adrianna, listing things that set her apart from others. Gina compiled these in a book that included pictures of Adrianna, a page filled with words, phrases, and pictures depicting fifty traits of Adrianna's character, lyrics from a song her father wrote for her birthday, a poem from her mother, a letter from her younger sister, a page of quotes, and a final family photo.

Adrianna was quite moved by this gift and read it carefully. Gina says it has caused her to reflect on who she wants to be as she reads the carefully crafted words of women who are encouraging and surrounding her with their letters.

The goal of female-affirming rituals is to name the blessing and responsibility of being women, to assert the right to guide how girls think about themselves as women, and to draw girls into a larger community. The female connection to others is a literal one. She gives life, nurtures the young, nurtures new mothers, and offers guidance and counsel to mothers of adolescent daughters. And she is a wellspring of wisdom in her old age, as one who has lived with the suffering of the world and seen a gracious God who is always working to draw people to God and to others. By surrounding each other in intentionally supportive ceremonies, women encourage the collective wisdom of walking with God to benefit each new generation. The task for women is to think creatively about how to facilitate these kinds of interactions in extended families, in churches, and in friendship groups.

Rituals that affirm sexuality by thanking God for and celebrating the gift of the female body reclaim menstruation as a blessing rather than a curse. I wear my grandmother's original wedding ring, which has a red stone, when I menstruate. The ring reminds me of and connects me to the lineage of women through whom I came and am a part and pass on through my daughters. I try to keep my schedule light during my period, to allow more time for reflection and rest. I honor my body and the way God made it in these simple rituals. Rituals that honor a body capable of giving birth, acknowledge a cycle that embodies our living, and welcome the wisdom associated with aging serve to rename a curse and call it blessing.

Contemporary Rites of Passage for Males

If menstruation is the curse in need of redemption for women, the definition of manhood as tough, invulnerable, and sexually uncontrollable is the curse in need of redemption for men. Traditional rituals addressed questions like these: What skills do I need to learn? What stories should I know? How am I to think about who I am? How do I fit into the larger community? Helping boys answer these questions in ways that affirm their desire to gain competence and to test their skills against others while drawing them into authentic relationships with others renames the curse a blessing.

Parents of all religious backgrounds create rites of passage for their sons. In most cases, they are unfamiliar with traditional rituals or programs such as Oldfield's Journey. We intrinsically know there are stories to tell, skills to pass on, and preparation for change and transition. Some relinquish the task to other cultural institutions; others desire to share their aptitudes and interests in athletics, history, mechanics, logic, or music with their sons, passing on a heritage their fathers gave to them.

Robert Lewis, author of *Raising a Modern-Day Knight,* dealt with the ambiguity surrounding raising his sons to be men by developing a contemporary rite of passage he adopted from medieval times.[25] He developed a code of conduct—a counterpart to the medieval code of knights—and identified three values he wanted to instill in his sons that he believed moved a boy toward authentic manhood: (1) a will to obey (God's will), (2) a work to do (according to his own unique design), and (3) a woman to love. Lewis uses a rite of passage ceremony, only after a period of instruction, to mark the completion of training and the readiness for a new set of responsibilities and rights. They are the exclamation point of training; he says they are the culmination.

Chester Higgins Jr. incorporated aspects of a traditional ritual in one he crafted for his twenty-year-old son. They went on a three-week trip to Egypt and Ethiopia, exploring the past and present of their heritage. While there, he thought about and developed a ritual he hoped would connect his son with his African roots. Inside one of the tombs of an Eighteenth Dynasty Pharaoh, he performed the ceremony. He faced his son and did the following:

> I poured the sand he had collected into the palm of my left hand, and with my right I anointed the top of his head with this sand. Looking into his eyes, I said:

"I, your father, anoint the crown of your head with the soil of Africa. This piece of earth is a symbol of the lives of your ancestors. It is a bonding of their lives to yours. Like your father, you too are African. We are Africans not because we are born in Africa, but because Africa is born in us. Look around you and behold us in our greatness. Greatness is an African possibility; you can make it yours. Just as the great ones before you have by their deeds placed their names on history, so can you by your deeds, place your name on tomorrow. You now have the rest of your life to benefit from this new awareness."[26]

An example of a community-based program for African American males is the National Rites of Passage Institute in Cleveland, Ohio. The founder, Paul Hill Jr., incorporates African-centered worldviews into extensive training of moral principles.[27] Unity, self-determination, collective work and responsibility, cooperative economics, purpose, creativity, faith, and respect are instilled during the training process. Boys are instructed two to four hours per week for one to three years. They are separated from other routines, taught by elders, connected with nature, taught peer cooperation, and given instruction in personal, sexual, spiritual, and political matters. An extensive African-centric ceremony marks their completion of the training. Jefferson Jones, who completed the program said, "Rites of Passage is a 101 Course. It gives us a reminder, a taste of what it is to be a part of a real community."[28]

In the absence of officially sanctioned rites, these emerge as efforts to pass on heritage, to strengthen boys for the challenge ahead, and to discover and make a claim on one's place and contribution in a broader, adult community. As boys shift away from a primary connection with their parents, these rituals give purpose and meaning, encouraging a thoughtful reflection on the connections and choices they make as they seek to become men.

A Personal Rite

My two sisters, my sister-in-law, and I are planning a backpacking trip for the women of the family: four aunts, six nieces, and our mother—a spry sixty-nine-year-old woman who is up for an adventure. We want to mark the transition of our daughters as they move out of our homes and into lives of their own. I envision something like the following.

The first night, we will have Grammy tell the story of our family and the women in our family. She will tell about strengths she admired in her mother and aunts and sisters. The morning hike will include pairing up an aunt to a niece, where the aunt listens to the niece, asks questions that allow her to get to know her better, to draw out her heart and her passions.

The afternoon hike also includes pairing up aunts and nieces, this time the aunt talking about how God has moved through life with her, through challenges, joys, and lessons learned along the way.

One day, we will send the nieces out on a twenty-four-hour solo trip; they will fast and pray and open their hearts to God as they reflect on who they are, who they are becoming, and how they are being called to fit in the context of this extended family and the bigger world that is also theirs. When the nieces return, we will celebrate and feast around a fire and listen to them talk about their solo time. We will prayerfully dedicate them in this next part of their journey to God. Grammy will name some strength she has observed in each granddaughter and offer a spiritual challenge or verse to each one that she, along with the aunts and mothers, have considered during their solo time. As she speaks to each granddaughter, the mother of that daughter will present a token reminder of this event, which will have been prepared ahead of time or perhaps picked up along the way—a ring, a stone, a carving from sticks, or a braid of grass and flowers.

Communities of faith could also organize such events for girls and boys at particular junctions—points of physical change corresponding to changing roles and identities. We are embodied souls and cannot separate our personhood from our body. God created us with longings. In the midst of physical change, we are not always sure how we are to belong and behave with the new possibilities maturing brings. Maturing also brings suffering and hard challenges, but even these can draw us to others, inviting us into a community bigger than ourselves. In that extended family, or church, or small group of committed friends, we can extend and receive grace and companionship for the journey. Although much of this occurs in the everydayness of life, occasionally we punctuate these transitions with ceremony.

Conclusion

The following five principles summarize what constitutes useful rites of passage:

1. Rituals are rooted in one's tradition, faith, and heritage, emerging out of values held by a community and being taught through the ordinariness of life.

2. Skills consistent with those values are taught and tested. Evidence of their being acquired is a necessary part of gaining the rights and responsibilities marking the transition to come.

3. Passages are punctuated with significant ceremonies that name the transition, clearly identifying what one is leaving and what one is moving toward.

4. Ceremonies have a before and after, that is, something has changed, some new right is bestowed that corresponds to skills acquired and responsibilities taken up.

5. Rituals occur in the context of a community, recognizing that individuals are connected to something bigger than they are and obligated to someone besides him- or herself. This connection brings both blessing and responsibility.

How adolescents imagine themselves as women and men will be reflected in the confidence they have about being and becoming adult females or males. How men and women transition through adulthood will also be reflected in the vision of manhood or womanhood crafted for them by the communities in which they live, worship, and work. Punctuating transitions with rituals helps us reaffirm our longings for connection and belonging and find our place in community, where we can pacify longings in ways that reflect our rights and responsibilities, as well as our obligations and blessings.

QUERIES FOR FURTHER REFLECTION AND CONVERSATION

○ What skills and stories were taught to me? What informal rituals do I remember? Are they the same skills and stories I want my children to learn?

○ How did I seek out affirmation or create ritual in the absence of formal rites of passage in my transition from childhood to adolescence, from young adulthood to middle age, and from middle age to mature adulthood?

○ If a ritual in the context of a community is more powerful than one focused on individual achievement, how can we take our celebrations of achievement and craft them into rituals connecting individuals to family or our community of faith?

○ Am I participating in a life-affirming and enriching community?

○ What is the balance between my rights as an individual and my obligations to others, to a community? Do I feel uncomfortable thinking I have obligations to others? If so, why?

○ What could a meaningful rite of passage ceremony look like for a daughter entering puberty? For the group of boys at church who start high school next year? For sisters and sisters-in-law who are entering menopause about the same time? For aunts and uncles, mothers and fathers who are about to retire?

○ If God made us for relationship and gave us longings to keep us striving for relationship, then how have my longings changed over the course of life thus far? To what am I drawn besides relationships? Are these life-affirming or hurtful?

○

ADOLESCENCE

AWAKENINGS AND CHOICES

---

*I was kind of one of those kids who was really
pissed off they missed the '60s.*

—Carol, high school student[1]

*One of the empowering things about the feminist movement is
that we're able to assert ourselves, to say no to sex and not feel
pressured about it.*

—Alice Kunce, college sophomore[2]

MEGAN, KYLE, KARA, KARA'S MOM, AND I were seated near the
front of Oprah's stage. The topic of the day: girls and their abusive
boyfriends. We talked about sex and the assumption that most teenagers
are having sex. Experts talked, and a sixteen-year-old girl who had been
with her abusive boyfriend for several years was interviewed and counseled, on live TV, to leave her boyfriend. They had been sleeping together
for the last year, and he had become increasingly possessive, jealous,
manipulative, and angry. Yet she loved him and could not imagine leaving him, in spite of her mother's and friends' counsel.

After the taping, Oprah facilitated an informal, off-air chat between the audience and speakers, including the sixteen-year-old. Kara raised her hand, and Oprah called on her. She stood up and told the audience that she and Megan and Kyle were seniors in high school and still virgins. "Not all teens are having sex, and we have guy friends who respect us, and themselves, and who aren't having sex either." Oprah commended her and the audience applauded her. Then to the young woman, Kara said, "I am sorry about the situation you are in. You deserve to be treated better than your boyfriend treats you. Don't settle for less; you are worth more." The girl nodded and then replied, "But have you ever been in love? Until you have, you can't know what it's like to leave someone who loves you. He really does love me, even if he doesn't always treat me well."

Adolescence is a time when sexual awakenings begin a lifelong journey of yearning and longing for intimate connection. Negotiating adolescence has long been perceived as dangerous, maneuvering through a field of landmines and hazards. Adults hold their breath and hope and pray for the best. Teens who live under our roofs and in our communities are not only our children but they are the next generation moving humanity into the future. We want them to reach adulthood spiritually, emotionally, and physically healthy and functioning well. But few teens understand what it means to be sexual or to explore and embrace their sexuality apart from having sex. Indeed, most of us struggle to articulate what it means to be sexual apart from sexual intercourse.

The first day of my Sociology of Sexuality class, I hand out index cards and ask students to write (anonymously) what it means for them to be sexual. Most of the students in this class are a few years out of high school but still negotiating the challenges of their awakening sexuality. One student wrote:

> It seems to me that there isn't really a way to be a sexual being at this point in my life, mainly because there are very few ways to appropriately express my sexuality since I am single. I know this probably isn't completely true, but I feel as though sexuality is about repression rather than expression, especially in the Christian subculture. I cannot just go out and have sex, pornography is out of the question, and masturbation is taboo in most cases. So mostly, my sexuality is about repressing the hormonal urges and battling all the media and culture that says sex is important. I really don't know how to be a sexual being at this stage in my life.

I develop the point in this chapter that Christian communities can offer something more satisfying to their youth—an adolescence that allows teens to embrace life and their personhood and moves them toward greater wholeness and health. We can start by recognizing and validating their longings and then offering ways of exploring sexuality other than sexually acting out with boyfriends and girlfriends. Adolescence is more than a time of danger when teens get pregnant or infected, or become addicted, depressed, or hugely rebellious. Adolescence is primarily a time of awakenings and choices, of opportunities and the refining of one's identity.

Teenagers are not so different from the rest of us. They long, as we do, to be connected, to be in relationship, to belong, to be loved and accepted. But teens in our culture typically separate from parents and disconnect from family and society. They fill the vacuum that is left by seeking alternative ways of connection. Gangs substitute for losses associated with the family and provide a sense of belonging, loyalty, and safety. Adolescents who try drugs and alcohol may be responding to peer pressure out of a desire to be accepted, to belong. They may be escaping the excruciating loneliness of an existence that is empty of life-affirming and life-giving relationships. Some may be doing this because nothing in adolescence engages them; others may feel driven to prove themselves as autonomous and independent.

Driver's education teachers cloak conversations about teen behaviors in fear, giving information about drinking and driving while showing bloody footage of accident victims. Sex education teachers talk about STDs and flash pictures of lesions on the screen. A healthy dose of fear-invoking consequences is not bad, but it is insufficient. We can offer adolescents something more. We can infuse teens with a desire to aspire to something ultimately more satisfying—an adolescence that allows them to embrace life fully while honoring and respecting their own and each other's lives and sexuality.

Cultural Ambivalence About Sex

It is not surprising that teens are uncertain about what they should be about during adolescence. Our culture, too, is unsure. A dramatic shift in ideas about teen sex and sexuality emerged with the sexual revolution of the late 1960s and early 1970s that led to a spectrum of perspectives. Some fight for greater sexual freedom and autonomy for teens, as do the authors of *Harmful to Minors: The Perils of Protecting Children from Sex*. The authors assert that teens should be allowed to unlock the door to sex and explore and embrace their sexuality. Teaching safe sex is more realistic, they say, and a better message than teaching abstinence based on puritan right-wing ideals.[3]

Others fight to empower adolescents to control their sexuality by embracing the sacredness of sex and respect for self and others by reserving intercourse for a committed monogamous relationship. Susan Browning Pogany assumes that teen sex introduces an assortment of problems adolescents could do without. She offers a pragmatic approach to sex that encourages teens to embrace abstinence.[4]

Both ends of the spectrum believe they have the best interests of adolescents in mind. Both want to smooth the road of adolescence and create confident, caring individuals who pass to adulthood unscathed by the dangers lurking in adolescence. Everyone's hope for adolescence is that teens develop healthy, responsible ways to be sexual beings. As communities legitimately concerned about life from conception to death, faith communities are well positioned to be participants in the process of developing sexually healthy teens. How people of faith believe that is best accomplished is influenced by assumptions and beliefs about freedom, choice, and responsibility as it relates to sexuality. Many of our assumptions and beliefs have been filtered down and shaped by our history, and stepping off the stage to explore them can inform and strengthen our approaches to working with teens during this time of sexual awakening.

Sexuality Before the Sixties

The physical and social costs for sex prior to the 1960s were high for teenage girls. Minors were not supposed to be able to walk into drug stores and purchase condoms. The pill was not yet available, and, for the most part, neither were abortions. Teen girls ran a high risk for getting pregnant, and once that happened, a girl's alternatives were limited. White girls who hoped for later marriage to a good man gave their babies up for adoption; black girls did not assume marriage was in their future and were more likely to keep their babies.

Middle-class boys grew up knowing they were supposed to get responsible jobs so they could take care of their families. Girls would become mothers and homemakers. The rigid role expectations perpetuated a double standard for sexual purity. Girls gained social status by being popular and getting asked out on dates but lost status if they let boys go "too far." Some degree of "petting" and "necking" was expected; intercourse would definitely damage her reputation and compromise her ability to secure a good husband later.

Sexually active boys, however, were not encumbered with the stigma of a damaged reputation. Indeed, having sex gained them status in the eyes of their peers. Prior to the sexual revolution, 47 percent of boys and 31 percent of girls reported having sex before their eighteenth birthday.[5]

Other developments preceded and set the stage for the sexual revolution; it did not occur in a vacuum. Upheaval defined much of the 1960s in Western Europe and North America, and television shrunk the globe. People in Wisconsin, Minnesota, Vermont, and Oregon could watch the injustices inflicted on blacks in the South and listen to Martin Luther King Jr. plead for justice on the nightly news. People in Nevada, New Hampshire, and Alaska saw soldiers trudge through the underbrush of Vietnam and watched antiwar demonstrations across the nation. University students became activists, adding people power and voice to the civil rights movement, the women's rights movement, the gay rights movement, and, most notably, Vietnam War protests. Television and the free press made people aware of each other and significant issues at home and abroad in unprecedented fashion. Protest movements and antiestablishment sentiments flourished and spread throughout Europe and North America.

The Sexual Revolution

The sixties youth began looking at the establishment and its values with disdain. Individual rights, self-expression and autonomy, and the pursuit of self-fulfillment set the ideological groundwork for a sexual revolution.

Contraception and Freedom

The introduction of the birth control pill in 1960, as well as the legalization of abortion in 1973, minimized some of the negative costs of sex outside marriage for women. Many were saying, "Down with the double standard that calls men who had sex studs and women who had sex sluts." Women could be as free to express themselves sexually as men.

Woodstock, a three-day rock concert attended by 500,000 people in August 1969, became an icon of the sexual revolution. Sex and music were dispersed freely in the name of love, along with a variety of drugs that enhanced the experience. The general parental response to Woodstock proved that parents would never, *could* never understand the groovy youth culture of the day. The Christian church was out of touch, too. Catholics refused to budge on the use of contraceptives. And although Protestants had reluctantly approved the use of contraceptives in the 1930s, they could not agree on the Vietnam War or civil rights. Some seemed to assume that any protest movement insulted the integrity of the nation and the Church, so down with the Church! Watergate confirmed the belief that the government could not be trusted. Authority attempted to sanction freedom in a desperate, illegitimate effort to cling to power. Down with the establishment! Down with government!

Equality for Women

Some proponents attempted to fit Karl Marx's ideas about class oppression and Freud's psychoanalytical themes of sexual repression into the fabric of the sexual revolution. They hoped that adopting the popular language of oppression and repression would give the movement legitimacy. Capitalism was perceived as that which sexually repressed the masses by being confined to a heterosexual family and packaged with moral puritanism, hard work, and sexual restraint. In contrast, spontaneous sexual expression was perceived to offer freedom, to break down the oppression of the masses. Defending the sacredness of sex was a tool of the oppressors, socially constructed "meanings" that could be as easily dismantled as they were crafted. Individuals, autonomy, and self-expression were the new sacred ideals. Predictably, the sexual behaviors and attitudes of youth changed as people determined new costs and benefits to the risks and rewards of premarital sexual activity.

During the sexual revolution, teen girls were told they could enjoy the same sexual freedom boys had. Girls too could have sex and gain status in the eyes of their peers rather than be stigmatized for it. Their obligation was to themselves, and commitments to religious or family values were optional, old-fashioned, and better left behind.

Having sex with multiple partners allowed girls as well as boys to explore their sexuality and learn what pleased them. Officially (though perhaps not unofficially), the double standard was demolished. In her book *Promiscuities,* Naomi Wolf tells stories of girls, including herself, who came of age during the sexual revolution, claiming their right to explore their sexuality.[6] The gap between sexual activity for boys and girls narrowed; 60 percent of males and 53 percent of females who came of age during or shortly after the sexual revolution said they had sex before their eighteenth birthday.[7]

Aftermath of the Revolution

The ideological engine driving the sexual revolution began sputtering out in the 1980s for several reasons.

First, AIDS emerged on the scene in 1980, sobering the world and introducing new costs and risks to sexual activity. In the 1950s, syphilis and gonorrhea were the primary STDs that doctors treated for teens. Thirty years later, doctors know about and can treat over twenty-five STDs, now generally referred to as STIs (sexually transmitted infections). Increased awareness about AIDS and other STIs has sobered would-be sexually active teens and their parents. Caution has become more important than sexual expression; sexual experiences are no longer assumed to be without cost.

Second, teens began seeing girl friends' aspirations for college and a career evaporate as they exchanged diplomas for diapers. Nine of out ten pregnant girls do not graduate from college.[8] Adolescents have less guarantee of the "good life" than their parents did, and some see what is happening around them and respond by focusing on achieving careers.

Third, welfare reform has made it more difficult for boys to walk away from the children they father. Now all fifty states require that every birth certificate include both the mother and father's Social Security number. A father's wages can be garnisheed to support any children he fathers. If he is unemployed, back payments build up until he is employed. Policy changes in welfare reform reflect a government that now expects boys to take financial responsibility for their children.

How much these realities have contributed to lower rates of both pregnancy and sexual activity is difficult to determine, but the numbers in the last ten years have been encouraging. In 1990, the number of teens becoming pregnant began declining. In 2001, we had the lowest teen pregnancy rate in the United States since 1976.[9] From 1991 to 2001, the percentage of high school students who had ever had sex decreased by 16 percent. Just over half of all high school girls were sexually active in 1991. This gradually dropped over the decade to about 43 percent in 2001. In the same time period, boys dropped from 57.4 percent to 48.5 percent.[10]

Postrevolution Morals

We are now in a post-sexual-revolution period, returning to something that resembles prerevolution morals. The return, however, is for pragmatic reasons, not ideological or theological ones. Postmodern ideology teaches us to acknowledge that there is more than one way to live well. We are taught to value diverse ideas and to give legitimacy to most of them. This is a good shift away from ethnocentric thinking that said our particular way of setting up an economic system, enjoying a church service, doing art or music, or having babies and raising them was best. It challenges us to be teachable, to embrace the wisdom that comes from diverse perspectives and backgrounds. But postmodernity is a double-edged sword for those of us committed to a single faith tradition.

Sex as Biology

When postmodern ideas extend to a theological understanding of the human soul, Christians wisely examine the differences in our underlying assumptions about what it means to be embodied souls. As Christians, we believe we are made in the image of God and are taught how best to live incarnationally by following the example of Jesus—the only perfect model for living as one bearing the image of God.

A contemporary example of a tolerant view that lacks a theological understanding of the human soul is *Sex Matters for College Students*—a handbook for students that describes normal sexual behavior. "As long as sexual behavior is found enjoyable, and is acceptable to the people involved, it is okay, whatever the behavior."[11] In a Q&A format, the author, Sandra Caron, helps students overcome shame and recognize that all sexual behavior is intended for pleasure and is normal and acceptable. She does admit that some behaviors introduce risk and says precautions ought to be taken (that is, condoms should be used). In a tolerant way, she discusses virginity and says, "It is important to remember that virginity, like sexual activity, is a matter of choice. Some men and women choose to wait until they are in what they consider a long-term relationship before they become sexually involved and some do not."[12]

A lingering belief from the sexual revolution is that sex is just a biological activity, without intrinsic meaning. If I assert that sex has meaning, I am only giving voice to one opinion among many. Prior to the sexual revolution, the Church taught, and it was broadly accepted, that sex was deeply spiritual. The sexual aspect of a person was an essential, integral part of being human, and an individual's sexuality had implications for society: people did not have the right to be sexually active in whatever way they wanted. Public policies and laws were enacted to control sex outside marriage. Some laws about premarital and extramarital sex and sodomy are still on the books, such as laws governing the conditions under which sex between two people is statutory rape, the age at which people can marry, prostitution, the limitation of men to one wife, and the steps for those pursuing divorces.

Sex as a Personal Choice

The more secular societies became (moving away from recognizing the Church's authority in determining matters of everyday life), the more sex came to be seen as a private matter between consenting participants. Under a new ideology supporting privacy and personal choice, public policy had no business in matters of private life. Changes in no-fault divorce law reflect this shift. As a private matter, any meaning given to sex was up to the participants. If participants wanted to view sex as just a biological activity of bodies, no particular significance had to be granted it. Shame was a leftover control trick of the Church and remnants of a puritan society, and the sooner people could shake shame, the more pleasurable they would find sex. Even though more teens began choosing abstinence, many of the teens choosing abstinence have acknowledged that their choice is simply one privately made choice among many other viable choices.

Boys still receive more peer pressure to become sexually active than girls.[13] Former NBA player A. C. Green became a spokesperson for abstinence, offering encouragement to boys who otherwise felt ostracized from their peers. Daniela, a twenty-year-old committed to abstinence, said, "My boyfriend's coach gave it [an article about A. C. Green] to him because the other guys sometimes say, 'Are you gay? What's wrong with you?' It's proof that if a famous man like Green can do it, so can he."[14]

The number-one reason boys gave for wanting to have sex was curiosity and feeling ready for sex. Girls said it was affection for their partner. Ninety-two percent of males in the National Health and Social Life Survey said they wanted their first sex to happen when it did. They anticipated, wanted, and felt ready for sex; only 71 percent of females said the same.[15] Most of the 29 percent who did not want sex were not raped but felt pressured and unable to say no.

A student in one of my classes wrote the following; she gave me permission to share it. Her story is a common one.

> My history is a rough one sexually. My freshman year my boyfriend said he'd break up with me if I didn't kiss him. After much debate and anger, I eventually ended up kissing him, and from there it went downhill. I completely related to the concept of "lost voice" in the Neal/Mangis article we read in class. He began to do things to me, while inside I was dying and hated it. Then he'd ask me to do things that I really didn't want to do at all, but eventually would give in. There was never any abuse at all physically, but definite pressure. I totally felt like I should please him and deep down I somehow felt that I owed it to him. At the end of my freshman year, we had done everything except intercourse and then he broke up with me. I was devastated. My junior year I started dating another guy and after a while he was pressuring me to do more than kissing, then more and more. I decided to break up with him because of this but then he apologized so I got back together with him. He was so nice that I felt bad and wanted to please him, so I did what he wanted. At the end of my junior year I lost my virginity and cried and cried. He said he felt so bad and promised it would never happen again. The next day he did it again, and I let him. I was raised in a wonderful home and my parents and I have always tried to figure out why I did what I did.

A study of one thousand high school students explored the circumstances of their first sexual experience: half of them were in an exclusive dating relationship; a quarter were casually dating someone they knew well; a quarter were also using drugs or drinking alcohol; three-quarters were either at their parents' home or a friend's house when they had sex. Perhaps of most significance, half say they wished they had waited longer before having sex.[16]

Awakenings and Choices About Premarital Sex

Sexual awakenings and choices are themes of adolescence, and a compelling pop media culture encourages teens to satisfy their curiosity and longings by exploring sexuality through sexual behaviors. However, seldom do teens hear messages from the media regarding how to make decisions about sex or potential consequences of premarital sexual behaviors.

In fact, not all teens do have sex; increasing numbers are choosing *not* to. The question often weighing on their minds is, "How far is too far?" It is a practical question, but finding a standard by which to answer it is challenging. Leonore Tiefer summarizes five standards, or underlying assumptions, used to answer similar questions about "normal" sexual behavior.[17]

Jill asks Jane whether or not she thinks "doing oral sex on a boy is going too far." Suppose Jane has given oral sex to boys and says, "It's not too far. You can still be a virgin and do oral sex." If she is basing her answer on her own behavior (and we justify our behavior this way all the time), she is using a *subjectively normal behavior* assumption. Anything similar to one's own behavior is normal.

If Jane says, "It's not too far. I read in our sex-ed textbook that almost all teens do it now-a-days," she is using a *statistically normal behavior* assumption. What is common equals what is "normal."

Now suppose Jane has not participated in oral sex and is deeply religious. She may say, "Oral sex is definitely going too far because my church [mosque/synagogue] says it's still sex. The Bible [Koran/Torah] says it's wrong to have sex outside of marriage," she is using an *idealistically normal behavior* assumption that measures all behavior against an ideal standard.

Jane may be an astute observer of cultural trends and patterns, as picked up in various teen magazines, reality TV shows, and movies, and may say, "Our culture says oral sex is normal. It didn't used to be back in our parents' time, but things change, they progress." This is a *culturally normal behavior* assumption.

Jane may have recently learned about STIs in her sex-ed class. She may have learned that oral sex, contrary to popular belief, does not protect participants from certain STIs, most notably the infamous HPV and, for girls, herpes. Thus she tells Jill, "It's going too far because you still might get infected with an STI." This answer uses a *clinically normal behavior* assumption. If the behavior causes unhealthy physical consequences, it is not "normal." According to Tiefer, only the clinically normal behavior assumption is an objective criterion for determining whether a behavior is considered normal and thus good.

The Christian View

To a large degree, the clinically normal behavior assumption supports Christian morals. But as Christians, we do not define our morals only on the basis of scientific data—in this case, on unhealthy physical consequences. Rather, we hold to a theologically informed standard shaped by our understanding of God and humans, and of God's intentions for human relationships. Although our understanding is not perfect, and some of our views change over time, Christians generally believe that God intends men and women to express their sexual freedom fully and freely within the context of marriage.

Adolescents get themselves in trouble when they do one of two things: (1) they confuse love with sex or (2) they are driven by the pleasure of sex. When they confuse love and sex (which they see happen in movies like *Titanic* and watch on television shows like *Sex in the City*) they engage in sex to get love, to keep love, to affirm love. "Sex is OK," they reason, "so long as we're in love." The other direction is to be driven by the pleasure of sex, as if love has nothing to do with it. So-called buddy sex is recreational sex among adolescent friends. Buddy sex carries no meaning, no commitment, no obligation.

When adolescents engage in sex to gain love and acceptance, or purely for pleasure, they seldom consider the physical or spiritual consequences of their choices. Instructing teens about consequences of sexual activity is an important part of instructing them about sex. Knowledge and information allow them to make informed choices. Yet information alone is insufficient—necessary but not adequate to inspire them to reach for something more satisfying. Inspiration then follows instruction, offering teens a vision for their adolescent years that encourages a full life, unencumbered by consequences of premarital sex.

Choices and Their Consequences

"My life is pretty much screwed up," Rachel told our Sociology of Sexuality class. She was a teen mom and a new spokesperson-educator for a community-based program that provides services and mentoring to teen parents and their children.[18] Rachel was nineteen, trying to finish her GED and working to support herself and Jacki, her two-year-old daughter. "I learned that you are more likely to get infected the earlier you start to have sex. I started at thirteen and slept around and partied and got pregnant at sixteen. I'm trying to make a life for Jacki and me. But I just found out I may have cervical cancer." She spoke in a matter-of-fact voice that did not betray whatever emotion lurked beneath her words. After the three teen parents left, a student asked if we could pray for them. Their prayers reflected a sense of concern and sorrow for these teenagers trying to parent well.

Teenagers confront choices about their sexual behavior at multiple points. For girls, the potential costs have always been higher than for boys. Because of biological differences, girls are easier to infect, and they carry the risk of pregnancy. A girl's first decision is whether or not to have sex; if she chooses abstinence, her future choices remain open to her. If she chooses to become sexually active, she needs to decide whether or not to use contraceptives. To use them is to admit that she plans to have sex, and that requires her to alter her definition of herself. Not using them increases her likelihood of getting pregnant.

A girl's choices are not usually easy for her to make; sometimes they are not even clear; examples can illustrate some possible results of being a sexually active teen.

The Dilemma of Pregnancy

Although some believe teens ought to be encouraged to be sexually active, and many assume teens *will* be sexually active whether or not they are encouraged to be, no one believes we ought to encourage teenagers to have babies. Teen pregnancy interrupts education for teens and interferes with their healthy development socially, physically, emotionally, and sexually.

If she gets pregnant, a woman can choose to have the baby or abort it. Neither is an easy choice; both incur physical and emotional costs. Aborting the baby is currently being chosen by 40 percent of teen girls who get pregnant (up to another 10 percent miscarry).

Two variables account for a teen's choice to have the baby or to abort: race and her parents' level of education. Black teens are more likely to choose to give birth than white teens. Single parenting is less stigmatized among African Americans, many of whom have less to lose economically and socially. In fact, many black women grow up assuming they will be single mothers. A teen's choice to have the baby is also influenced by her parents' level of education. The more education her parents have, the less likely it is she will give birth.[19] These parents perceive their daughter as having much to lose by having a baby. By encouraging her to have an abortion, they protect her future and perhaps their reputation as well.

If a teen chooses to have the baby, she decides whether to raise it herself or to place it for adoption. Again, both choices are costly. Some believe the greatest sacrifice a teen can make is to give up educational and career goals, and potentially marriage, and assume the responsibility of parenting and caring for her child. Four out of five mothers who choose this path will live in poverty for at least ten years. Most of these women (along with their children) will live below the poverty line for the rest of their lives. The stigma for keeping a child has diminished greatly since the sexual revolution, and currently almost all (97 to 98 percent) teens who choose to have their babies decide to keep them.

The 2 to 3 percent who place their babies for adoption believe the greatest sacrifice they can make is to give their child a family and, with it, the hope of emotional and financial stability. But giving up one's child to another woman to mother is a costly sacrifice. The young mother bears whatever shame there is of pregnancy, as well as the physical and emotional cost of pregnancy and birth, knowing she will not keep the child for herself. Mothers who do so are going against the current trend, and some face criticism for relinquishing their child.

Adoption

Marcia is one mother who felt certain that adoption was the best thing she could do for her son.

Marcia became pregnant at fourteen and faced only bad options, so she tried to have an abortion. She was lying on a table at a clinic, her feet in stirrups, before the doctor determined she was too far along in her pregnancy for that particular abortion procedure. By the time she had rescheduled another appointment for a different procedure, she was again too far along for that procedure. Six months pregnant and unable to get an abortion, Marcia and her boyfriend decided she would have the baby and place it for adoption. "Raising the child was never an option—I was fifteen; my boyfriend was seventeen. I came from a crazy home, and I wanted a normal home for my child."

The young couple found The Cradle, an adoption agency in Evanston, Illinois, where they pursued an open adoption. Marcia's son is now seven and she sees him every few months. "My son's adoptive mother is great. She became a mentor for me through some pretty tough years. I was my son's primary babysitter for a while."

I asked if now that she was married she had any regrets about placing her son for adoption. "I have no regrets at all. My son has a wonderful family. I could not have provided that for him at fifteen."

I asked Marcia what she would say to a pregnant girl now. "I am against abortion now, but am still unsure whether or not it should be illegal. I talk to them about the grieving process of abortion. Every woman I have talked to who has decided to have her child has also decided to keep her baby. Sometimes I have a problem trying to pressure people to do what I did. I feel like I did the best thing for my son's future, and also for mine."

Girls who place their babies for adoption make a sacrificial choice for the sake of their children. They could assert their right to keep their babies; they have, after all, given much to these children by carrying them to term and giving them life. Adoption is an unpopular option these days, yet it is a redemptive option that allows birth mothers a chance to finish growing up before they attempt to mother a child and children a chance to grow up in stable families.

STIs

While pregnancy may be a parent's worst fear as a consequence of their daughter's sexual activity, it is far more likely she will contract one or more STIs, some of which are life-threatening. A legacy of the sexual revolution has been an explosion of sexually transmitted infections. One out of every thirty-two graduating seniors in the class of 1967 carried an STI, and one could have sex with a number of partners before contracting a disease. In 1996, one out of four high school seniors carried at least one STI; the average sexually active teen carried two or three.[20]

Most adults who graduated from high school before 1975 have little knowledge of the increasing STI rate and explosion of varieties of STIs in the last thirty years. The sexual landscape for teens today is significantly different from what it was for my generation. For their sake and for the sake of our communities, adults are wise to become familiar with the new landscape. That way, we will better understand the questions that shape the conversations we have with adolescents.

Although AIDS might have started a scare that slowed sexual promiscuity, AIDS is not the greatest threat to teens' health. Far more common yet far less discussed are several easily transmitted STIs that have life-threatening and life-altering implications. Some of these STIs are viruses and cannot be cured; once they are contracted, one has them for life. The most common STI is the human papilloma virus (HPV), which causes genital warts. In males, this means that warts appear on the genitals periodically throughout life, but these can be burned off at the doctor's office. Genital warts are not life threatening for them. However, these warts can develop on a woman's cervix, and without routine gynecological exams and Pap smears, she may never know she's infected. HPV is the leading cause of cervical cancer, resulting in hysterectomies for women in their twenties and early thirties; 90 percent of cervical cancers are caused by HPV. More women die of cervical cancer every year than AIDS; almost half (47 percent) of sexually active teens are infected with HPV. Intercourse is not required to pass on this virus; any contact with the genitals can infect an uninfected person. Increasingly, teens are substituting oral sex and mutual masturbation for vaginal sex, assuming these behaviors will protect them from pregnancy (which they do) and STIs (which they do not).

The most common bacterial STI is chlamydia. Although bacterial infections can often be treated and cured, 85 percent of those who have chlamydia do not know it and are not treated. Thus the infection can cause pelvic inflammatory disease, which scars fallopian tubes and the lining of the uterus. Eggs (both fertilized and unfertilized) have difficulty moving through scarred fallopian tubes, which increases the risk for tubal pregnancies. Fertilized eggs, or embryos, that make it to the uterus need to attach to the uterine wall, but embryos cannot attach to scar tissue. If a girl contracts chlamydia once and is treated for it, her chances of getting pregnant later in life have been reduced 25 percent. She gets it twice and her chances of getting pregnant drop to 50 percent. If she gets it three times, she will likely be infertile.[21]

Other common bacterial STIs include gonorrhea, which can lead to infertility, and syphilis, which if untreated can lead to nervous system, brain, or heart problems, or possibly death. Herpes simplex virus or (genital herpes) is another common viral infection; one out of every four women and men will become infected with herpes during their lifetime.[22]

HIV has been given much attention since its emergence in the 1980s. In the United States, the disease spread rapidly through the homosexual male population and among drug users who injected with shared needles. Currently, the greatest increase in HIV infections is in the heterosexual population. In 1996, the Centers for Disease Control and Prevention estimated that one out of every three hundred individuals over the age of thirteen tests positive for HIV. This means they carry the virus, even if they do not yet have symptoms of AIDS, which is incurable. About half of those infected since 1992 develop AIDS within ten years of being infected. Research continues for an effective vaccine, and meanwhile other research has led to the development of drugs that inhibit the virus from developing into AIDS.

Although AIDS is of grave concern in the developed world, it is of graver concern in parts of Africa and Asia where it has decimated populations. We need to continue to teach teens about AIDS in the United States, and we must bear our responsibility to address AIDS elsewhere as members of the global community. But to focus sex education prevention primarily on AIDS in the United States is shortsighted. AIDS affects only one in three hundred individuals in the United States, whereas HPV is carried by about half of all sexually active teens.

Abstinence

Many teens choose *not* to have sex. Some adolescents say religion plays a significant role in determining their choice to be abstinent before marriage. Others say they do not feel ready for sex yet. Some stay away from sex for fear of pregnancy or STIs. But an understanding of sex that is inspired by Christianity should move beyond information about negative consequences. Christians are to treat sexuality respectfully and sacredly, because our spiritual life is an embodied life. We see God and embrace ourselves as image-bearers who reflect the character of God. Our proper response is to emulate God—to mature and to conform to the character of God. Inspiration can help us frame our sexuality around a bigger, transcendent picture. Inspiration, given with accurate information, can empower adolescents by anchoring their embodied lives in lived realities.

An Inspirational Vision: Abstinence and Sexuality

Our culture is in a transition stage. The explosion of STIs and an increase in the numbers of children born to teen mothers were unanticipated outcomes of the sexual revolution, and society is eager to find some better way. Most of us have rejected the sexual revolution of the 1960s and are moving cautiously toward some greater moral conservatism. But as a society, we have not yet figured out where we stand or on what we stand. We are unlikely to come to consensus. We still value individualism, and with individualism comes the expectation that the self defines and finds its own form of sexual expression. Authority is not given much swaying power.

This transitional era is a vulnerable time as well as a good opportunity for instruction. We can tell our adolescents that sex outside of marriage is a sin and inside of marriage a gift. We can show them pictures of lesions, boils, and warts. We can give them numbers about infertility and cervical cancer. We can warn them about the dangers of compulsive masturbation. But unless we help them embrace the beauty and sacredness of the image of God within them, encouraging meaningful engagement with others through bodies that are sensual and sexually alive and awake, we stop short.

Our challenge is to reclaim a sacredness of personhood that is wrapped up in adolescents' sexuality but moves beyond sex. Communities of faith can help them find appropriate ways to celebrate the awakening of their desires for sexual intimacy. Desires that are acknowledged and celebrated can be channeled in directions that bring joy now, usually accompanied by the hope for sexual fulfillment later.

Most high school students expect to marry, so when psychologist Pam Stenzel gives a group of high school students the choice to, "Play now and pay later," or to "Pay now and *play later*," she assumes that most will marry. She lingers over those last two words, raising her eyebrows, offering a secret smile, and inviting teens into the mystery of something richer, deeper, and more satisfying after the disciplined cost of choosing to wait for sex.

Although I applaud Stenzel's work, her challenge to adolescents, and her approach to sexuality, I would caution against putting marriage on a pedestal as the Final Good. Some high school students will not marry, and the expectation that genital sexuality is the reward for earlier abstinence reinforces the idea that marriage ultimately fulfills all longings and that singleness is a sign of failure to find love. Sexuality is expressed in personhood, apart from whether or not people eventually marry.

Christianity rejects the idea that the only meaning given our bodies and our sexuality is whatever is determined by a given culture or subculture. Although we cannot easily separate the meaning ascribed by our culture from that inspired by our faith, Christians nevertheless believe that there is meaning to our sexuality that transcends the arbitrary and fluid ideas of society. This belief in some transcendent truth inspires us to try to conform to God's image. But defining what that looks like when watching an increasingly boring movie while snuggling with a date in the basement family room is difficult. To help teens out, Christian churches and parents have traditionally offered a list of "dos and don'ts."

Friendship and Dating

The assumption underlying the list of dos and don'ts is that teens will have boyfriends and girlfriends—a fair assumption in the twenty-first century. That they long for a connection like a boyfriend or girlfriend flows from their embodied yearnings. To assume that they *must* or *should* or that this is *good* comes from embedded cultural assumptions. I have asked a few teens and college students what changes when two friends decide to date instead of stay friends. They generally say that dating partners have greater expectation to be exclusive socially and greater permission to "be physical" with each other.

Friendship dates back to the beginning of human relationships, yet dating is a relatively new phenomenon in history. Immediately prior to our current patterns of dating, men courted women. After seeking and being granted permission to do so, young men visited young women in their homes and, with help from parents, determined over time whether or not they were suited for marriage.

Emerging trends associated with independence and autonomy shifted teens away from courtship toward dating at the turn of the twentieth century. Automobiles gave freedom and offered a symbol of independence and autonomy. As cars became increasing available to teens, the venue for courtship shifted away from homes and out from under the watchful eyes of parents. Boys could pick girls up and take them out, increasing the variety of activities, as well as the time alone, to explore the delights to which their bodies were awakening. Our vocabulary expanded as well. "Lovers' lanes" and various "look-out points" became code words for places to "park," where "necking" and "petting" took place.

Dating initially involved casually going out with a number of people simultaneously. This smorgasbord approach to dating allowed for sampling a little of this and a little of that. Teens transitioned away from the smorgasbord approach, exchanging casual dating with going "steady." Teens still had variety, but moving from one steady or exclusive relationship to another marked their relationships. Among other things, this exclusiveness granted them permission to engage with each other more physically.

Teens today seldom assume they will marry their high school boyfriend or girlfriend, but they recognize the relationship as a temporary, though exclusive, relationship that is sometimes considered practice for later. Speaker and writer Jonathan Lindvall critiques the current dating system:

> Western culture has, for some time, been experiencing an ongoing epidemic of broken marriages. Is it possible that although, "breaking up is hard to do," the more you do it the better you get at it? I have come to the conclusion that dating is preparation for divorce rather than for marriage. We learn to attach to one person after another. Give emotions first to one and then another in such a way that we wound each other, and learn to break up.[23]

Although much of dating today is characterized by serial dating relationships, adolescents also go out on *dates,* where they may or may not have any physical contact. Sometimes they *hang out* (usually implying an emphasis on friendship). The array of possibilities regarding how physical two people get in any of these situations is, in most secular material, a matter of personal choice. How far one goes depends on how comfortable one is. Some Christians writing about adolescent sexuality are hesitant to draw lines short of sexual intercourse, not because they do not believe there are any but because they recognize various meanings and contexts associated with physical and sexual touch. They give principles to consider and questions to ask instead.[24]

Aspiring to More

Part of what we long for in our desire for relationship is the intimacy of full-body sharing. Intercourse allows us to give and take with our bodies, to be *fully* present in body to another person. Priests, philosophers, and ethicists have described the purposes of sexual intercourse and tend to reach similar conclusions. In its ideal form, sex bonds people to each other, recalling an exclusive, lifelong commitment they made to each other. Sex is pleasurable and is intended to signify mutual submission to please each other in all areas of life. Procreation occurs through intercourse, so sex is an expression of openness and of willingness to invite life if life is conceived. Sex is a spiritual metaphor for our consummate longing for God. It is an act that can draw our hearts toward God, in whom all our longings will one day be met.[25]

From a Christian vantage point, these purposes of sex assume a committed marital relationship. Sex still may have profound meaning to those participating in it, though without commitment sex cannot express an exclusive bond, make claims for mutual submission, or be fully open to receiving life. But sex can still be an act God uses to pursue our hearts. All longings go unfulfilled this side of heaven. In our experiences of sexuality, whether within marriage or without, we ultimately recognize that what we long for will not be experienced this side of heaven. God pursues people through broken sexuality, drawing them toward the mercy of the One who created and loves them.

Sexuality is about more than sex; it is about experiencing the world through bodies that are male and female. The exploration of relational feelings, desires, and experiences is appropriate and healthy. For instance, we can celebrate a choice of refraining, for a time, from pairing up sexually or romantically with another. Dare I call this adolescent celibacy? Rather than saying we are "abstaining from sex," we actively "choose celibacy." Celibacy may close some doors, but primarily it is about opening others. To be celibate so that one can focus on attaining particular goals is an affirmation of personhood and calling. To be celibate so that one can establish deep and meaningful friendships with both sexes affirms personhood in others. Celibacy frees people to love widely, to serve lavishly, to focus on the needs of others. Celibacy grounds friendship in mutual respect and warmth. For one who chooses celibacy, there is freedom to use touch to nurture and affirm friends without fear of compromising integrity, or the future relationships of those friends, or one's own future marriage.

Teens can be sexual without participating in genital sexuality. Developing friendships, appreciating the company of the other sex, enjoying the beauty and sexual appeal of the other sex, affirming touch that is nonsexual or asexual—all recognize and validate sexuality. Admitting longings and desires to oneself and to God affirms sexuality. Choosing to wait until one is in a committed, lifelong relationship to explore genital sexuality acknowledges that sexuality is core to personhood, not to be given and taken lightly.

Adolescents choosing celibacy can still hang out and go out on dates. Our youngest daughter, Megan, chose this approach throughout high school. She invited boys to the Turn About dances and accepted invitations to prom and homecoming dances. She went out to dinner, to movies, and on coffee dates with boys. But she did so as friends, committed for this time to friendship. As a result, Megan developed a good set of friends among both boys and girls. She was a "safe" girl for boys who wanted someone to talk to as a friend. She learned much from her friendships with boys about how they experience their world; sometimes she learned what they think about their futures and even what they think about girls. She also spent a lot of time with girlfriends, going into Chicago, shopping, going out for coffee, or hanging out at each other's houses. Because she was not investing time in boyfriends, she had interest and energy for both friendships and other extracurricular activities. She entered college confident in her ability to be a friend and to choose friends.

Falling in love is a combination of attraction and choice, though our pop culture suggests love is a destiny—a combination of attraction and fate. We experience attractions, interests, sparks—and then make a series of choices in response. The urge to fall in love does not disappear with marriage, but because of marriage's exclusive commitment, people make different choices in response to attractions toward others who are not their spouses.

And the sixteen-year-old girl on *Oprah* had choices: she did not *have* to fall in love with her boyfriend, and once she did, she did not *have* to sleep with him. She kept making choices that moved her toward an exclusive and sexual relationship. Kara, too, could have replied to the question about whether or not she had ever been in love by saying, "I have chosen *not* to fall in love during high school, not to be in an exclusive relationship."

Choosing to be celibate throughout adolescence is also a choice. This is a valid choice for our adolescents, but they need to see it as a choice for something ultimately more satisfying. Celibacy is a choice that moves adolescents beyond deciding to abstain from sex because they fear getting an STI or getting pregnant by offering them an alternative that respects their own and others' sexuality and opens the door for receiving rich benefits of friendship.

Given that societies are concerned about the well-being of their youth, sex education programs are put in place to educate teens about all their choices. Some religious groups and parents are concerned that the vacuum left by our move toward secular education is being filled with moral relativism— an attempt to avoid judging any sexual behavior. The fear is that such programs pass out values embedded in handouts about sexual choices and adolescent relationships. The curricular content of the sex education that schools offer is hotly contested. Meanwhile, some churches are adding their own sex education programs for teens, and civil and religious groups are establishing programs to encourage and educate parents about becoming active participants in the sexual teaching and training of their young people.

The Role of Sex Education and Faith Communities

Most parents do not want their teens to be sexually active yet are unsure how best to persuade them to wait for sex. The majority of parents support what are called comprehensive sex education programs. The idea is that parents do not want their children to be sexually active, but they want them to be using contraceptives in case they choose to be anyway. A smaller group of parents have become politically active in the support of "abstinence only" sex education programs in schools. They have the support of the deputy secretary of U.S. Health and Human Services, Claude Allen, who says that sex is a risky teen behavior and abstinence is the only way to sufficiently reduce the risk. "Condoms may be effective in preventing transmission of HIV/AIDS and, in some cases, transmission of gonorrhea in men, but beyond that they do not protect adequately against other sexually transmitted diseases."[26]

Advocates for comprehensive sex education worry that telling teenagers that condoms do not work will decrease the number of sexually active teens using condoms. They argue that abstinence is naively idealistic, and the better approach is to talk to teens about how to minimize their risk as they explore their sexuality.

Both sides agree that teen sex is risky sex but that the *other position* introduces greater risk. Abstinence programs seem risky to parents concerned primarily about preventing pregnancy and AIDS. Comprehensive sex-ed seems risky to parents concerned about preventing STIs in general, especially for girls who are more easily infected.

Communities of faith could come alongside the sex education mission of schools by helping adolescents figure out how to think about and act on their yearnings and their desire to explore intimate relationships and sex. In a national study of Protestant, Catholic, Unitarian, Jewish, and Islamic faith communities, 68 percent of the clergy said they believed it was possible for their congregation to do more than they were currently doing regarding sexuality education and that they would like to make that a greater priority than it currently was. A quarter of the clergy agreed that more should be done but felt unable to make it a priority at the present time.[27]

Encouraging teenagers to fill their lives with other good things is a strong starting point. High school students who had high daily attendance at school and were involved in various extracurricular activities were less likely to have sex than other students. These kinds of activities help by satisfying inquisitive minds and by fulfilling the desire to be stretched, to test skills, and to gain social, academic, athletic, or artistic competencies.

High school students in the study who had a peer group that supported their decision to abstain from sex were also more likely to abstain than students who did not. For committed religious students, their beliefs influenced decisions about their sexuality. The national study of faith communities found that seniors involved in congregational life had had intercourse half as often as high school seniors nationally (31.0 percent compared to 60.5 percent). Seniors who were especially involved in their faith communities and reported a deep faith were half again as likely to have had sex (16.5 percent). Congregations that provided their young people with information about contraceptives and sexually transmitted diseases (8 percent of congregations did) had no reported pregnancies or cases of sexually transmitted diseases; 11 percent of girls in other congregations who had intercourse had become pregnant; 9 percent of teens who had intercourse or oral sex knew they had an STI. Half the girls who had become pregnant aborted their babies, even if their faith community was pro-life. The study concluded,

> Teens were virtually unanimous in wanting their faith-based institutions to do more to help them relate their faith to dating, sexual decision-making, marriage, and parenting. They are very open to more help from their congregations, and they are frustrated with the overall failure of adult society to give them the help that they need.[28]

Some churches are becoming proactive in teaching teens about sex and developing curricula focusing on the sexual choices of teens and preteens. Trevecca Okholm, director of Children's Ministries at St. Andrews Presbyterian in Newport Beach, California, has provided a curriculum titled PFA (Preparing for Adolescence). She offers a class for fifth-grade girls and boys using *Preparing for Adolescence* by James Dobson and *Created by God: About Human Sexuality for Older Girls and Boys* by James H. Ritchie Jr., which openly deal with issues of male and female sexual development and address questions that teens typically ask. One session in the PFA series is a panel made up of Christian teens from the congregation who wrestle with living out their faith in a public school environment. Okholm said, "We divide into girls' and boys' groups, and no questions are off-limits for our fifth graders to ask our teens. Questions dealing with dating, sex, dress, sports, flirting, first kiss, French kissing, and peer pressure come before our panel." Okholm believes parents should be the primary sex educators, and the church should function to facilitate that process. A mandatory meeting for parents who want their children enrolled in PFA brings parents onto the team that educates youth about sexuality.

Other parents work to infuse their children with their own (the parents') values about sex. Some find help from book series such as that by Brenna and Stan Jones that begins with *How and When to Tell Your Kids About Sex*. Parents who can move beyond the discomforts of talking about sex to having frank conversations with their children are able to influence their teens' choices. Teens who live with both parents have a strong connection to their parents, family, and communities of faith, and those whose parents disapprove of teenage sexual activity are less likely to engage in sexual activity than those who do not.

Following is a list of suggestions for parents, youth leaders, and those working with youth about filling the vacuum.

- Encourage your community of faith to offer sexuality education for youth. Become an active participant in gathering information, curriculum ideas, and potential discussion facilitators.
- Encourage good friendships among adolescents. Learn about their friends; this is most effectively done when your home is the kind of home adolescents would invite friends to.
- Encourage adolescents to discover and try out various activities and develop the building of confidence and competency through extracurricular activities to which they are drawn.
- Consider preparing a rite of passage in the context of a group of girls and mothers and a group of boys and fathers that opens the

door to dating after a time of preparation that is characterized by conversations about longings, sex, and relationships.

○ Encourage participation in volunteer opportunities. Better yet, serve with the young people in volunteer ministry. Through serving, we connect our place in the world to the larger community outside us. Serving the underserved exposes us to suffering and to the Church's important role of serving.

○ Encourage unstructured time alone—personal time to walk, bike, read, hike, play, or listen to music, or to write while reflecting on who one is and is becoming. The goal is not to make adolescents so busy they do not have time to get into trouble (though this outcome may have some merit) but to help them make meaningful investments that satisfy their longings for connection, for a sense of purpose and for relationship during these years of adolescence.

The Role of Masturbation

Males and females are capable of having sex by 13 or 14 years of age, yet at this point in history the average age at which males marry is 27.5 in the United States and the average age for females is 26.5. Does this mean that for more than a dozen years sexually alive and awakened young adults are to forgo sexual gratification?

When we discuss masturbation as a topic worthy of reflection in Sociology of Sexuality, we are very much aware this is not a discussion that would be had on most college campuses. Masturbation is an assumed sexual behavior. Yet for many Christians, masturbating is clouded by shame and doubt. In our class, we talk about perceived needs being met by masturbation, expected benefits, unintended consequences, and assumptions about the body-soul connection that are at work in one's views on masturbation. They wrestle to make a body-soul connection. They talk about needs, benefits, and consequences with a level of sophistication that reflects thoughtfulness about this issue. After our discussion, a male student wrote the following in a response paper:

> In the movie *Mulholland Drive*, there is this scene where a woman who recently broke up with her lover is seen masturbating and crying at the same time. A friend of mine who had seen the movie told me that he felt like that before. His act of masturbation was a reflection of his loneliness as well as his deeper desire and yearning for love and intimacy. In all honesty, I resonate with his comment in the sense that

on days when I feel connected to the world and the people around me, having intimate, spiritual, and intellectual conversations with friends and people, I do not have the desire to masturbate.

Males and females say they masturbate as a sexual release, to relieve stress, to help them fall asleep. This male identified a deeper motive: *His act of masturbation was a reflection of his loneliness, as well as his deeper desire and yearning for love and intimacy.* When we understand that we are made for relationship, that we are existentially alone in our embodied state, yearning for a powerful connection that is fundamentally expressed in our sexuality, then we see masturbation as an attempt to fulfill a longing for intimacy. As a substitute, it is poor and sad, but masturbating represents a longing that is good.

Students identify unintended consequences of masturbation; they experienced those consequences and suffered from them. Masturbation can take on an obsessive character that becomes a habit, sometimes interfering with the development of meaningful relationships. When people masturbate, they are engaging the self instead of engaging with others. Masturbation is isolating, and the shame often associated with it drives people into secrecy. The possibility that masturbation is sin is problematic for students; most consider masturbation a sin if it includes lusting, though many also believe it is possible to masturbate without lusting.

A student asked if we could meet, and over lunch he shared his struggle with masturbation. He assumed masturbating to mental images was lustful and thus sinful but wondered if it was worse to hold a mental image of his girlfriend or of a stranger when he masturbated. The first, he feared, objectified his girlfriend; the latter, sex and women generally. He felt much shame and told me he had never struggled until this year. I learned then that his girlfriend was overseas for six months. They had always been careful with physical boundaries, and he felt like he betrayed her in this struggle. He spoke of his longing for her, his missing their face-to-face, hand-to-hand personal relationship. The separation had stretched and prodded them to develop other forms of intimacy in the absence of physical proximity.

This student's urge to masturbate seemed to be an embodied response to his longing for his beloved, yearning for her presence. We talked about whether or not a person could invite God into moments characterized by shame and longing, not primarily to ask for forgiveness but to acknowledge the suffering that came with joy. Could he thank God for the gift of this woman for whose presence he yearned, rejoicing in the growth brought through the suffering of separation? Rather than coming to God only to seek forgiveness for what felt shameful, could he bring God into the joy that longing for her represented? Could he masturbate and give God his feelings, emotions, and confusion? Together we asked questions rather than answered them. But he left knowing that I thought God would welcome him in that place, fully understanding his longings and yearnings.

Identifying assumptions about the body-soul connection as it relates to masturbation is not something most of us think about. Many of us are neo-Gnostic without realizing it, holding on to a dualistic idea about the body and soul, believing we can separate the two. We rank the body as less valuable than the soul, as something useful and good but also base, crude, in need of chastisement and discipline so that the desires of the body do not lead the soul astray. Thus many people attempt to control or manage their sexuality by boxing up their sexual self and storing it away. Some manage their sexuality by spending hours in prayer, asking God for "healing" from their sexual struggles. Others concede the struggle with masturbation, yet are overwhelmed by shame and guilt when they allow bodily desires to win out over their will.

An incarnational perspective does not accept this separation of body and soul. Indeed, our soul's longing for connection and intimacy is expressed in the body's desire for sexual fulfillment. We hunger and satisfy our hunger with the means available to us. When masturbation is understood as a reflection of one's aloneness and loneliness, it takes on significance for the soul. Our redemption is for our bodies as well as our souls, not because they are two separate entities but because they are one.

The redemptive challenge becomes finding healthy ways to engage the self with others so that the need to satisfy longing by engaging with one's self in masturbation is minimized. Some develop accountability groups, where they share sexual struggles and hold each other up to a standard they agree on. Some people come up with a strategy, like the male student who scheduled Thursday nights for masturbation. He said this kept him from obsessively thinking about it the rest of the week. By allowing himself this sexual outlet, he was able to let it go and not obsess about masturbation the rest of the week. There is something sad about that, yet also good. It is good to recognize we long for something we cannot have and search for an appropriate way to speak to that longing rather than boxing it up or denying its existence. God made our bodies to experience sexual pleasure, and God delights in our experience of sexual pleasure. God intended sexual pleasure to be most fulfilling as experienced in the context of marital sex. When self-pleasuring can be done so that it recognizes longing, celebrates sexual pleasure, and is neither exploitative nor a substitute for relationship with others, then it can be a way to stretch toward authentic sexuality.

To redeem our sexuality, we move beyond simple and assumed answers and seek to understand how sexual needs reflect spiritual longings. We encourage each other by asking questions such as these: How else can I meet these longings? What relationships can I develop? Who is a safe person to talk to about my struggles? What fears keep me from getting too close to other men or women? When accountability groups are successful (and they frequently are reported as being very satisfying relationally), it is because these groups legitimate intimate friendship; they are a place of safe vulnerability where people are known. Grace is granted and received in the midst of suffering and struggle.

Awakenings: Upward, Outward, Inward, and Other-Ward

We inspire awakenings associated with adolescent sexuality along three directions. The first awakening is upward. We walk with them toward the mercy of a God who knows we will fail and forgives us our failings. God creates all that is beautiful and redeems and mends that which is broken. When we see God, *truly* see God, we are awed by the beautiful and broken by the awareness of our own limitations. The beauty and sacredness of God's image resides in frail human vessels created for greatness, yet also doomed to sin. In that honest place before God, we find the capacity to focus not only on our littleness but also on the greatness of being image-bearers of a powerful and loving God.

The second awakening is outward. We can show adolescents other teens or older young adults who have maneuvered adolescence and have stories of victory. Dustin just graduated from high school and is the son of dear friends, Jeff and Cindy Crosby. As I entered their house one day during his senior year, the aroma of freshly baked chocolate chip cookies met me at the door. My salivary glands began to anticipate one of Cindy's home-baked treats, but alas, Dustin had made them for his girlfriend, Lauren, whose week had been full of stressful last-week-before-performance play practices. He thought she needed a little encouragement by way of freshly baked cookies and a letter. Dustin had dashed off to deliver them before meeting his fellow folk-band players for a schoolwide solo and ensemble competition. Most competitors performed classical numbers—not so the Frozen Moldy Biscuit Band. Dustin had written, "An Ode to Davy Jones Liquor Locker" for the band. His banjo accompanied the washboard, an upright double bass, guitar, and claves, and an ordinary bread-toasting toaster in the performance. They were dressed in overalls and cowboy hats, and the toaster player handed out toast to audience members. The second night, students crammed into the back aisles of the auditorium to watch.

Dustin said singer and writer Michael Card reinforced his perspective. "God is the center of creativity and we are called to use our gifts in creative ways." Developing his creativity was a significant focus for Dustin in high school and a way to reach out to others through example and friendship.

Dustin talks to his parents about his relationship to Lauren, and he graciously spoke with me. She is the first girl with whom he has entered an exclusive relationship. He says, "She's my sister in Christ before my girlfriend and encourages and builds me up in my faith. We were friends for a year and have been better friends in these last six months. She is a blessing to me." I asked about physical and emotional aspects of their relationship. "We want to move slowly. When I first asked her to go out with me, I made a commitment to God, Lauren, and myself to draw the line physically above the collarbone." He says it is harder to know where emotional boundaries should be drawn. "There are not clear boundaries about emotional closeness. We want to earn each other's trust, not freely give it away. And we don't want to rely too heavily on each other for all our spiritual and emotional needs. It's important to us to keep other friendships healthy and active."

Dustin intentionally approaches opportunities and challenges of adolescence. He exudes life and energy, love and compassion. Often we hear only the colorful testimonies of those redeemed from brokenness. These are important stories but alone are insufficient to inspire a vision of awakened life. Victorious stories of people living vibrant lives in which creative energy is building, celebrating, playing, and ministering to others awaken and inspire us.

A third awakening is a simultaneous movement inward and otherward. We encourage teens to explore their own thoughts, feelings, fears, and longings as they connect to relationships with others, while also being mindful of potential thoughts, fears, and longings of others.

Blake, a student in my Sociology of Sexuality class, used a class presentation to remind us our bodies are sensual, alive, and able to meaningfully engage with others in a bodily fashion. He led us through an exercise he adapted from a drama group. The desks were pushed against the wall, giving us a big open space. Blake told us to close our eyes and keep them closed throughout the exercise. "Now take deep breaths. Be aware of your body as you inhale and exhale." Blake spoke slowly, intentionally. "Move slowly around the room, and go to a place in the room that expresses something of what you feel today." I headed for the window, wanting to feel the warmth of sunlight on my skin, especially feeling the call of the outdoors on an early spring day. He had us think about what we were feeling physically for a few minutes and then instructed us to move around the room until we bumped into someone. "Hold each other's hand and wait until everyone has found a partner." We did so, clumsily, hesitantly, sometimes needing Blake to help isolated souls find each other. He then had us sit down on the floor, facing our partner, our eyes still closed. "Explore your partner's hands," he instructed. I could tell I was holding the hands of a male and wondered if he could tell by my hands that I was the professor. He'd surmise I was one of the married or engaged students by the ring on my finger. "Tell each other about your day, using your partner's hands. After a few minutes I'll have you switch." Blake watched our feeble attempts to pantomime our day using the hands of our partner. Let's see, I exercised (I take my partners hands, moving two fingers across his palm to stimulate running). I prayed (I put his hands together in a position of prayer). I wrote, taught, read, and tried to express all this with his hands. "Try to express how you *felt* as you walked through your day, not just what you did."

We spent ten or fifteen minutes communicating through touch, growing increasingly comfortable and skilled at the tasks given us. Eventually, Blake said, "Now, put your hands in your lap. Keep your eyes closed." Slowly, with time to reflect silently, he asked a variety of questions. "How did it feel to have your hands examined so closely through touch? What was uncomfortable about it? Did it get more comfortable? Why or why not? What are you anticipating as you think about opening your eyes and finding out whose hands you have been touching?"

We opened our eyes and, as partners and then a class, talked about the experience and concluded touch was powerful, sexual, and sensual without having to be erotic. We had engaged in an experience that celebrated being created as sexual beings that longed for connection and were capable of connecting in a variety of ways, including nonerotic touch.

Conclusion

Making our way through life clothed in the particulars of our human longings is a lifelong process. It begins before adolescence but is keenly awakened to new possibilities in adolescence. Our sexuality draws us toward connection to others, but we are existentially alone in our bodies. Communities of faith and parents can guide teenagers toward embracing the aloneness and welcoming this time of celibacy before marriage. Adolescents are primed to learn and experience multiple ways of connecting meaningfully to others that leave future options wide open while preserving the dignity and personhood of others and of oneself.

○

QUERIES FOR FURTHER REFLECTION AND DISCUSSION

○ How did the sexual revolution of the sixties indirectly or directly affect your beliefs about sexuality, girlfriends and boyfriends, necking, and sex? Refer back to Tiefer's list of assumptions people use to determine normal sexual behavior. How were your own thoughts about adolescent sexual behaviors shaped by these various assumptions?

○ Did the discussion of STIs surprise you? What might you do with this updated information about changes in the sexual landscape?

○ Are you inclined to think any differently about high school boyfriend-girlfriend relationships after reading this chapter? How might you talk to adolescents about their longings, about what is potentially harmful and what alternatives look like?

○ By the way, what was the nature of your communication with your parents during adolescence? How well did they know you? Did any adult know you? If you have children, how is your communication similar or different from your parents?

○ A related query: If sex-ed were no longer offered in the schools, would you be prepared to take over the sex education of your children? Does the thought make your stomach ache? If so, what does that say to you?

○ A sign of good parenting is *not* that adolescents talk to their parents about everything. A more realistic goal is that teens have *some* adult they can talk to about their longings and sexuality. Do your children have such an adult in their life? Are you such an adult to another parent's child? What would it take to put you in a position where you could be?

○ Do you know the names of your children's closest circle of friends? How might you learn them and learn to recognize their voices on the phone and their faces at the door?

○

SLEEPING ALONE

SEXUALITY AND SINGLENESS

---

*I used to chew on ice. After years of ice-chewing, a friend
told me that people deal with sexual frustration that
way. So, okay then, I chewed on ice.*

—Naomi, a seventy-five-year-old, never-married woman

A WOMAN CALLED IN DURING A RADIO INTERVIEW when I was
talking about raising strong daughters. She had been listening to radio
talk shows a long time and wanted to know what I had to say to single
women like her, who felt invisible in most conversations, like the one we
were just now having. If I talked about parents raising strong daughters,
what did that mean for her—a woman who was not a mother and no
longer lived at home with her mother? She looked to the church for her
primary fellowship and community, even though she felt almost invisible
sitting in a pew Sunday mornings, participating in services geared for families and married couples.

According to the 1970 census, about twenty-eight people out of a hundred over the age of eighteen were unmarried. This grew to forty out of
every one hundred by the year 2000. The population of single people in
the United States is not small, even if it is, by some measures, invisible.
Absorbed in that invisibility are the experiences, losses, hopes, and fears
during years of singleness.

The fullness of God's nature cannot be captured in one human who
bears God's image, or in marriage as a model of God's love for the Church,

or in one of Christianity's traditional emphases on evangelism or holiness or contemplation. God's nature is most fully represented in the diversity of community—male, female, married, single, Protestant, Catholic, young, old, Asian, African. We are incapable as individuals of carrying or experiencing the fullness of God. Yet as we come to understand and validate different elements of God's diversity, we see our own distortions and false assumptions. We become aware of our own incompleteness.

Richard Foster explores the diversity of Christianity in his book *Streams of Living Waters: Celebrating the Great Traditions of Christian Faith*. Foster examines dimensions of the Christian faith as reflected in six historical traditions. He shows us how each tradition contributes a piece to the whole and encourages us to learn from and integrate pieces of traditions that are not ours. In a similar way, single people reflect a different aspect of God's nature than married people; they're an important piece of the whole. Faith communities will be enriched and will reflect a greater fullness of God's nature as they better understand, learn from, and integrate single people and their experiences into the life and rhythm of the Church.

Who the Single People Are

Men and women are single for a variety of reasons, and more adults are single now than in the past, partly because we marry later. In 1970, the average age for marriage was about twenty-two; by 2000 it had increased to twenty-six. About 4 percent of adults now sixty-five or older have never married.[1] A few who never marry choose celibacy and invest their lives fully in ministry, career, or service.

The reasons vary: some people never find a spouse, though they would like to be married; some are homosexual in their orientation; others have been married but are now single; some are widows or widowers; others are divorced. Some single people are childless, and some are raising children, increasingly so since the second half of the twentieth century.

The yearnings and needs of people who are single are not identical, that is, they do not share one common experience. An isolated, single mother of a three-year-old child generally experiences greater loneliness than a seventy-year-old widow surrounded by family. The sexual frustration of a thirty-two-year-old unmarried person who wants to be married is generally greater than the sexual frustration of a fifty-two-year-old divorcee at peace with the divorce. Needs and desires, expectations for life and relationships, and self-perception determine how single people see themselves as sexual and express their sexuality; this differs from person to person. A poignant challenge for all who live alone is finding contentment, joy, and fulfillment in their situation. Singles live in a culture that assumes they cannot be complete alone, and many experience this as a self-fulfilling prophecy: to live alone is to be incomplete, unfulfilled.

God breathed a desire for bonding, for connection, into our beings by making us inherently incomplete. Longing is fundamental to our sexuality. We continue to long for completion, whether married or single, because nothing this side of heaven will fill us completely. In this anticipation of fulfillment, we seek bonding with others. A challenge of the contemporary Church is to claim a theology of sexuality that names, validates, and embraces the sexuality of singleness. Redeeming sexuality for singles includes challenging the belief that God as bridegroom and parent captures the ultimate and full picture of God's relational love.

On the one hand, God's love as depicted in marriage shows an exclusive love of a husband and wife—the beauty of difference and similarity coming together in "one flesh." Faithfulness, permanence, and the welcoming and nurturing of children born of their parents' sexual union teach us about God as lover and life-giver. On the other hand, singles reflect the inclusive love of God—a love for everyone. Married people cannot reflect God's inclusive and open love as fully. God's love is at once *exclusive* (we are commanded to worship no other gods [Exodus 20:3]) and *inclusive* (God loves and wills that all would be saved [I Timothy 2:3–4]). In the freedom singles have to love others freely and openly, they reflect this expansive, universal love of God. They reflect a God who is unencumbered and free in expressions of love that can be given to all without a sense of betrayal or infidelity.[2] In the movie *Dead Man Walking,* Sister Helen Prejean visits Matthew, a man on death row, and becomes his spiritual adviser for his last week of life. At one point Matthew asks her, "Don't you ever wish you had a husband to go home to, and children?" She answers, "If I did, I'd probably be home with them instead of here with you." She is free and unencumbered in her love and loves him well during his last week of life, being the agent God uses to ultimately draw Matthew into a relationship with God.

Christianity makes this exclusive faith claim: Jesus is the only way of salvation. If we elevate marriage (also an exclusive relationship) as the only picture of God's love of the Church, we diminish the inclusive, universal, and unencumbered love God has for all people. The community of faith reflects God's nature more fully when this expansive and inclusive aspect of God's nature is celebrated in harmony with our desire to be faithful and undivided in response to God's faithful love of us.

In marriage, sexuality is expressed through an exclusive relationship that includes genital sexuality. But in all of us, sexuality is broader than sex. Stanley Grenz says, "This drive to bond with others in community is an expression of our fundamental sexuality, a sexuality that goes deeper than body parts, potential roles in reproduction, and genital acts."[3] The community of God will function more fully as we understand and think differently about God's nature and love through the diverse experiences of those living alone.

The Experience of Being Single

The Church, like society, reinforces marriage as the better and preferred path for individuals to take as they make their way through life. How people experience singleness is influenced by cultural and religious values, beliefs, and meanings. We get the idea that the goal of all single people is to find others to hook up with, and the goal of all friends of single people is to help them hook up. Sleeping alone, we've come to believe, is bad. Fear of being alone, being marginalized, questioning one's completeness, and dealing with unmet needs come to characterize the malady called singleness. Not surprisingly, national surveys show a higher level of unhappiness among singles than among those who are married, particularly for never-married and divorced singles.[4]

Fear of Singleness

A student wrote this in a class journal:

> I went through a period of time when my greatest fear in life was imagining my life single—forever. At that time I saw having a boyfriend as an outward symbol of being lovable. So that meant being single had a stigma attached to it. If I were to be single for life people would look at me and wonder what was wrong with me. Maybe they'd think I didn't have the social skills to be in a relationship or that I was overly clingy or needy.

The fear of being single is exacerbated by a high average age of marriage, combined with the belief that women over thirty seldom get married. In 1986, Yale University sociologist Neil Bennett offered predictions on the likelihood that educated women would get married. Still single at thirty? There's only a 20 percent chance of getting married; at thirty-five it drops to 5 percent; at forty to 1 percent. The numbers were picked up by *Newsweek, People Magazine,* and Phil Donahue, and they reinforced what women already feared.[5]

That the reliability of these projections was questioned did not make it to the pages of *Newsweek* or *People,* but current projections suggest that social conditions have, in fact, changed. Economic independence is associated with higher, not lower rates of marriage for women of all races.[6] The newest predictions assure college-educated women that they are still capable of "finding a man." College-educated women marry at higher rates than women without a college education, even though they marry later. We live in an era of economic and job uncertainty, as well as a high standard of living, and people choose marriage and particular partners for reasons that appear pragmatic or rational to them. Yet the myth and the fear persist: once a woman turns thirty, she is doomed to the sorry state of singleness.

Men generally escape the tyranny of time and worry less about being thirty-five and unmarried than women do. We are still largely a culture that grants men the initiating power to pursue and propose and women the less powerful role of accepting or rejecting proposals. The infamous biological clock ticks away, reminding women their fertile years are passing by.

Marginalization

"My singleness helped me be very empathetic with minorities on campus," said Naomi, a seventy-five-year-old, never-married woman who had spent her career ministering to college students. "They were marginalized as I was. We were outside the norm, the expected life of everyone else."

Marginalization means living at the edges, outside of what is perceived by society as the normal, everyday existence. Those who are marginalized are often misunderstood, stereotyped, and seen as inferior in some way. "It is socially less acceptable to be single," forty-five-year-old Rebekah, said. "So I think most people see me as incomplete, especially in the religious community. We are set up as a couples-oriented world. People have internalized a couples-world, even if they don't intentionally conceive of it that way."

Our world is indeed set up for couples and families. One indication of the way our society adds stability by institutionalizing family life is that married people receive tax benefits, as well as medical, Social Security, and retirement benefits from spouses who work. Adults also have rights and obligations that are recognized by the state when they are parents and spouses. In addition, hotels that promote a "kids stay and eat free" weekend, offer companion airline tickets, and give two-for-one deals attract families and couples and reinforce the idea that this is a couples-oriented world.

Well-meaning friends and family try to set single friends up on dates, and they may inquire into a single friend's love life, implying that a state of singleness should be temporary because it is inferior to being married. Often associated with marginalization is a sense of incompleteness.

Incompleteness

Our couples-oriented world appears to contribute to the overall well-being of married people, reinforcing evidence that the married life is the better life. And being married, in fact, has measurable health advantages over being single, especially for men. Married people live longer than single people, thus some conclude that married people are more complete, living the life God designed. But numerous studies find that those with good social ties have less heart disease and are less likely to develop physical impairments as they age than those without them.[7] So friendship rather than marriage may be what contributes to better health and longer life.

Our sexuality, whether expressed as married people or singles, draws us toward others. Good bonds in friendship among singles are more satisfying than poor marital bonds or purely sexual relationships. Gary's case is a good example of this.

Gary's wife left him after twenty-five years of marriage. He felt shock, anger, and depression but ultimately came to peace. "I had a number of years in my marriage where my sexual needs were being met but not my intimacy needs. Now I have intimacy needs being meet and not sexual needs. I prefer this; I feel more complete with this. My soul has been enlarged. My completeness is more in community now, in meaningful relationships. My friends affirm that I seem healthy and stable, and I feel that, too."

Scott, thirty-four-years-old and never married, also feels complete, though Scott imagines he will marry someday. "Marriage does not fill a hole but adds richness. A spouse empowers you to do more good, to be more of who you are. Yet not being married, I have built strong relationships with friends and found other ways to partner with people. I've used my singleness to grow, to invest in others, in learning, in becoming and being."

Rebekah is also content with her singleness, even given the couples-oriented world she lives in. Yet she acknowledges some missing pieces. "I know that I am not experiencing all the fullness life has to offer because I'm not married or a parent. But not all married people experience the fullness life has to offer either. Having the full experience of being a woman is not just about motherhood and marriage."

Doubts about one's completeness are confounded by questions concerning needs and desires. Much in our culture suggests that sex is the primary need of unmarried people—one they should meet any way they find helpful so long as it does not hurt or exploit someone else. Movies, TV, and music all assume that fulfillment is achieved through sex. Christians committed to abstinence struggle to determine what sexual fulfillment means for them, particularly those without hope of ever being able to marry. One man, whose sexual attractions are for other men, said this:

> I hope to marry a woman someday, but as long as I'm attracted to men I can't rightly pursue a woman; it would not be right or fair to her. I have not been able to make myself be attracted to women, even though I very much want to be. So when I express my sexuality it's with men and it's in the bedroom. Yet it leaves me feeling blah at best; it's never the epiphany or catharsis I expect it to be. As much as I idolize men and admire their masculinity, you'd think that being with them physically would give me a boost that would last beyond the bedroom. It never does. I don't know what sexual fulfillment can look like for me since I'm not attracted to women and do not find sex with men ultimately satisfying.

Others suppress their sexuality as a way to contain desires. "Expressions of touch are always limited, boundaried," a woman said. "I am aroused by images, seeing people touch, kiss. If I avoid it all, I can become deadened to desire. That's an easier place to live sometimes, but I don't think a good one, a healthy one. I've occasionally used masturbation as a way to express my sexuality, but it's not fulfilling; it's just a reminder of what I don't have."

Unmet Needs

All people have relational needs, bonding needs. We are, as Ronald Rolheiser says, "Grand Canyons built for the infinite." Relationally, we are ultimately unfillable. All the people I spoke with about perceived needs talked about relationships, either longing for them or thinking of them as the way to have their needs met. Married or single, we all long for connection—to fully love and be loved, to know and be fully known. Marriage does not guarantee that kind of fulfillment; neither does being single and able to pursue meaningful friendships with any and all. We are presumptuous to assume that either singleness or marriage will fulfill us, yet we despair if we assume we will not find some fulfillment either in our marriage or our singleness. Single and married people are alike in our longings, only different in our avenues for fulfilling them.

Ginger's husband died six months before their fiftieth wedding anniversary. She is an eighty-year-old, active, charming woman who, along with some friends, identifies herself as a WOW—Winsome Old Widow. Loneliness is her biggest challenge. She has no family nearby, and though she has good friends and stays active in church and clubs, she is still very lonely at times. When I asked how she dealt with loneliness, she said this:

> I don't "deal with it." It's just my life. I suppose that growing up as an only child I have always been somewhat lonely. I believe it was Augustine who said, "God has made us for Himself and our hearts are restless until they find their rest in Him." That is certainly true for me. When I stop to realize that Christ is always at my side and in my heart, it is like a "balm of Gilead."

Some are single because of brokenness—past experiences that have shaped their view of marriage. Rebekah, now forty-five, said, "After my one-year marriage in my early thirties, I doubted I would remarry. I don't have a preference for being single, but I've made peace with it. I learned marriage could be really bad and didn't crave it in the same way anymore."

Yet even given a painful past regarding relationships with men, Kate, a forty-two-year-old single mother longs to be married. "My intimacy need leaves a huge hole. No matter how resourceful I am, how much I go to the cross with this, how much I pray that God take this desire out of my heart, I still want to be married. I want to see the wisdom in staying single, but the desire doesn't leave."

Others, like Greg and Thad, had no desire for intimacy with someone of the other sex, yet both wanted to be married to a woman someday. Greg eventually married at thirty-nine; Thad is single. Greg said,

> I had no roadmap that could take me from where I was to the point of marriage. My inability to get married was a sign of failure. I couldn't muster desire or confidence that someone would love me. I spent sixteen or seventeen years in a process of healing that moved me toward the potential for marriage. I needed to work through issues of trust, intense neediness, self-hatred, fears of abandonment, and my tendency to be clingy to males. I wanted to *want* to be married but didn't know how to get there.

In addition to needs for intimacy, connection, and companionship, Ginger, Rebekah, Kate, and Gary talked of the pragmatic needs of partnership, such as having help doing the ordinary tasks of living like computing taxes, raking leaves, taking out the garbage, changing the oil in the car, handling furnace and plumbing crises, earning an income, and parenting children. The four who mentioned it had all previously been married, and two were parenting children. Kate said,

I have friends who let their husbands handle the finances because it's just not their thing, or they let them handle "bedtime ritual" with the kids because it frustrates them too much. They have permission to be balanced, not to be an expert at everything. But when you're single, and particularly a single parent, there's both a societal and a self-expectation that you should be good at everything. It's not an option for me to not be good at my finances. That increases the burden and the guilt.

Christian singles talked about three primary relationships that met some of their needs for connection: (1) church and family, (2) close friendships, and (3) their relationship with God. Rebekah said,

I've created family by developing good relationships with my nieces and nephews and by becoming close to the children of my friends and some of my students. I create intimacy through meaningful friendship, including male-female friendships. Male friends are important to me—I learn how they perceive life. I gain some understanding of the male perspective in safe friendships with men.

Naomi also expressed the significance of friends:

I need friends, and some of my early friendships went through vulnerable stages. Did I need them too much? Become too enmeshed in them? I met intimacy needs by staying close with family. I feel very loved and accepted by them—my sisters, their children, and now grandchildren. Knowing how important the Church is in meeting my needs, I sought to be in mixed groups, to be around couples, around men so that my experience as a single woman did not isolate me.

As the celibate saints before us, some of those I spoke with talked of God as their lover and pursuer, as One who embraced and held them. They spoke of wanting to deepen their love relationship with God. Seventy-five-year-old Naomi said, "I've always wanted greater intimacy with the Lord. I finally have less guilt about not being where I want to be in that, even as I continue to yearn for God."

Even though intimacy needs were met for many of those I spoke with, specific sexual desires remained unsatisfied. For some this loss was keenly felt. Some spoke of their longings for sexual intimacy and the pain of shutting themselves off from sexual desire they did not know if they would ever experience, or ever experience again.

What It Means to Be Sexual and Single

Definitions of sexuality are constructed, not entirely arbitrarily, but the nuancing and clarifying dimensions are up for grabs; those with the loudest or most powerful voice often determine how a thing comes to be understood. Definitions that are too broad render sexuality meaningless. If we say sexuality is simply being drawn to relationship, we diminish the meaning of the genital sexual element. This definition denies sex as a unique experience and part of sexuality. However, if we say sexuality is only expressed when it involves sex, or the genitals, than we reduce sexuality to only one aspect of being male and female.

Several people defined sexuality as having sex. When asked what it means to be sexual, one man said, "I don't consider myself a sexual person because I'm not having sex. Satisfying sexual desire has a negative connotation. Right now my sexuality needs to be contained and controlled."

A woman said, "To be sexual is to be frustrated. I've had years shut off from sexuality and am enduring the pain of that."

"It's an important and beautiful part of life that's not for me anymore," another said.

Many people are unsure what it means to be sexual. We have a vague sense that we are, whether or not we're having sex, but do not know how to define it or express it. One said, "This is still a confusing part of being single for me. I'm not sure who I am as a sexual person or how I express my sexuality."

For some, the definition of sexuality constructed for them in childhood is full of shame and disgust. Greg despised his body and believed both it and sex to be shameful and dirty.

If a key dimension of sexuality is that of drawing us toward others so that we experience the life-giving affirmation of being with others, then we are sexual whether or not we are having sex. Scott saw his longing for someone to share his life with, both in erotic and nonerotic dimensions, as an expression of his sexuality. Similarly, Thad said,

> On a very basic level, sexuality means to have an attraction to someone. On a higher level, though, a healthy sexual person should feel no inconsistency between their wants and desires and actions. They are attracted to a person on a physical, mental, and emotional level. You don't have to have sex to be sexual. I think a virgin can be just as sexual as someone who is regularly having sex.

Our sexuality is bigger than sex and more complex than just wanting intimate friends. Sexuality is also about being attracted to difference—to that which we are not. Being sexual means that we notice the other sex, even when there is no specific attraction. When we hold hands in a circle of prayer, we notice if the hand we are holding belongs to someone of the other sex. Physical attraction is an element of sexuality that goes beyond the desire for the comfortable intimacy of friendship. It adds a spark.

Although Freud has been misunderstood and criticized for saying so, he saw sexual energy as the life force that motivates all human behavior. Sexual attraction is powerful. We look forward to being with people to whom we are attracted because in their presence we feel energized and more alive. Married people feel sexually attracted to men and women other than their spouses, but as people in an exclusive relationship they guard their hearts, watching their boundaries and expressions of sexuality. Whether or not people are married, they still experience relationships as sexual beings. But singles are free to pursue attractions with other singles they're attracted to. They have more freedom to flirt, to be drawn toward, and to welcome the energizing presence of others than married people have.

Ginger, who had been married almost fifty years before her husband died, said she does not want to marry again but would like to date—to have a man to go to movies with or out to dinner. She wishes men and women could date more easily. Ginger travels with women friends, goes to plays, and takes classes with them at the local community college. Yet she also desires male companionship. Her desire for a male friend is an expression of a sexuality that longs not only for the intimacy found in her female friends but for the rounding out of experience, the pleasantness, the spark that comes with exposure to difference found in companionship with the other sex.

Christian singles committed to celibacy outside of marriage struggle to determine appropriate expressions of sexual desire between two people who are mutually attracted to each other. Touch is important for all humans. Some touch is explicitly sexual in that it moves two people toward genital sexuality. Other touch reflects a desire to reach out of our aloneness and connect to another. Touch finds meaning within a cultural context, and how it is experienced and understood varies widely between cultures and individuals.

Generally, our culture looks suspiciously on touch, especially between men and increasingly so between women. Holding hands, hugging, being held, and kissing on the cheeks or lightly on the lips are ways touch has been used across time and cultures between men, between women, between parents and children, the old and the young, siblings, and courting pairs. Yet touch has often been used abusively, and our sensitivity to that means most forms of touch in our culture are assumed to be sexual, and they come under scrutiny.

With the plethora of possibilities for how touch is interpreted, those desiring to be responsible with touch work to clarify meanings and ensure consensus. Honestly and openly exploring and naming the purpose, intention, and potential unintended consequences of explicitly sexual touch demonstrates respect for the other and a desire to make responsible and moral choices about the use of touch among singles.

Naomi understood the complexities of touch and sexuality and embodied an inclusive, expansive love of God for people.

> I have different opportunities to interact with people because I am a woman, and now an older woman. Generally that means I'm safe, and that's part of my sexuality. It's fun being an older woman. I can express my love to people safely. I can walk down the aisle at church and bend over and whisper something affirming or loving and not be held in suspicion. My age and gender make me safe. It's easier to touch people's lives, either momentarily or on a regular basis.

Gary, the man divorced after twenty-five years of marriage, also thought our definition of sexuality needed to be bigger.

> We need a broader, fuller understanding of sexuality. It's helpful to talk to people who are celibate to gain a better understanding of what celibacy means. Intimacy and creativity are part of what it means to me to be sexual. Companionship is more important to me than genital sexual expression. This is what I long for, especially when companionship comes with shared values, vision, and mission. That expresses my sexuality. Letting go of narrow definitions of sexuality has been very liberating.

Broadening and changing definitions of sexuality help some move beyond the pain of brokenness toward healing and wholeness. As an adult, Greg sought to change his negative definition of sexuality and consider what might be good about it. He began by affirming that he was created as a male rather than cringing from his maleness.

> I learned to thank God for every part of me—to stand in front of the mirror and thank God, even for the parts that I felt shame about, or despised. Changing my perception was an incremental process. I learned to curtail my self-incriminating remarks. I found areas to express my masculinity where I could achieve—like running. Running connected me to my body, gave me appreciation for what my body

could do. I realized God had made a divine imprint on me—*divine imprimatur*—and that my body was good. If I was created in the image of God, how could my body be disgusting? The journey of my life has been a battle with despair, dealing with the doubt that I would ever feel whole. I've learned to let life be a process, to keep yearning for, hoping for, fulfillment.

Outlets for Sexual Desires

The desire for and possibility of engaging in some form of genital sexual expression calls to us from billboards, television commercials, and our computer screens. "I want my desire to be localized, to be less random than it is," thirty-four-year-old Scott said. "I'm amazed at how easily the male sex drive can be turned on, apart from being in relationship with someone. Gratuitous sex has never appealed to me, and I don't like that my body can respond to a billboard. But on one level, even that reminds me I have a healthy sex drive, that I long for something good."

People, whether married or not, make decisions about their involvement in or outlets for genital sex. Three kinds of attributes influence how single people in the United States generally make choices about genital sexual involvements:[8]

1. *Individual preferences:* primarily referring to how much one thinks about sex and notes individual differences in sexual drive or interest
2. *Physical health:* variables that influence the ability to engage in various sexual activities
3. *Social competence:* communication and people skills and resources such as time and money that make one able to attract potential partners

These three attributes influence the opportunities one has to get married or to meet potential partners. One's social class, religious preferences, location (rural or urban), sexual identity, and racial group all contribute to the opportunities and the choices a person makes regarding the expression of their sexuality. Religion is a significant variable for those who have faith commitments. That Christians believe sex has meaning apart from the biological act, that it represents a covenantal commitment—a sacred union, a symbol of mutual openness to life and each other—is lost on those who see it primarily as a way to express affection or fulfill a biological drive.

Our culture gives men and women who are not married numerous avenues for genital sexual outlets. We do not live in the days of Hester Prynne from Nathaniel Hawthorne's *The Scarlet Letter.* Rather than mark people with some outward sign of their sexual sin, our society accepts or at least tolerates people who choose to have sex outside marriage. In 1992, about two-thirds of unmarried women and three-fourths of unmarried men said they had sex in the last year—some in cohabiting relationships, some with dating partners.[9] Both men and women masturbate and use other means of erotic stimulation.[10]

Those committed to abstinence outside of marriage may feel they are alone in their pursuit of healthy expressions of sexuality that do not include having sex, viewing pornography, or going to strip clubs. Masturbation is the genital sexual outlet that Christians leave open for discussion. The men and women who talked about masturbation generally felt it was an acceptable outlet but still sometimes accompanied with shame and doubt about its appropriateness, or was performed with a sense of resignation. None felt as though masturbation was fulfilling; it did not satisfy a longing to be in a meaningful and sexual relationship with another person.

Often people said that the intimate bonds they had with others and God assuaged their longings for sexual intimacy. On some level, they understood God to be the ultimate One who fulfilled their deepest yearnings, and they wanted to experience that as true.

Churches' Ministry to Singles

The ministry of churches extends to those who are single, particularly to younger people. Although singles may find some common bond with other singles in their churches, organized singles groups were not spoken of as being particularly encouraging or helpful. Scott, who at thirty-four has participated in a number of singles groups, said having a critical mass of singles was important but having organized singles groups was not. Several people said that classes and groups that "single singles out" are a bad idea. Michael, a twenty-six-year-old, said, "Singles groups are there for people to meet each other, and that's OK, but it's like a meat market. There is too much pressure to meet someone."

Some singles feel marginalized and stifled by segregated classes; others prefer the segregation of similar-age-based Sunday School classes and grieve the loss of good connection and comfort without it. Both reflect two basic human needs: the need to be with those most likely to understand us and the need for the stimulation of being with those who are different from us. Both produce growth; both are necessary and meaningful connections. Understanding the experiences of those whose lives unfold differently from ours stimulates growth and helps us overcome awkwardness and discomfort.

Church leadership may not be taking advantage of the training and abilities of singles. Some felt their gifts and abilities were underused *because* they were single; they were assumed to be less mature and to have less to contribute than married people. Although singles are recruited to work with youth or other singles or to volunteer in the soup kitchen, they are seldom invited to be senior pastors, recognized as elders, or given leadership of adult Sunday School classes or small groups that are marriage- and age-integrated. A relatively untapped resource of potential leadership and giftedness waits for validation, discovery, and invitation.

In eternity, we will transcend barriers of age, marital status, socioeconomic levels, sex, race, and national and political affiliation; we will interact with each other freely and fully. Yet a social fact about humans is that we tend to congregate with people who share our life experiences and backgrounds. This tendency to be homogeneous in our social circles explains why few churches are as racially diverse as they would like to be and why we seldom see the impoverished sitting in pews beside the wealthy. It also explains why some singles feel they are outside an inner circle made up of married people and their children.

Churches are active in responding to the visible needs of singles. Many churches offer divorce recovery groups, support groups for single parents, and vibrant singles groups. The invisible needs are harder to identify. Ginger felt like her church did not attempt to serve widows and widowers but looked to them as mature people in life and faith to provide spiritual guidance to others. "That's not a bad thing, but churches have so much on their plate that they fail to see that we also have social, physical, and emotional needs."

Religious communities are powerful places for love and fellowship to be practiced. The Church does not function perfectly but is a primary tool God uses to meet the longings of people intrinsically drawn to relationship. Most faith communities are committed to learning how best to serve and to respond to needs of their given cultures and eras. They wrestle with how to strengthen marriages, encourage abstinence among the unmarried, respond to unmarried couples living together, and relate to those who have homosexual desires. Understanding the social milieu and experiences of singles offers a context for communities of faith trying to meet the particular needs of single people.

Singleness and Life Experiences

Not everyone who is single lives alone; some are single parents, living in a house with children; some have moved back home and live with their parents. Others share life with same-sex roommates, sometimes sleeping alone and sometimes not. Some share a bed with people they date; others choose to cohabit for a time in a monogamous, sexual relationship. The contexts and issues for each of these people change as they move from one situation to another.

Singleness and Cohabitation

As people began waiting longer to marry, more chose to cohabit with a partner. From 1970 to 2000, the numbers of cohabiting couples increased by 900 percent and now make up 5 percent of all households.[11] Although cohabiting used to occur primarily among never-married college students, now this group accounts for about one-fifth of all cohabiting couples; people forty-five and older account for another fifth.[12]

Some factors influencing this change are as follows:

- Less stigma is connected to living together without marriage.
- Young people are testing relationships or cohabiting for convenience.
- Middle-aged and older people cohabit to avoid the complexity of merging families and finances.
- Living together has become a temporary or transitional step between being single and getting married, increasingly seen as a normal pathway to marriage.

Cohabiting couples come from all social classes, ages, and ethnic and racial groups. In the 2000 census, one in four women said they had cohabited before their first marriage.[13] Yet cohabitants live more like singles than married couples. Their employment patterns, enrollment in school, and home ownership resemble other singles more than married couples.

Although cohabiting before marriage has become part of a normal progression toward marriage for many couples, people who cohabit have lower self-esteem,[14] are less happy, have poorer relationships with their parents, and report lower levels of commitment than married couples.[15] People who cohabit and later marry are more likely to get divorced than couples who do not live together prior to marriage. The divorce rate for people who cohabit prior to marriage is 50 percent higher than for couples who do not. Choosing to cohabit does not alone account for this higher divorce rate; people who are more likely to divorce may also be more likely to choose cohabitation. Because commitment is not assumed, negotiating life together is less essential.

For some people, maintaining a sense of autonomy and freedom is an attractive aspect of cohabitation over marriage. As a result, cohabiting couples tend to disagree more on issues that make up life: money, recreational choices, household chores, and work.[16]

Although some couples live together because it is a convenient next step in their relationship, others avoid marriage because they have seen so many fail and want to avoid a divorce if their relationship does not work out. The expectation that the relationship will last tends to be higher for married couples than for those who cohabit.[17] The expectation for fidelity is also higher for married couples. Cohabitation does not assume an explicit commitment to stay together or be exclusive sexually, especially for men. Men who lived with partners sought out other sexual partners more often than did the women they lived with. Men reportedly felt less obligation or need for fidelity than women.[18]

That cohabitants struggle with stability and happiness is not surprising. Living together is not institutionalized and recognized like marriage. And although people tolerate cohabitation, couples do not have the support structures or norms of marriage that could offer these relationships stability. Medical benefits and tax breaks continue to be aimed at encouraging people to be married rather than single, even when they are cohabiting.

Cohabiting couples present a timely opportunity for faith communities to help grow and stabilize these relationships. Although cohabiting couples who attend church are often not obvious (they do not wear scarlet letters on their chests), churches wrestle with responses to couples living together who come to them seeking to be married in the church. Some of these couples know the Church believes they are living in sin; others are surprised to find condemnation still in the Church when they assume everyone lives together before they get married.

In *Authentic Human Sexuality: An Integrated Christian Approach,* Jack and Judy Balswick discuss ways the Church can respond to cohabiting couples. At the center of their discussion is a goal of moving couples toward a permanent covenant commitment before God (whether or not that is ultimately marriage) for the purpose of bringing depth and stability to their relationship.

Singleness and Parenting

In the 1960s, my classmates and I lined up for class, sat in our assigned desks laboring away at phonetics and math, and played four-square on the playground. At the end of the day, only two or three of my thirty classmates went home to a one-parent family. The 2000 census showed that today ten or eleven out of thirty go home to a single parent. Fifty-five percent of those children live in homes where parents have divorced or separated; 41 percent are in homes where their mother or father never married, and 4 percent are in homes where a parent has died.[19]

I ask my Introduction to Sociology students, "Who are the poor in the United States? Give me three primary categories." Usually, they mention the elderly, minorities, perhaps the handicapped. Sometimes they jokingly say, "college students." The answer, once they hear it, does not surprise them: racial minorities, primarily African Americans and Latinos; women, particularly those who are the single heads of their households, and the children of those women constitute most of poor in the United States. By 1990, more than half of all people who lived in poverty lived in mother-only homes.[20]

The term *feminization of poverty* describes the social climate that leaves more women in poverty than men. When parents are not together, mothers are more likely than fathers to be providing for and raising their children. Even though women are earning more than ever before, they still earn significantly less than men. Three years after a divorce, a man is usually better off financially than he was while married. Three years after a divorce, a woman is usually worse off financially. Women without college degrees earn less than those with college degrees, and women without college degrees are more likely to be single mothers.

Financial challenges are paramount for many single mothers. A lack of social support and a feeling of being overwhelmed with the sole task of providing financially, emotionally, and physically for children are other challenges confronted by single mothers.

Kate said, "I looked at my four-month-old son in his crib and knew I couldn't do this on my own. Even though I saw celebrity single moms and other women I knew around me doing it, when I saw my son, being single became a big deal. Literally broken and on my knees, I came to Christ. I looked to the Church to help me and God to be my partner and my son's father." In choosing to put her son's needs before her own, she compromised her financial security and social opportunities. She worked around her son's schedule, taking jobs that paid less but allowed her flexibility. "I didn't want him to grow up in day care, and I'm committed to being there for him before and after school. So he doesn't have as much as other kids, but he's a great kid—and so appreciative of everything he does have."

Many churches have rallied around single moms, developing networks to help with pragmatic needs and support groups. Kate felt upheld by the church, even though she also felt like the Samaritan woman at the well (Luke 4).

> There are a lot of women out there trying to claw their way into the Church. Churches don't intend to make us feel like the woman at the well. It's just that when they find out we weren't ever married to the father of our children. . . . I had to stop thinking about my image if I wanted to be part of the Church. But I don't want my status as a single mom to be my sole identity in the Church. But part of me wonders, does God give me credit for working toward emotional and physical purity, or does God condemn me when I don't succeed perfectly?

Kate has been deeply wounded by Christian men she has dated. As one new to the faith, she felt betrayed, assuming she could trust men who called themselves Christians. Another single mom spoke of Christian men who dated her and assumed she would be willing to have sex with them, since she had a child out of wedlock. Given the depth of Kate's wounds and desires, she still expressed hope and blessing. "I'm not bitter. I'm not under the illusion that I'm the only person in pain. I know my bad choices got me in this situation. Yet I feel full, content, and blessed in every realm of my life except for my relationships with men."

Singleness from Death and Divorce

When I visit my parents in rural Pennsylvania, they take me to Summit Quest to exercise with them. One day, we arrived to the news that Ruby's husband, a man in his eighties, had died the day before. He had been failing for some time. People speculated about whether or not Ruby would still come that morning. Most thought so, not primarily because she was committed to her workout but because the people of Summit Quest were Ruby's family. She did come, and I watched members approach her, hug her, talk with her. A sympathy card circulated quickly through the aerobics class, and several offered to go with her to the visitation that night. They surrounded, upheld, and comforted Ruby in her loss.

Death is an acceptable loss. Some losses, like those experienced because of a homosexual orientation, are hidden because of shame or fear of rejection. Other losses we cannot hide, like divorce, and we bear the shame and hope that acceptance will come. One does not need to hide when one's spouse dies. No sin has been committed and giving comfort is uncomplicated.

Fifty-eight out of one hundred women over sixty-five years of age are single, and forty-five of those are widows. Half as many men at that age are single (twenty-seven out of one hundred), and fourteen are currently widowers.[21] Some widows and widowers remarry; others live alone; some move in with family. These choices depend somewhat on age, sex, and race. The younger a widow is, the more likely she is to remarry. But age is not relevant for widowers, who have more potential mates to choose from, given the cultural norm of men marrying women their own age or younger. Thus men are more likely to remarry than women, and many tend to do so within a few years of their spouse's death. White and African American widows are more likely to live alone than Latino or Asian widows, who are more likely to live with family members.

How a widow or widower adjusts to the loss of a spouse also depends on overall health, connections with others, and financial status. Ruby will likely do well, as Ginger has. Neither has significant family connections, but both have a strong social support through friends. Both stay physically and emotionally engaged and active. They are in good health and have an adequate financial base to cover their needs. In contrast, Ralph, a seventy-year-old Christian widower, lacked social support. He committed suicide several months after the death of his wife. Suicide rates are highest among white elderly men, many of whom are divorced or widowed and are without strong ties to family and friends.

Divorce and death require a major realignment of identity. Yesterday she had a husband; today she is single. The process is complicated or eased by the relationships one has (or does not have) with others and involvements that are life-giving or life-draining. Death of a marriage suggests failure in a way that physical death does not, adding another element of pain to the process of adjusting to loss through divorce.

Perhaps because divorce has become common both inside and outside the Church (slightly less than half of all marriages end in divorce), many churches have learned to embrace those suffering or recovering from the loss of a marriage because of divorce. One in ten people over eighteen were single in 2000 because they were divorced.[22] A longitudinal study that looked at factors of adjustments to divorce found that those who were younger, had an adequate income, were in a relationship with someone else, and had initiated the divorce adjusted better.[23] Gary is an exception to this study.

Gary, fifty-two years old and divorced, is not currently in a relationship, nor is he seeking to be. However, his perspective on loss and growth and his relationships with friends and God have moved him toward healing and forgiveness. "I don't think people ever heal completely," he said.

They are forever different. But loss and growth come in phases. Loss is a pivotal experience of life. I've had more growth since my divorce than during my whole life. You make choices whether to stay in a bad place or to work toward forgiveness. Sometimes you work for forgiveness more for the peace it gives you than because it's the right thing to do.

Singleness and Homosexuality

Communities of faith are unsure how to rally around single people whose sexual attractions are for others of the same sex. Students who have talked to me in past years about their same-sex attractions feel very isolated in their singleness, as did Greg, Thad, and Margie. Friendships were not safe. Someone of the other sex might become romantically or sexually interested and introduce awkwardness and shame. They may not handle friends of the same sex right, and their desire might be discovered. Even when Margie was not attracted to a same-sex friend, she feared that if the friend found out she struggled with homosexuality, it would introduce an awkwardness that would doom the friendship. Many of those struggling with orientation questions build walls of protection to keep people from discovering their secret or getting too close. Thad said,

> Having to hide, or rather choosing not to be completely open about my attraction to men, makes me feel less than honest. Then again, I really don't consider myself gay so it would be foolish for me to "come out" when perhaps I'm not even "in." If I did come out it would just make things worse. People would start expecting more of certain things and less of certain things. I would end up being more uncertain. I like it that not many people know about me. It's like if I tell people, I become committed to that identity or to how they view that identity.

For those who struggle with a homosexual orientation, issues of completeness are not related to marriage but to a personal crisis of sexual identity and the subsequent inability to relate authentically to others. Feeling complete for Thad meant having congruency between his attractions and beliefs and his actions. Greg said,

> Completion for me would come with a man—though not sexually. I knew a sexual relationship wouldn't satisfy what I longed for. But I had idealized men who had permission to be strong men. I wanted to be in relationship with someone like that. Yet at the same time I felt a

fear of men. I knew I couldn't compete with them and could be crushed by them. I had so much ambivalence toward men, so much distortion about what being in a relationship with a woman would be and no sense of what completeness could look like.

Margie felt like a leper—one who was an abomination, unclean, and likely to contaminate anyone to whom she got close. Margie, Greg, and Thad all said they longed for a heterosexual friend of the same sex who could love them in a nonsexual way for who they were, maintaining appropriate friendship boundaries to keep at bay tendencies they had to become enmeshed or overly dependent but who would not reject them or abandon them. Like all humans made in the image of God, they longed for relationship.

People experience homosexual desires to varying degrees. Few people are completely homosexual in their attractions, or completely heterosexual. Sometimes sexual attraction is described as a continuum with exclusive homosexuality and heterosexuality at the extremes and bisexuality (attracted to both equally) in the middle. Most of us fall somewhere along the continuum and most of us on the heterosexual half of the spectrum. Many people never act on homosexual desires and still consider themselves gay or lesbian; some who do participate in same-sex activities do not consider themselves homosexuals. An increasing number of people experiment with others of the same sex as part of exploring their sexuality. A same-sex experience does not mean one is homosexual.

Labeling someone homosexual is a relatively new development in human history. People have participated in homosexual acts throughout history, but they were not called homosexuals. Many people are surprised when they find themselves attracted to same-sex friends, and because of our all-or-none thinking (one is either gay or straight) and our love affair with labels, college students struggle with their sexual identities, wondering if same-sex desires means they are gay.

Because we do not know who counts as a homosexual, it is difficult to determine how many people are gay. Consider these questions: Have you ever had a sexual experience with a member of the opposite sex? Do you exclusively engage in same-sex sexual experiences? Do you consider yourself gay or lesbian? These questions yield different numbers. A large national study of Americans' sexual behaviors found 7.7 percent of men and 7.5 percent of women expressed homosexual desire; 2.8 percent of men and 1.4 percent of women identified themselves as gay or lesbian.[24]

Many Christians believe that homosexual behaviors are sinful, using biblical references condemning homosexuality to support their position.

At the core of the debate is a question about what makes a person gay. Christians tend to fall into one of four categories regarding the cause of homosexuality. What they believe about homosexuality flows from their beliefs about its cause.

Those in the first category believe, as do Coral Ridge preacher James Kennedy and psychologist Paul Cameron, that homosexuality is a sinful lifestyle choice that can and should be un-chosen.[25] Cameron claims that nothing causes homosexuality except an obsession with sex, self-centeredness, and the desire to be rebellious. Those choosing homosexual behaviors are an abomination to God and should be rejected until they repent. Cameron does not use credible research methods, so his work is dismissed by most academicians, both Christian and secular.

Those in the second category acknowledge homosexuality as more than simply a choice; it emerges from one's social environment. They consider homosexuality a disorder—the result of gender confusion and bad, wounding, or abusive interactions with parents or others—but ultimately one decides to live a gay, straight, or celibate lifestyle. God heals those who seek healing from the wounds received in childhood that lead to homosexuality. One can and should seek healing and un-learn the habits and inclinations of homosexuality. Psychologist James Dobson, Reverend Jerry Falwell, and Exodus Ministries are examples of those who view homosexuality this way.[26]

The first category sees homosexuality simply as a choice to sin; the second sees homosexuality as emerging from brokenness and requiring healing, not simply the will to stop sinning. However, both see the behaviors and the orientation as sin. In the first case, repentance is required; in the second, repentance for past sins and healing are necessary.

The third category includes sociologist Jack Balswick and family counselor Judy Balswick—Christian social scientists who assert that homosexuality is not only an interaction of social environment and social learning but may include a biological predisposition for homosexuality. They see homosexuality as a result of a general brokenness that permeates all of our bodies as well as our characters. One person may become gay; another who is not biologically predisposed to be gay might come from the same social environment and have similar experiences and not become gay. Because causes of homosexuality are complex and some aspects are rooted in biology, healing may not be possible for all who seek it. Homosexuality is not merely a choice that can be un-chosen nor a childhood trauma that can easily be healed. Most in this position suggest celibacy is the best response for homosexual Christians, though some accept committed monogamous homosexual relationships as a viable choice.[27]

Scientists like Simon LeVay[28] and religious leaders like the Reverend Mel White represent a fourth category. LeVay is a neurobiologist who claimed to have found evidence that sexual orientation, at least in males, is biological, linked with prenatal sexual differentiation in the brain. White is a gay rights activist and an official in the Metropolitan Community Churches in America. Christians in this category believe homosexuality is primarily rooted in biology. God made homosexuals as God made heterosexuals, and so gays and lesbians are God's children and should be free to embrace their homosexuality and live in loving, monogamous unions. Sexual sin is present in exploitative sexual encounters, whether homosexual or heterosexual, and not in committed, loving relationships, whether homosexual or heterosexual.

Some who have a homosexual orientation embrace their homosexuality; others struggle to change it; some continue to live with discontinuity, neither embracing it nor continuing to struggle to change it. How one defines successfully "dealing with" or living with a homosexual orientation is part of the challenge, which is again driven by assumptions.

Success for Jerry Falwell and for many in evangelical communities of faith is a complete redirection of one's orientation. Of those who seek to redirect their orientation, no more than 30 percent succeed,[29] and this may be an optimistic figure. People most likely to succeed are those toward the middle of the continuum of sexual attraction who are able to engage in a loving, heterosexual marriage and who felt less embedded in a homosexual orientation and lifestyle. Even so, success seldom means all homosexual desires are gone for good. Exodus, a ministry that helps gays toward healing, took a hit to its credibility in 2000 when John Paulk, a married ex-gay and then chairperson of Exodus International, was discovered in a gay bar. The media fostered a feeding frenzy that condemned Exodus-type ministries for being unable to change sexual orientation, even though they claimed to do so.

Yet Paulk's experience would not be surprising if we saw success as part of a lifelong journey of striving for wholeness. Healing does not have to be defined as complete redirection. When healing means moving toward maturity, through God's grace becoming more holy and virtuous, then anyone can change and stretch toward a hope for redemption. Greg, who is now married and contentedly so, said this:

> When I finally heard God say, "I'm not surprised by your feelings toward men, I don't hate you for your desires, I know where it is rooted, I love you," it opened the possibility for choice. Is this how I wanted to feel? Could I think differently? I needed to refuse to see myself as a label. I was not gay, but experiencing a common response

given my past. People need to know that there is always potential for sexual growth and development. That means different things for different people because they start from different places in terms of their life experience and degree of sexual wounding. But at any point, they can use whatever remains of their life journey to grow and mature, to become more holy and virtuous.

Greg found a support group of other Christians dealing with homosexual issues to help him begin a journey toward healing. Later he became part of a ministry team (all of whom were straight) who prayed for each other, encouraged each other, and embraced each other, even knowing his struggle with homosexuality. He also belonged to a group in his church that met together for prayer and friendship—ordinary people with ordinary challenges, who opened themselves and journeyed alongside each other toward the various ways they each sought wholeness. These groups sustained and blessed him on his own journey toward healing.

At least 70 percent of those who desire to exchange a homosexual orientation for a heterosexual one are unable to do so. Most psychologists and psychiatrists, a few Christians among them, believe it is unethical to try to redirect a homosexual orientation.[30] They believe that the defeat experienced by those 70 to 90 percent who fail leaves them worse off emotionally and sometimes spiritually than if they had never tried. Self-doubt, depression, and guilt accompany their failure, and facing members of a faith community who prayed for them leave them with no good place to go. Success for those who do not pursue, or do not continue to pursue, redirection is striving toward peace by living with integrity.

Success for Henri Nouwen was living a celibate life, letting God use his struggles to deepen his spirituality and minister to others. Michael Ford, his biographer said, "I sensed that Nouwen's struggles with his sexuality had been integral to his life and his spirituality, probably even inspiring his writings on loneliness, love, and alienation."[31] Some of Nouwen's friends wanted him to come out, leave the priesthood, and satisfy the longings of his heart for a relationship. A subtle nuance of the biography suggests that Ford thought Nouwen was trapped by the deformed position of a Church that did not have a healthy theology of homosexuality. Yet Nouwen's call was to celibacy. He believed people with homosexual orientations served a unique purpose in the Christian community and endorsed Carl Jung's view that "homosexual people are often endowed with an abundance of religious feelings, and a spiritual receptivity that makes them responsive to revelation."[32] For Nouwen, success was daily taking his feelings and his confusion and offering them to God, affirming a desire to serve God well through his writing, teaching, and ministry, and to remain celibate.

Christians with a homosexual orientation have a number of choices that correspond to the Church's traditional responses to homosexuality. One choice is to leave their faith and embrace the homosexual lifestyle. Condemned by the Church and driven by the incongruence between their longings and beliefs, they have no more to lose. Change eludes them, and God's wrath and judgment are poured out on them. God hates them; hell awaits them. Better to leave that behind and embrace what fulfillment they can find elsewhere.

Another choice is to leave the Church officially, while continuing to struggle privately with homosexuality and with maintaining a relationship with God. Thad said,

> I no longer blame God for "allowing" things to happen to me when I was young or for "cursing" me with being gay. Instead of looking to Him as a cause or as a silent criminal, I now look to Him as a possible way of "getting out" of the lifestyle. If things do change for me there will be some sort of spiritual awakening associated with it, and I think it will mean a return to a modified version of my earlier Christian roots. I don't blame Him anymore, and I don't hate Him; I'm not angry with Him. He's almost become a motivation for me—another reason to "change" if that's possible. I used to think that there was no way He could accept me if I was gay, and while I still think like that a little bit, I've decided that He's probably not all-out disgusted with me. But still, given that, He's not really a huge part of my life or my thinking right now.

Many Christians choose a third option—to stay with the Church and live celibate lives, although most keep their orientation a secret. Some get married, desiring the life of heterosexuals. An anonymous husband and father wrote the following for *Christianity Today:*

> At 19, when I found myself in the throes of suicidal depression, Christ seemed to be my best choice of last resort. I thank God that much about my life changed as a result of that choice. I recovered from my depression . . . and straightened out my sexual life enough to begin a healthy relationship with a wonderful woman. In time this led to my marriage to a person who *knows* and has supported me more than I could ever deserve. But as great as all this was, my sexual orientation did not change. . . . God has given me the power to live a fulfilling heterosexual life, together with the grace to live with the fact that I'm still homosexual. It hasn't been an easy victory. . . . Yes mine is a victory in the sense that I have managed to maintain life, love, and fidelity in my

marriage, but it is a victory that has required almost daily battle . . .
and I am frequently angry that I have had to do this on my own, without the support of friends or of a caring Christian community. . . . Why
haven't I told my story to my church friends? Because despite all the
claims by my heterosexual friends to "love the sinner but hate the sin,"
I do not trust them. I do not believe that they could know this about
me and still want me to be their congregational president, their youth-
group leader, their sons' coach.[33]

Greg's experience with the Christians and communities of faith brought
life-sustaining support. This author's experience has led to isolation and
a secret struggle for victory. Christian heterosexuals who are able to walk
alongside those striving for victory and wholeness are willing to accept
the complexities surrounding homosexuality and healing. They have
learned to extend grace by sitting with suffering and walking with others
down a road that has holds no promise for complete healing and fulfillment this side of heaven.

A fourth choice for Christians with a homosexual orientation is to
join a church that embraces homosexuals as children of God who are
created by God to be homosexual, even though rejected by the world. The
Metropolitan Community Churches of America is a denomination that
believes homosexuality is an acceptable lifestyle and calls people, whether
gay or straight, to live in committed, monogamous relationships. Some
Christians embrace homosexuality as God's best choice for them, even if a
difficult choice, given the rejection faced by a world too broken to embrace
them. Others believe that in God's understanding of human frailty and brokenness, God accepts monogamous gay relationships as a second-best choice.

Mel White, who has lived with his partner, Gary Nixon, for over twenty
years, founded Soul Force—an organization that seeks to use nonviolent
means to confront religious leaders who hurt gay and lesbian people with
their antigay messages. Many in the Church largely dismiss White, though
White's accusations could be used as a prophetic message to explore
the Church's insufficient response to those who struggle with homosexual
orientations.

Christians who disagree with White's theology can accept the challenge
to find ways to extend grace while upholding traditional Christian values
of celibacy and faithfulness. If Christians challenge their implicit assumption that celibacy in general is an inferior option to marriage, would it
change the ability to embrace those with homosexual orientations,
whether or not they continue to try to redirect their orientation?

I believe that homosexuality is an aspect of broken sexuality; it's not
the way it's supposed to be. When students struggling with homosexual

orientations or lifestyles talk with me, my goal is not to get them to live a certain way. Rather, I hope to be a conduit of God's love, to help them see God is not surprised or disgusted by their struggle and wants to be in relationship with them. That said, I still think celibacy is the best option for those who cannot come to a place of healing (which is the majority of homosexuals). The Church needs a better theology about healing and celibacy. Except for gay and lesbian churches, most churches are failing to love homosexuals well and support their struggle for victory. A redemptive view of victory or success is to see it as a consistent movement toward God, toward virtue, and toward authentic relationships. Communities of faith wanting to walk alongside people attempting to live victoriously and find some measure of relational fulfillment will need to be willing to change their assumptions about homosexuality and their definitions of healing and victory.

Just Single

A colleague who read an earlier draft of this chapter commented that the experiences of people who were just single—not divorced or widowed, or who are not parents, cohabitants, or gay—are still largely invisible. Indeed, the expectation is that those who are "just single" will marry, and because most do, married people feel justified to move on to other matters. Yet the singles themselves, many of whom hope to marry, wonder about how best to find potential mates. A thirty-four-year-old, never-married woman said, "I no longer expect to find a spouse through the traditional singles dating scene. If I marry, I assume it will be to someone I am introduced to through a mutual friend."

Some singles looking for a relationship use dating services like eharmony.com—a Christian organization that promises to match people on character qualities essential for a successful and satisfying marriage. Rebekah looked into signing up but thought it was a desperate thing to do and wondered if the men who signed up might also be desperate. She wasn't sure how to think about using Internet technology to find someone with whom to share her life.

Rabbi Yaacov Dyo wanted to make it easier for Jewish singles to find Jewish mates and established "speed dating" in 1999.[34] Dyo claims that half the participants find mates. His template has been picked up by numerous organizations in the last few years, most of them secular. Participants pay a fee, are given a number, and gather with about thirty other singles (fifteen males and fifteen females). They have a timed three- to ten-minute conversation with each participant of the other sex. On a card, they mark "yes" or "no" after each conversation to determine whether or not they would be interested in future contact. At the end of the night, they turn in their cards, and when matches occur where both people marked "yes," they are given each other's information and can pursue further contact if they so choose.

A woman who participated in a speed-dating event said she likes how it lightens up dating; it helps people take dating less seriously and gets people out to meet others, infusing some energy and enthusiasm into the process. However, she also said that speed dating has the potential to reinforce people's feeling like losers if no one they are interested in returns their interest.

Never-married singles, whether by choice or circumstance, contend with others' perceptions (or *perceived* perceptions) that something is wrong with them because they are not married. Some wonder if others think they might be gay. People who are not married, for whatever reason, need authentic communities and relationships where they can talk about their sexuality—what it means and how to embrace it, given their singleness.

Marriage has the potential to bring great blessing, but perhaps the emphasis of Protestants on the ultimate good of marriage continues to keep celibacy or singleness from being seriously considered as a viable or good choice for singles. A few choose celibacy and singleness for life, though only the Catholic church has honored this choice through a vocational call to serve as nuns or priests. Finding honor for the celibate life is challenging for people without legitimate or ceremonial recognition of singleness as a valid choice.

Communities of faith face two challenges, which are seemingly at odds with each other, when it comes to never-married singles. The first challenge is to validate singleness as a good option that has potential for great blessing. The second challenge is to provide opportunities for singles to meet each other and form bonds of friendship and perhaps marriage.

Loss is part of life. Loss comes with singleness, and loss comes in marriage. Some losses stay hidden or unspoken, such as the hopelessness of a woman or man who can never have children or be married or that of a man in a homosexual orientation who desires to live a life complete with wife and children. The world is broken; it is not as it should be. We are incomplete, single or married, and we long for what we do not have.

Hope for Fulfillment

German Catholic philosopher Josef Pieper said hope is the longing for something not yet realized. Hope believes fulfillment will come someday and holds the tension of not yet finding fulfillment. Hopelessness—the rejection of hope—exists in two forms. In one case, it gives way to despair, no longer believing that fulfillment will ever come. In the other case, hopelessness is *praesumptio*—presumption that fulfillment has already fully come.[35] A married woman may believe she is fulfilled now that she is married. Once she realizes her marriage is not perfect, that she still longs for something she has not received, hopelessness sets in.

We lose hope once we give up on the possibility of fulfillment. Although fulfillment will not fully come until our pilgrim journey on earth is complete, we get a taste of it on earth and so continue to hope. Those who are married get a taste of fulfillment through a bond that allows them to give and receive love as expressed fully and freely in their sexuality. Together they bring children into their union and experience different capacities for love that mirror God's love of us, as children and lovers of God. Marriage brings certain rights, with corresponding limitations and obligations.

Those who are single get a taste of fulfillment in an inclusive embracing and welcoming of others, unrestrained by obligation. Singles have the freedom and ability to pursue possibilities, dreams, and callings unencumbered by limitations of family and spouse. The celibate life keeps choices open, with corresponding limitations in sexual expression.

The celibate life also offers a beautiful picture of redemption—of what life will be like when we are in communion with God in heaven as those neither married nor given in marriage (Matthew 22:30). The Catholic church has been criticized in recent years for continuing to demand the celibacy of priests, particularly in light of sexual misconduct. But Pope John Paul II stands by the Church's position. Celibacy reminds us that our deepest longings cannot be satisfied on earth and is the choice to wait for the fulfillment of heaven rather than pursue a partial fulfillment now. However, the Pope urged people to refrain from assuming that the choice of celibacy is the more complete and perfect choice.[36] Those choosing marriage and those choosing celibacy complement each other; they explain and complete each other, giving us a fuller picture of God among us, as evidenced in a community of both married and unmarried people.

For most, singleness is a temporary state. Yet during that time, single people can embrace this unique way they reflect the inclusive nature and love of God. They can name the yearning for what they do not have, grieve the lost hope of having it, yet hold the desire for fulfillment lightly, knowing that full fulfillment is yet to come. Grieving reminds us that we all are incomplete in the end. We all sleep alone at night in our own skin, existentially alone. Yet there is also an abundance that comes from singleness— the unencumbered ability to love and live freely. We have the hope of future fulfillment and a taste of fulfillment now. When singles celebrate their lives—the fulfillment they have now—they enrich and bless the community of God. When married people within the Church see single people yearning toward, waiting for a future state of fulfillment while living fully the life they have, married people are instructed, reminded not to focus overly much on what singles do not have but to celebrate the abundance they have and to yearn for fulfillment yet to come.

Conclusion

Where one lands at the end of the journey is partly determined by choices one makes along the way. Naomi, who spent much of her life serving students, inspires me. I want to be like her when I'm seventy-five. She says,

> I wouldn't change who I've become in my seventy-five years as a woman. That's been a special gift. My life has been meaningful and full of relationships—even if I'm not married with children. We go through passages of life—changes through the years. If you don't pay enough attention to your vulnerabilities and to the work of God within you to ask, "Is this the way I want to be?" you lose opportunities to grow.

May we all, like Naomi, pay attention to our lives, recognizing and savoring the taste of fulfillment we have, even as we stretch toward hope—the fulfillment that is to come. May we encourage and minister to each other, drawing each other toward community and peace in the places and situations that fill our days and lives.

———— o ————

QUERIES FOR FURTHER REFLECTION AND DISCUSSION

o How did the chapter stretch your concept of singleness, both as a category of people (divorced, widowed, gay) and as a state of being that uniquely reflects an aspect of God's character?

o If 40 percent of people over eighteen are single, why are they largely invisible in our communities of faith? Are they in yours? Why or why not?

o What might faith communities do to integrate single people and their experiences into the life and rhythm of the Church? What can communities of faith learn from singles, and how might they be enriched in the learning?

○ If you are married, are single adults (who are not related to you) an integral part of your life? If single, are married adults an integral part of your life? If over sixty years old, are younger adults part of your life? If under thirty, are older adults part of your life? What would it take to widen the scope of people with different life experiences into your life?

○ What did you think of the anonymous gay father and husband? How would you respond if someone like him disclosed his story to you? What questions did the section on homosexuality raise for you?

○ Given the higher instability of cohabiting relationships and higher probability that cohabiting couples will divorce if they marry, how might faith communities move cohabiting couples toward greater stability and commitment? What cultural barriers keep the Church from having a greater impact on cohabiting couples, and how might Christians overcome those barriers?

○ If you were to pay attention to your vulnerabilities and to the work of God within you, as described in the chapter, what kinds of questions would you be asking? What are your vulnerabilities? What work is God doing within you? Is your experience of sexuality life-affirming? Where do you savor the fulfillment you have, and where are you stretching toward hope—toward the fulfillment that is to come?

───────────

○

BIRTHING BABIES

THE ESSENCE OF EARLY MOTHERHOOD

(AND FATHERHOOD)

Sexuality has always been studied separately from maternity, as if sex has nothing to do with maternity or keeping infants alive.

—Sarah Blaffer Hrdy[1]

"TELL ME ABOUT WHEN I WAS BORN," five-year-old Megan said, as we settled into the rocker to read. I put the book down, held her hands in mine as she sat with her back against my chest, and told Megan her story. "You came late—at least we thought you were late; Grammy had already come and gone. She wanted to be here for your birth, but she couldn't hold out as long as you could."

"That's too bad," Megan said.

"The night you were born, we were at church watching a missionary slide show. I started having the light contractions I'd been having that told me you were getting ready to be born. I told Papa, and soon after that we decided to leave. We stopped at Winchell's for donuts, like we always did, and came home and put your sisters to bed. Finally, we went to bed, too. But you didn't want us to go to bed, because you wanted to be born. The contractions got closer together and lasted longer. They were a lot harder, too. Papa needed to talk me through them to help me relax. We called Dr. Uma to tell her I thought you were finally going to be born. She came to our house and checked me about midnight, and we still had a long way to go. Uma suggested I soak in our bathtub to help me relax, but I couldn't relax well there either. Papa told me to think about being calm and to remember each contraction was bringing you closer. About an hour later, I felt like I wanted to push, and sure enough, it was time for you to be born! It took about fifteen to twenty minutes to push you into the world. I felt your head as it started coming out—it was great to touch you!"

"Ewww!" said Megan.

"Uma was very good at helping you be born. And Papa was very good at helping me relax. After you were born, Uma put a little purple hat on your head to keep you warm and gave you to me to hold. You opened your eyes and looked at me. And when Papa held you, you looked at him, too. Sarah met you first, coming downstairs in the morning. Her eyes were big, and she said "baby" softly, as she pointed to you. We sent her up to get Rae, who welcomed you with big-sister enthusiasm. We were all a bit awe-struck to have you finally join us."

"Hmm," Megan said as she snuggled deeper into my lap. "That's a nice story."

A woman makes a rather large physical investment in the reproductive process. Every month she ovulates, and if the egg is fertilized she conceives; then she spends nine months growing the baby. As the baby grows, it demands increasing amounts of room, taking up space hitherto occupied by such organs as lungs and intestines, putting pressure on the heart and kidneys to provide extra oxygen and remove excess waste. Hormone levels rise and fall throughout her pregnancy, during birth, and following birth, sometimes influencing her emotions and behaviors. The mother accommodates these demands until her uterus, in response to hormonal cues, begins the contractions that will bring about the birth of the baby.

The prediction of this date is only approximate, and whatever she has planned for the day takes a back seat, as she turns her attention to the laborious work ahead. All this for someone she has not met, who will give nothing tangible in return (and the intangibles are uncertain), and who will become yet more demanding once he or she is born and takes up residence (for the next twenty years or so) in her home. She literally embodies change, as her body and soul expand to make room for another.

When a woman becomes a mother, she enters a stream of women who have become mothers before her, reaching back thousands of generations. It is not surprising that after giving birth, women often tell each other their stories and eventually tell them to their children. Women recount their experience, which is filled in by others who were present, adding details and substance to the emerging birth story that will be filed away in memory, shaping perceptions of birth and parenthood. The experience alters her body and her identity; she becomes different from the way she was before.

In the telling, we develop our ideas about how babies should be birthed, how women should experience childbearing, and how motherhood and fatherhood should be defined. In other words, sex produces babies; cultural beliefs and values produce ideas regarding what to think about it all. So it is indeed odd that we often talk about sexuality separately from maternity, in Hrdy's words, as if sex has nothing to do with maternity or keeping infants alive.

To embrace the physical aspect of birth is to welcome the whole embodied experience of pregnancy, birth, and parenthood that profoundly changes women and men. Women who embrace childbearing learn how laboring bodies do the work of birthing babies and are spiritually and emotionally aware of, in tune to, and working with the changes and demands of a pregnant, laboring, and nursing body. Women in faith communities actively participate in the physical and spiritual process of growing and strengthening community bonds when they support each other through pregnancy.

Throughout generations, some aspects of childbearing remain unchanged; others accommodate to new technologies that change perceptions and approaches to childbearing. Perceptions of motherhood depend on place and time. At times, women have fostered a strong awareness and connection to their bodies and to each other through childbearing; at other times, a woman's identity has been separate from her body and the experience of childbearing.

What a woman believes about childbirth and motherhood affects how she sees herself as a mother, a woman, and a sexual being. What a man believes about birth and motherhood shapes his expectations and ideas about the woman who becomes the mother of his children and his own view of himself as a father. Childbearing is a beautiful expression of sexuality—the fruition of a life-perpetuating process God put in place that expands the love a woman and man have for each other to welcome and embrace new members of the human race.

Faith communities are key players in training and instructing about marriage and family; however, except for abortion, they are often silent on issues related to reproduction. We have relinquished most of the training, decision making, and caregiving associated with reproduction and childbearing to the medical community. But our particular time in history gives the Church unique opportunities to reintegrate physical aspects of childbearing with the beauty and mystery of spiritual longings for connection.

Communities of faith wanting to reclaim an active role in discussions about reproduction and childbearing will find it useful to look back down the road humanity has traveled. Understanding our cultural history, as it relates to childbearing, helps us know where we have been so we can better see and choose the road ahead.

A Brief History of Birthing Babies

Two features distinguish our history from the present day regarding the birthing of babies. The first is that for most of human history women helped women birth babies. The only men to attend births were the fathers of the babies being born. Mothers—generally women who had stopped having children—became birth attendants for others. Women particularly skilled at assisting in births were recognized by a village or town as midwives and were asked most frequently to assist young mothers in their births.

A second distinguishing feature is that for most of history, women had babies in their own homes or the homes of their mothers. In the normal cycle of life, babies were born and old people died at home or in the homes of their relatives. Both events were perceived as being deeply spiritual yet belonging to the ordinariness of life. Relinquishing the events surrounding the beginning and ending of life to the care of strangers, primarily technicians who worked out of places intended to cure the sick, did not fit with beliefs about how life should begin or end. Turning birth—a spiritual, physical, and sexual life event—over to the medical community happened gradually, with significant watershed moments.

One early watershed moment, far back along the path down which we have come, occurred with the great bubonic plague. The plague killed about one-third of all people living in Europe in the fourteenth century. Some thought it a scourge of God. Rich and poor died, as did political figures and priests, bringing change to cultural and religious institutions. People died whether or not they put their hope in God. God had scourged Europe, and after the fact some were left wondering what kind of God would do such a thing. The introduction of religious doubt opened the door for science to offer more satisfying answers. A contest would be waged during the Enlightenment between the new ideas of science and the old traditions of religion: which of the two could better deliver the good life? As the black plague (another name for bubonic plague) subsided, people began to look beyond the Church for answers.

Over the next six centuries, scientists continued making breakthrough discoveries or building on previous ones. Penicillin allowed victory over bacterial infections, reducing deaths from pneumonia and other infections we now take for granted. Medical knowledge about nutrition and hygiene led to improved health and longer life, and fertility treatments allowed infertile couples to have children.

Increasingly, normal aspects of the sexual life (particularly reproduction) that had been overseen by skilled midwives in the community came under the supervision of doctors in medical institutions. The perception of childbirth as a natural and normal extension of one's sexual life shifted to that of a temporary state in which, for a time, a woman's normal nonpregnant state was altered by becoming a high-risk pregnant one. Sociologists call this shift in perceptions and childbirth attendants from midwives in homes to doctors in hospitals the *medicalization of childbirth*.

Benefits and Losses with the Medicalization of Childbirth

An upside of the development of medical intervention for childbirth was that some mothers and babies lived who otherwise would have died. Indeed, women and infants *had* died in childbirth, at times at alarmingly high rates. A downside was that pregnancy and birth came to be identified as high-risk physical states in need of medical supervision and, increasingly, medical intervention. Women began to lose an intrinsic connection to, awareness of, and knowledge about how their bodies did the work of growing and birthing babies.

Medical communities in industrialized countries had reshaped perceptions about and experiences of childbirth by the 1950s. Women went to hospitals to be *delivered*. Husbands, mothers, and other female support were kept out of the delivery room. Not surprisingly, the introduction of various interventions made delivery of the baby quicker and easier for the doctor; rupturing the membranes or the "bag of waters" helped labor progress. Giving women pain medication made them more comfortable and passive but often meant that greater intervention was required to deliver the baby. Episiotomies—surgical cuts to make the vaginal opening larger—decreased pushing time and helped get the baby out quicker, but sometimes forceps were needed to pull the baby out of a mother too sedated to push.

In traditional birthing positions, women squatted or used birthing stools; they were active participants in the birthing of their babies. Traditional positions were replaced with the lithotomy position, which put women on their backs with their feet up in stirrups—a position that gave doctors easier access to babies they were delivering. Babies were whisked away shortly after birth and kept in nurseries; they were brought to the mother according to a schedule set by the hospital.

These procedures became routine in the 1950s and 1960s. In 1968, with the introduction of the fetal monitor (an instrument that allowed for continual monitoring of babies' heart rates), the number of cesarean section deliveries increased dramatically. In 1970, 9 percent of all births were by cesarean, increasing to 20 percent in 1980 and hovering around 24 percent since 1990. In the current climate of litigation for malpractice, doctors protect themselves from lawsuit by quickly taking a baby by cesarean that appears to be in stress.

By one measure, we are a society that protects the lives of newborns and birth mothers by offering excellent medical care. Many life-threatening complications are resolved so that infants and mothers survive. Yet the United States, one of the most progressive and technologically advanced nations of the world, ranks 34th worldwide in infant mortality rates (6.76 deaths for every 1,000 births).[2]

The United States does not have a better infant mortality rate for a number of reasons—the most likely being that the United States is the only industrialized country without national health care, which would ensure that every pregnant woman has access to good prenatal and birth care. A second explanation is the greater prevalence and use elsewhere of alternative ways of birthing babies that promote better mother and baby health by keeping women connected to the process of conceiving, carrying, and birthing infants.

A Christian View

By and large, contemporary Christianity sees value in integrating the body and soul, rejecting dualistic ways of thinking that suggest the soul is spiritual and good and the body is crude and bad. We live enfleshed spiritual lives, as Henri Nouwen says. The Church expands a vision for an enfleshed, or embodied spiritual life by re-examining patterns and beliefs about childbearing, seeking avenues for fostering connection between a woman's physical experience as she participates with God in the deeply spiritual task of creating and sustaining life. The most obvious avenue of connection is between women in families and communities of faith where seamless modeling and training and care and instruction can be given and received from generation to generation. We do so by remembering and relearning something we forgot along the way.

Reclaiming the Birth Experience

Dr. Grantley Dick-Read delivered babies in England in the 1930s and found that women labored more effectively when they knew what was happening to their bodies and learned how to relax their muscles and work with the laboring process. His book *Childbirth Without Fear* laid the foundation for later efforts to reclaim birth experiences. In the 1960s, women began to reflect on the history of childbearing, and a natural-birth movement began, with the goal of women helping women get through labor and delivery without medication. Ina May Gaskin, founding member of The Farm, a community in Summertown, Tennessee, is credited with starting the homebirth movement in the United States in the early 1970s. She was a self-trained midwife who started attending births for women belonging to The Farm. Gaskin became a writer and educator for the homebirth movement, and lay midwives once again began offering the option of homebirths to pregnant women.

Birthing in the United States

By 2000, women had a number of childbirth setting options; most were recognized as legitimate and were covered by insurance. At one end of the spectrum are women taking charge of their birth experiences, believing childbearing is a normal process that can be carried out at home with the skilled care of a midwife; high-risk cases are referred to the medical community. In the rare cases when complications occur, women are transferred to hospitals for care. Fewer than 1 percent of women in the United States choose to have their babies at home.[3]

At the other end of the spectrum are options emerging out of the assumption that childbirth is an unpredictable and potentially life-threatening event that requires close medical supervision and care. The use of fetal monitors is routine, as are the insertion of intravenous lines in the laboring mother and the use of a flat bed and stirrups for delivery.

In the middle are the birthing centers, which are set up so women labor and deliver in the same room, keep their babies with them after delivery, and allow for the presence of family members and friends. The assumption of birthing centers is that childbirth is almost always a normal process requiring no medical intervention. Some hospitals are trying to move toward the middle by providing birthing rooms that blend the offerings of birthing centers with the technologies of medicine. Assumptions about childbirth at hospitals with birthing rooms vary considerably.

In light of new research coming from nations with better maternal and infant outcomes than the United States, some standard interventions used in the States are being reconsidered by medical professionals, with efforts to decrease the frequency of their use. Cesarean rates are often compared to determine whether a hospital or country overintervenes in childbirth. The World Health Organization set a global goal of reducing the cesarean rate to 15 percent by 2000; in the United States, cesarean rates continue at about 24 percent. The routine use of episiotomies declined in the 1990s with the publication of studies that showed no significant benefit to episiotomies and increased difficulty in healing and postpartum pain, compared to women without episiotomies, even if their tissues were torn. However, at some hospitals episiotomies are still performed on 80 percent of mothers. In hospitals attempting to avoid the routine use of episiotomies, they are used approximately 30 percent of the time. Midwife rates at hospitals and birthing clinics are below 10 percent for episiotomies.[4]

Hospitals can provide state-of-the-art medical treatment and still be sensitive to timeless needs of laboring women, as is true of The National Maternity Hospital in Dublin, Ireland. When a woman arrives at National Maternity, medical personnel determine whether or not she is in active labor. If not, she spends the day in the antenatal ward or returns home until she goes into active labor. Inducing labor at National Maternity Hospital occurs infrequently. Once a woman is in active labor, she is assigned her own nurse-midwife (in Ireland this is a midwife-in-training), who stays with her throughout labor and birth, providing her with one-on-one continuous care. She encourages the mother to walk, assuages her fears, builds her confidence, massages her as she labors, encourages her as she gives birth, and celebrates with her afterwards. Ninety percent of first-time mothers have babies in less than eight hours—50 percent of them in about six hours. The cesarean rate ranges from 5 to 6 percent. These numbers are attributed to the hospital's low-intervention approach and the assumption that women labor and give birth more effectively when helped by another woman offering continuous support and care.

Birthing centers in the United States come closest to resembling the National Maternity Hospital in Dublin. As of 2000, 145 communities in the United States had birth centers that were not in hospitals.[5] Medical equipment and personnel are available when needed in these facilities, and unless complications emerge, midwives assist the mother giving birth. Family members come and go, and the baby stays with the mother. Monitors, intravenous lines, episiotomies, and flat beds with stirrups are only used when complications emerge. A study of birth centers and hospital births, published in the *New England Journal of Medicine,* shows that the outcomes for mothers and infants were as good, if not better, when they gave birth in centers and that mothers' satisfaction with the birth experience was higher at birthing centers.[6]

Women Helping Women

The use of doulas has been on the rise in recent years—a return to early eras when women helped women give birth. A doula (Greek for "women helping women") offers continuous emotional and physical support to the mother before, during, and just after birth. Although they do not assist in the actual birth, doulas are experienced and trained in childbirth. Studies have consistently found that the length of labor decreases for women who use doulas, epidurals are used less frequently, and 50 percent fewer of these women have cesarean sections.[7] Although these outcomes might reflect a connection between women inclined to use doulas and those hoping to have a natural childbirth, they also suggest that the presence of doulas, or other attentive women experienced in childbirth, creates a comforting environment for the work of labor, easing the anxiety and pain of childbirth.

Women without specific training can also help other women during childbirth. I speak from personal experience. Some friends asked me to be present with them during the birth of their first child; they wanted me to film the birth and offer support to them during labor and birth. The birth took place in a hospital-based birthing center. I wish I had known better how to assist Joy. Her birth experience was difficult, and I did not know what to do to help ease her discomfort and discouragement. Women in my generation and for several generations before me have not grown up expecting to need to know how to help other women labor and give birth. Joy ultimately needed some of the medical interventions available to birth Garrett. In spite of the difficulties, Garrett's birth was a deeply meaningful experience that I felt honored to have been invited to share.

Twice I was a support person for a friend in labor, and during one of my own labors, a friend supported me. These are key memories for me— times of strong connection to other women. We lived in a rural Tennessee town far from family when Sarah was born. I asked my friend Leslie to come help with the birth. My husband, Mark, called and woke her up sometime after midnight and told her it was time. She came to our house, willing to assist my midwife and me in any way she could. One of her most meaningful tasks was to meet Rae, who woke up when she heard Sarah's newborn cry, and to bring Rae in to meet her new sister. Relationships are strengthened and bonded through shared, intimate life experiences.

Fathers can also play an important role; they can be terrific coaches. Mark held my hand and squeezed it tight during contractions, just the way I wanted him to. He told me that I was doing great and that he loved me; I needed to hear that over and over. Mark counted the toes and fingers of our newborn daughters, and his awe and wonder blessed me. A father's presence cements his role as father and husband. His presence affirms his identity as father, allows him to honor his wife, and gives him immediate bonding opportunities with his newborn. But fathers, however dedicated and doting, are as inexperienced at birth as first-time mothers, and expecting them to know how best to help a laboring woman is asking a lot. Women who have experience and training are naturally suited to bless and minister a laboring and birthing woman.

Strengthening Community

Throughout history, as women have helped other women give birth, family and community ties have been strengthened. Laboring mothers who have an experienced woman present to offer continuous assistance and comfort find that this reassures her, decreases fear and anxiety, eases her pain, shortens her labor, and minimizes her need for medical intervention. How much more of a blessing is shared when this woman is someone a laboring woman knows. God created us for relationship, to help each other during significant life events.

What if faith communities started offering childbirth classes where spiritual, sexual, physical, and relational dimensions of childbearing were woven together? What if churches maintained their own list of doulas or women with experience in childbirth who are available to advise women throughout their pregnancy and care for them as they labor and give birth to their babies?

The Influence of Culture

Certain elements of motherhood are embodied, that is, rooted in a woman's body and essentially unchanging throughout history. Other elements are embedded, that is, given interpretation and meaning from culture. And motherhood is an interaction between the physical (biological) realities and the meanings given to physical events (socially constructed realities); the sum of embodied and embedded experiences makes up what we call motherhood. The two pieces are inseparable and beautiful expressions of sexuality—the culmination of a man and woman's sexual union, a bond that unites them literally in parenthood.

As communities of faith look toward possibilities for actively reclaiming a role in shaping and ministering to women during childbearing experiences, we are wise to first observe taken-for-granted assumptions of parenthood that are present in our culture.

Sometimes at a park I walk by, I see a couple of pregnant women sitting on a bench or standing by the swings with a couple of other children. As they talk, occasionally resting a hand on their wonderfully rounded abdomens, they are mindful of their other children sliding, swinging, and climbing around them. I find them sensuous—a beautiful picture of sexuality as depicted by motherhood. A woman's changing perception of herself as mother, a father's emerging perception of himself as father, and the mysterious process of attaching and falling in love with an infant all reflect physical and spiritual realities interpreted and given meaning by culture.

Self-Perceptions and Motherhood

How a woman perceives her pregnancy and birth experience affects how she sees herself. The inverse is also true: how she perceives herself affects how she experiences pregnancy and birth. The two reinforce each other, creating either a negative cycle that distances her identity from her body or a positive cycle that integrates her physically, emotionally, spiritually, and socially.

The Childbearing Center Morris Heights, a birthing clinic in the Bronx, offers an example of how this cycle is being used to empower women. Low-income women receive good-quality prenatal and childbirth care at the center. "I think the essence of the midwifery model of care is that birth is a body process and through it you can really grow," said the director of midwifery services, Jennifer Dohrn. "It's not just about suffering; it's experiencing how your body works and working with it. And that can be rewarding for someone to go through." The goal of the center is to empower women in the childbirth experience. Women weigh themselves, check their urine, record their progress, and participate in decisions. Mothers who take control of their pregnancy care come to believe they can also be empowered in other areas of their lives.[8]

Whether a woman believes pregnancy ends with her *being delivered* or *giving birth* is a subtle yet significant issue. If she is *giving birth,* she is an active participant in the decisions and processes of pregnancy and childbirth; if she is *being delivered,* she is a passive recipient of a process over which she has little control. She depends on the advice and decisions of medical experts. It stands to reason that afterward she may feel less of a woman and less attractive, her sexuality forfeited by the demands of pregnancy and a baby. One who chooses, participates in, and relishes the amazement of her body may well feel more sexy, more sensual, more of a woman for having given birth. Women can enjoy the process of being pregnant and having a baby, of participating in a timeless experience that connects the past to the present and will take humanity into the future.

Women can also be resentful and fearful, and feel cursed for the burden they bear. Research suggests that women who feel positive about their birth experiences and spend a lot of time with their newborns tend to have more positive feelings about mothering, feel like more competent mothers, and have happier, better-adjusted children.[9] All women want that, as do communities of faith concerned about the well-being of families. Because culture shapes perceptions, positive responses can be planted and cultivated, passed on by mothers to their daughters or to women in faith communities and then to younger women as a legacy of blessing and empowered creativity.

I interviewed a number of women regarding how they felt about being the person who gets pregnant, gives birth, and nurses her young.

Responses varied significantly, but they clustered into two groups consistent with other research looking at women's participation in the birthing process and perceptions of themselves as women and mothers.[10]

Ambivalent and Eager Mothers

The first group, "ambivalent mothers," is summarized by Allison, a mother of two: "Sometimes I feel like it's really unfair. My pelvic floor is shot. It stinks that I give up my body to this thing. I know it's a miracle and beautiful, but women make all the sacrifices. We give up so much of our lives to this process. I wish men would understand the sacrifice better. Whenever I hear men batter women about losing their figure or gaining weight after having babies it makes me mad." Allison continued to be unsure about her ability to mother well. She wanted children and loves her children but is unsure about her identity as a mother. She felt like her body was invaded, used, engulfed, and consumed in this thing called motherhood.

The second group, "eager mothers," is captured by Maggie: "This is very positive to me. It's a huge gift. I'm most proud of my body in its role in giving birth and nursing. My body has never let me down in that arena. Because of birthing four kids, I have a rather positive view of my body, even though it isn't culturally the norm or the ideal." Maggie had four children in six years, all of them at home. She home-schooled, working part-time in various jobs she could fit around her children's lives, and then, as her children left home, went back to school to become a nurse.

Many life events and social circumstances influence women's perceptions and experiences of pregnancy and childbirth. Allison went through a number of years of infertility diagnostics and treatments and eventually had a daughter. Several years later, she went through more treatments and had a son. The home she grew up in had not been safe physically or emotionally; puberty and menstruation brought shame and discomfort. In contrast, Maggie grew up in a home where she felt loved and secure, and observed a mother who enjoyed mothering. Childhood home, self-perceptions of motherhood and womanhood, problems or not with fertility, ease or difficulty with pregnancy and birth, their husband's perspective—all shape women's emerging identities as mothers.

The Church's Role

The Church beautifully affirms the positive role of mothers yet is largely silent on the decisions and processes that take a girl from womanhood to motherhood. The void left by the silence is filled with expectations woven together by our backgrounds and histories. These become self-fulfilling prophesies, either positive or negative. If women are told that childbirth, like menstruation, is a curse and that women bear the burden of producing children, then women will experience pregnancy and childbirth as an ordeal to be endured. If women believe bearing children allows them to uniquely reflect God's image as Creator and Sustainer of life and partner with God in continuing the chain of human life, then they might experience pregnancy and childbirth with awe and amazement.

During each of my three pregnancies, though especially the first, I remember frequently being struck with awe. "So this is the havoc a new pregnancy can cause a woman," I thought, while reeling from the smell of ham and retching at the smell of toothpaste. "So this is what it feels like to have a baby hiccup inside me! This must be a foot," when the kicking catches my breath. "Ha! Now I see what belly buttons do when the stomach is stretched as tight as a big rubber ball! So this is what a contraction feels like!" I had a deep sense of satisfaction and connection in identifying with physical and emotional feelings that every woman giving birth had experienced before me.

Experiences are embedded in cultures that give them meaning. Our technological advances have changed the meaning given to childbirth, in some cases isolating body from personhood. Sexual health and wholeness includes embracing and celebrating this miraculous thing women's bodies do. Faith communities can participate in the naming and reclaiming of this experience, recognizing and honoring the spiritual, psychological, and social significance of childbirth and motherhood.

Fathers and Fatherhood

"I knew that our relationship was changing," one father told me as we talked about his response to his wife's pregnancy. "We were going from a kind of romance relationship to a family. I wasn't sure I was ready for that or that I could do fatherhood well. I'm glad my parents divorced *after* I had kids, because if it had been before I might have had more fears about whether or not I'd be able to stick with it—something my father ultimately could not do."

Men do not stay outside the circle of life created between mothers and infants. Their sexuality also links them literally to their children. Fatherhood, too, is shaped by embodied (his sperm contributes half his children's genes) and embedded realities. Men experience a variety of feelings when their wives get pregnant. Some, like the father quoted, fear the baby might displace him or otherwise interfere with his relationship with his wife. Some fear their ability to father well. Some are reluctant, unprepared, or unwilling fathers—men who contribute biologically to the process but are subsequently not part of the child's later life. Many men have waited for fatherhood with great anticipation and greet it enthusiastically, whether or not they also have fears. Some feel a profound sense of amazement and appreciation for what their wives accomplish. Others worry whether or not their wife will lose the weight gained during pregnancy and feel shame for even thinking about it.

Men can feel some or all of these, their experience being shaped by their culture, their observations of their fathers, and their relationship with their wives. Fatherhood is as culturally embedded an experience as motherhood.

Culture also defines the good father, and so do communities of faith. Because in general men want to be good fathers, they want to know what fatherhood requires of them. The father of the 1950s may have been banned from the delivery room, but he knew his role as provider and protector, even if his work meant long separations from his family.

The New Father emerged in the 1970s—a father who was physically present, supporting his wife as she birthed their child, changing diapers, and getting up at night to feed the baby or bring the baby to his wife for nursing. Options are still opening for men, making this an exciting time to be a father. A few choose to be the at-home parent while their wife works, increasingly a possibility because women are obtaining better-paying professions. Even though the average woman's wage is still lower than a man's (she earns about 75 cents for every dollar he earns), in almost one-third of households where a wife works, she makes more than her husband.[11] Some fathers prefer being home with their children; for others it is the pragmatic option. Still other fathers attempt to provide well financially and still be physically present.

God made us for relationship, and our sexuality draws us to others. Some truths are simple; we clutter simple truths by layering them with culturally derived rules and regulations. We have complicated the simplicity of our longings by assigning particular parenting roles along gender lines to be fulfilled by mothers or fathers. If fatherhood is defined by being strong, self-sufficient, and economically successful providers, fathers may well be alienated from relationships meant to nourish them. Faith communities that encourage fathers to be interdependent, vulnerable, and engaged invite them into deep communion with their partners in parenting—the mothers of their children and the children intended to bless them and be blessed by them.

Attachment: Instinctive or Learned?

Animals of all kinds exhibit complex instinctual behaviors. They make webs, honeycombs, and nests; they travel miles back to their birthplace to lay and fertilize eggs, gather nuts, and migrate south for winter. Except in the rare cases of some fish (salmon, for example) and spiders, when mothers are not around after their babies hatch, mothers of all species provide for and protect their young, almost always with the help of a mate or other kin. Their behavior is embodied.

Hardwiring in Babies

Anthropologists, psychologists, and sociologists all speculate about how much of maternal behavior is instinctive. In the 1960s, British medical doctor and psychoanalyst John Bowlby demonstrated that newborns are genetically wired to attach to a trusted caregiver, usually the mother who just gave it birth. They instinctively look around for nourishment and for a face to stare at. I remember the surprise and the deep satisfaction at having my new baby daughters gaze fixedly into my eyes as they nursed. We would often hold that gaze until she dozed off; I was as drawn to this deep, contented eye-gazing as she. My daughters, it turns out, were not special. This gazing is instinctual among newborns. Infants, when nursing, are drawn to their mother's eyes (or to the eyes of whoever is holding the bottle that feeds them). A newborn infant's best range of vision is about the distance between a mother's breast and her face. Although their eyes will wander around the room and her face somewhat, they usually come to rest on her eyes. Babies are hard-wired to attach.

Learning in Mothers

But whether mothers respond to their infants because of instincts or social learning is debated. Her breasts fill and begin to leak milk when her baby cries. Does that mean the attachment is biological? Social learning theory says not necessarily. Maternal attachment may well be a learned behavior. Mothers respond to their babies' cries by picking them up; the baby stops crying and gazes into her eyes. Maybe all the baby wants is some attachment and some supper. But the mother is reinforced by all this positive attention and is snookered into attaching to her child. And we call that attachment love.

An evolutionary biologist would say that attachment is a maternal instinct that comes primarily from the fosB gene and the hormone oxytocin. When the gene is absent in mice (removed from them at an embryonic state), they grow up normally, can mate and give birth to pups, but do not care for their pups as any good mother mouse should. Humans have a fosB gene, but we do not know whether or not it influences human mothers in the same way.

Levels of the hormone oxytocin (sometimes called the peace and bonding hormone) increase when a mother nurses. Evolutionary biologists say this hormone functions like a mild sedative, weaving warm feelings of satisfaction between the mother and her child. Attachment follows, guaranteeing the mother will keep nurturing and taking care of her child.[12]

Because we cannot see hormones or genes directly at work, we can maintain a level of skepticism about how much human behavior they explain. Examples of biological connection between mothers and infants also have social learning components. Ask a nursing mother or a mother who has ever nursed whether or not she ever experienced a let-down reflex of her milk a moment *before* her baby began to whimper. Perhaps the mother's breasts are full and have "learned" the baby's nursing schedule. As they begin to leak in anticipation, babies smell the milk, which whets their appetite, and they whimper. Perhaps, as anthropologist Sarah Blaffer Hrdy suggests, the mother and child have a biological connection that allows the mother's body to anticipate her baby's hunger. Both biology and social learning are probably at work. Either way, the relationship is embodied and it is physical—a God-created reality that intrinsically links mothers and infants.

We see our sexuality at work, drawing infants toward life and connection, and mothers responding by connecting and giving sustenance. Societies build on biological connections, defining the specifics of the motherhood task, reflecting needs and values of particular generations and geographies.

Societal Influences on Perceptions of Parenthood

Parenthood is experienced individually, but parenting experiences are shaped by beliefs held by a society. Policies, values, and beliefs about childbearing are reflected differently in nations looking to increase their population size, compared to nations wanting to stabilize and slow population growth. Economic and political needs come to shape individuals' perceptions about family size, adoption, contraception, abortion, and the role of caregiver, thus influencing the choices men and women make about their sexuality, particularly their reproductive capacities and responsibilities.

Pronatalism: Valuing Children

According to sociobiology, men and women are driven by the instinct to reproduce themselves. When societies are *pronatalist,* they believe married couples should have, and should want to have, biological children.

Throughout history, children have been highly valued, and religious ideas have often supported pronatalist values. The world was full of empty spaces, and tribes and nations were eager to fill the spaces with people so they could make claim to and protect their staked territory from invaders. So having babies, and lots of them, has been perceived as a good thing—a sign of blessing of God, Allah, or the gods. Children also brought personal fulfillment and filled one's obligation to reproduce the next generation of workers, leaders, artists, priests, and parishioners. Societies trying to build their populations offered intangible rewards (like social status) and tangible rewards (like tax credits) to married couples for having children; sometimes they sanctioned efforts to limit children by limiting the access to contraceptives and abortions.

Antinatalism: Slowing Population Growth

The increasing awareness of a global population explosion in the 1950s convinced some countries (most notably China and India) to implement *antinatalist* policies by the mid-1960s and early 1970s. Policies now rewarded couples who conformed and limited family size or punished those who did not, effectively slowing population growth in both China and India. However, in India pronatalist ideas were so deeply entrenched (many founded in religious beliefs) that the people rebelled against the policies of Prime Minister Indira Gandhi and removed her from office in 1977.

Couples in the United States have gradually decreased family size to about two children per household. They do so primarily for economic reasons—to maintain a standard of living difficult to achieve with large families. Although the official stance of the Catholic and Mormon churches is against the use of contraceptives, many members of those faith traditions use them. Spain and Italy—two predominantly Catholic countries—have the lowest birth rates in Western Europe.

Declining birth rates in the United States and elsewhere do not mean people no longer want to have babies; they just want fewer of them. A strong element of pronatalism is that the biological bond between parents and children is essential. People want to have their own biological children, and the strength of their desire, coupled with technological advances, has driven the development of reproductive technology. One woman said of infertility, [it is] "an admission that you're not a whole person . . . either sexually or anatomically or both. That there's something wrong, and I guess reproduction, the ability to reproduce, strikes at the very essence of one's being."[13]

Infertility: Making Ethical Choices

Infertility has traditionally evoked shame in pronatalistic cultures. In the Old Testament, a barren woman was without honor, unable to provide what her husband most counted on her to provide—heirs, particularly sons. Infertility continues to cause pain, loss, and self-doubt. The scientific and medical community has developed a booming industry: fertility treatments that enable many infertile couples to have biological children. Artificial insemination (the use of donor sperm or the use of highly concentrated partner sperm that is deposited through the cervix into the uterus), in vitro fertilization (harvesting eggs surgically, mixing them with sperm in a petri dish, and then implanting embryos in the uterus), and fertility drugs are treatments that have become increasingly popular among couples who can afford them.

Some of these treatments introduce ethical questions like this one: What is the moral responsibility of a sperm donor to children he anonymously fathers when they come looking for him eighteen years later? People opposed to abortion need to consider multiple issues raised by in vitro fertilization. Do embryos have a right to life once they are conceived? Is it morally acceptable to create many embryos, knowing most will not survive the implantation process? What are the implications of putting multiple embryos in a woman's uterus? If five embryos are implanted and all survive, what risk is she introducing to herself and her babies if she refuses to "reduce" the number of fetuses once it is determined how many are developing? And what of frozen embryos not implanted?

Creators of the technology assume consumers of their treatments will apply their own ethical standards when they choose to use or not use available fertility treatments. Those assumptions mean ethical questions are left out of many conversations about fertility treatment choices. The Catholic church has been more active in these conversations than Protestant churches. Communities of faith, by their nature concerned about ethical and moral questions, should not stay silent on this issue. Christians need help negotiating the options, knowing the important questions, sifting through the information. By bringing the conversation into faith communities, infertility options and their implications can be explored from within the context of religious moral convictions.

Adoption: Considering the Issues

A related issue in pronatalist cultures is their views about adoption. Most adolescent girls who get pregnant and choose to have their babies also choose to raise them. In part, these girls are acting out of a *collective consciousness* of the culture—a shared belief (even if unstated) that babies should stay with their biological mothers. Some pronatalist cultures (and subcultures within the United States) take care of this dilemma by having a relative adopt or raise the child, keeping the family lineage intact. Family bloodlines are protected, and children are raised in stable homes.

Adoption is largely perceived as a second choice in pronatalist cultures, both for birthing mothers and for couples desiring to adopt. Birth mothers who give up their children are the unfortunates who could not provide adequately for their young; adoptive parents are the unfortunates who could not have their own children. Even after adoptions have taken place, court cases have demonstrated a preference for biological ties over adoptive ones in several high-profile cases where biological parents were given custody of children they had earlier put up for adoption.[14] Adoption is largely perceived as a less legitimate way to create family—an interesting irony for Christians, for whom adoption language is central to our heritage. We are the gentiles, that is, those not naturally included in God's family but adopted as sons and daughters into the family of God.

Most Americans are aware of a burgeoning world population, though they do not personally experience it and do not consider their family size choices as being relevant to population problems in Asia and Africa. Few Americans realize that people living in industrialized countries consume as much as *ten times* of the world's resources (water, food, electricity, oil, textiles) as people in other countries, particularly nonindustrialized countries. Every American leaves a big footprint, that is, we consume more than our share of the world's resources. Some couples who want large families but are concerned about their almost unavoidable overuse of resources as Americans have none, one, or two children biologically and adopt the rest. The vision is a good model for seeing beyond a preference for biological children and recognizing that we make reproductive choices based on assumptions that can be challenged and changed.

Faith communities concerned about representing God's grace and mercy will enter this critical conversation. Christians make reproductive choices, and they can do so being mindful of our call to serve and minister to the needs of others, both near us and distant from us. The Church helps people understand and negotiate changing social landscapes and realities as they journey with others through life. We can talk about our desires for large families or about our reasons for wanting small ones in the context of something bigger than our personal preference— big enough to recognize our desires for connection, for belonging, and our needs and obligations toward others in a larger community, even a global one.

Family Planning: Contraception and Abortion

Contraceptives allow women to postpone pregnancy and limit the numbers of births they have, and throughout history women and men have found ways to limit and control reproduction. Not surprisingly, people from religious communities do not agree about the morality of controlling reproduction. The Anglican church cautiously affirmed the use of contraceptives in the 1930 Lambeth Conference but only where there was "clearly felt moral obligation to limit or avoid parenthood," so long as the method was chosen with Christian principles in mind.[15] Protestant denominations followed suit, though the Catholic church has stood by its anticontraceptive position.

Pope Paul VI saw four potential problems with the adoption of contraceptives: (1) a widespread potential of lowering morality both inside and outside of marriage; (2) the potential for husbands to view sex for pleasure only and turn their wives into an instrument of selfish enjoyment; (3) the potential for governments to force contraceptives or sterilization to control powerless populations such as the poor or the mentally disabled; and (4) the promotion of a delusion that people can control their own lives.[16]

The Pope's concerns are well taken, and people choosing to use contraceptives are wise to consider the implications of these potential problems. Promiscuity did accelerate with the availability of contraceptives; the government did force sterilization on several groups of people during the middle of the twentieth century, and contraceptives do give people a false sense that they can control their lives and destinies. The conversations and questions emerging from the Pope's concerns are instructive, yet these potential problems are not necessary outcomes of responsible choices to limit family size.

Increasingly, adolescents are abstaining from sex, and most husbands and wives stay faithful to each other. We no longer force sterilizations on people, though some agencies encourage the use of implanted hormonal contraceptives among sexually active teens. We have a multitude of technologies, not just contraceptive ones, that give us a false sense of control. This issue is much larger than reproductive choices.

Janell Williams Paris's book *Birth Control for Christians* describes and explains major forms of birth control; she explains how they work to prevent pregnancy, as well as their physical and moral advantages and disadvantages. Her book is an excellent resource for faith communities and individuals seeking to be well informed in their contraceptive choices.

The following questions can start conversations for couples desiring to make contraceptive choices in the context of Christian beliefs:

○ What are our priorities: Ease? Safety? Side-effects? That it be natural? Ethical considerations? Financial considerations?

○ What do I believe about when life begins? If life begins at conception, does this method prevent conception, or does it work by destroying fertilized eggs or keeping them from implanting in the uterus?

○ What are the health and safety risks of this contraceptive?

○ Does this approach allow husbands and wives to share the responsibility of contraception?

In the early 1970s, the U.S. Commission on Population Growth determined that continued population growth in the United States would not be beneficial. Legalizing abortion was one of three recommendations to slow population growth; abortion became legal in the United States in 1973. Currently in North America, twenty-six out of every one hundred pregnancies are aborted; 82 percent of women getting abortions are unmarried or separated.

Abortion continues to be debated, even among communities of faith. The Catholic church, the Mormon church, and conservative Protestants continue to reject abortion, although thirty-five mainline Christian and Jewish organizations are members of the Religious Coalition for Abortion Rights.[17]

Pro-Choice Theory

The pro-choice argument stands by the constitutional right of people to make personal decisions in marriage and reproduction, parenting and education. Abortion is an exercise of that liberty; it is a woman's right to determine what she does with her body. Her "bodily integrity" is violated if she is forced to continue an unwanted pregnancy. Abortion also creates greater sexual equality between men (who can escape the responsibilities associated with pregnancy) and women (who without abortion cannot escape the responsibilities of pregnancy).

The fetus is biologically and morally inseparable from the mother, so abortion is not against the interests of a fetus, given that a fetus does not yet have interests at the time of abortion. A fetus is not a person from conception and does not have rights to the same degree as an adult, or even a child. Even if fetuses have a "right to life," this does not guarantee the right to use another person's body, even one that is needed to sustain life. Women cannot be forced to offer life-support to a fetus, even as no one, no matter how ill and needy, can force another to donate bone marrow, blood, or a kidney. Some pro-choice proponents say that abortion may be immoral but should not be illegal—that society should not mandate a moral code. No law requires that one be a Good Samaritan.

Pro-Life Theory

The pro-life argument says that constitutional rights do restrict personal decisions that bring harm to others. Laws prohibit infanticide, the abuse of children, incest, polygamy, and suicide. Sanctity of life trumps personal choice for bodily integrity. Women are not just making a personal decision when they choose abortion; they are deciding the fate of another. There is a clear difference between one's duty to save a life (a moral issue) and one's duty to not take a life (a legal issue). Abortion is the taking of life, and thus it is an appropriate legal issue.

Adoption is an option for women unable to provide financially or emotionally for their child. So not being able to provide for a child does not justify abortion. Neither are the dangers of illegal abortions an excuse for legal abortions; the focus needs to be on preventing abortion through education and the availability and use of contraceptives, not abortion. The issue of sexual equality is about equal access to education and employment, not abortion. Men should be held legally responsible for children they father, and states are increasingly demanding that a father's wages be garnisheed to support children he is not raising. The argument continues: civilized society is one that takes care of and protects its most vulnerable, including the old, sick, young, poor, imprisoned, homeless, mentally and physically disabled, and the unborn.

Rights Versus Moral Obligation

Embedded in the pro-choice and pro-life debate are values of freedom and rights for women (who have long been denied them) versus a moral obligation to fetuses without recognized rights. Our culture values individual freedom, and most Americans are reluctant to pass legislation that limits it. Pro-choice advocates fear that if women lose the right to choose abortion, they risk losing other hard-fought rights as well. Pro-life advocates might have more productive conversations if pro-choice advocates believed people fighting against abortion were as concerned for women's lives economically, politically, and socially as they are for the rights of the unborn.

Medical advances allow us to know more about fetal development than we used to know, so also embedded in the debate is a question of when a fetus is given the right to life. At what point in a pregnancy should an abortion no longer be an option? Pro-life proponents argue that the full potential for human existence is present from the moment of conception, and thus the right to life begins at conception. Others believe abortions are appropriate until the eighth week, at which point brain activity can be monitored. Some suggest abortions are appropriate up until the twelfth week because the fetus is not a fully formed human until that point. Others argue for the twenty-fourth week, when the baby could survive outside the womb. Still others argue that abortions are appropriate until birth because the fetus has no identity apart from the mother, thus is not yet recognized as an individual with rights until birth. Cultures that practice infanticide do not recognize young infants as having a right to life because they are completely dependent on the care of others. Infanticide is therefore not always about killing a baby but about allowing it to die.[18]

As a sociologist concerned about the rights of women and other groups of people who have historically been powerless, I still conclude that the sanctity of life trumps the right for bodily integrity—the right to abortions. My belief is based on an assumption that the potential for life that is captured in a fertilized egg represents a calling forth of life, an opportunity to participate with God in the creation of life. The emphasis in our culture on individual rights has made it difficult to think about our obligations to others, particularly voiceless others who are out of our line of vision. I count the unborn among these.

Consistency and Caring in the Christian Community

What would it look like for communities of faith to see this issue in the context of a broader need to think about our obligations to others, particularly those who are powerless? What would consistency look like? If we care for the unborn but not for the poor, the disenfranchised, the marginalized, then are we inconsistent in our care? Conversely, if we care for the poor, the disenfranchised, and the marginalized but not the unborn, are we inconsistent in our care? How much are our views of abortion and adoption shaped by pronatalist or antinatalist assumptions? Can communities of faith find consistent ways to reflect *imago Dei*—the One who made us for relationship, who calls us to love inclusively and who bound us together on one planet that we might care for, protect, and love each other as fellow bearers of *imago Dei*?

The Role of the Caregiver

Because women get pregnant, give birth to, and nurse their babies, a commonly held belief is that mothers are naturally better nurturers and more capable of being a child's sole caregiver than fathers. The "good mother" in the 1950s stayed home and nurtured her children. Mothers and fathers today have multiple opportunities to combine careers with parenthood, bringing men back into an active role in fathering and sending women into an active role in the public sphere. But in some communities of faith, such parents feel they are perceived as bad parents, compromising their roles as nurturers and providers. Ironically, mothers on welfare (women who accept a government subsidy, thus sacrificing a better economic position in order to stay home and care for their children) also feel they are labeled as bad mothers. Good-mother and good-father images are embedded in cultures, shaped by various political, economic, and religious values.

Cultural traditions help answer the ambiguous questions about what is best for children. To spank or not to spank? To nurse and for how long? Should one force potty training or not? Should parents shape their children's character or let character emerge spontaneously? In the United States, many of the current answers to these questions reflect values of individualism and independence that seem odd and wrong-headed to cultures that focus primarily on family and community.

Inasmuch as motherhood reflects the character of God, mothers are to love and nurture children to adulthood, teaching them what they need to know to connect meaningfully with others, to belong, serve, and live in a community. When doing what is thought best for one's children includes killing the newest one (either through infanticide or abortion) so the others can be provided for, we need to look at larger social issues created by unjust or evil social systems. If we did not have such great disparity between the rich and the poor, if parents could provide adequately for their young, if personal choice and freedom were not the supreme value for Americans, if dowries could indeed be eradicated from India, then mothers would not be constrained to choose between bad options.

For generations, cultures were communities of interconnected extended families where grandparents, aunts, uncles, and cousins resided near and participated in each other's lives. The opportunities and choices of modernity meant families began to dig up their roots, pack them along with their toddlers, TVs, and Tupperware into their Chevrolets and move them across the country. Job opportunities and choice led to a shift in focus from the extended to the nuclear family that consisted of mother, father, and children. The independence of the nuclear family was applauded; the launching of adolescents became the end point of parenting. We embrace this notion of independence and freedom from familial obligation so readily that parents who continue to help their adult children are sometimes criticized for not insisting on greater independence.

A friend of ours welcomed her pregnant daughter back home. Now, almost two years later, she gets the impression that some people think she should be working harder toward helping her daughter achieve independence. "Why don't people realize that extended families are the norm in most parts of the world?" She asked as we discussed our lives over lunch,

"What does it mean to empty oneself as Jesus did, to sacrificially give of oneself for others? How is it 'enabling' for us to provide a secure home for a daughter and granddaughter who need it?"

Some communities of faith fill the gap left by loosely connected extended families through small groups, where people provide each other the care, nurturing, and support that families used to provide. Those without the support of either extended family or some type of small group often struggle to do alone what they used to do with the support of aunts and uncles, siblings and grandparents. Culture is fluid, changeable, open to discussion and reconsideration that allows for ongoing redemption—the possibility to be drawn forward, crafting ways of living connected lives in changing circumstances. Grace calls us to learn from mistakes, adapt to change, and eradicate structural evils that perpetuate bad options. Communities of faith are active in this process. The more they are aware of how cultural trends and currents shape beliefs about individuals, communities, rights, and obligations, the more intentional they can be in crafting relational, connected communities that reflect changing cultural landscapes.

Work and Motherhood

An example of a changing cultural landscape is the relationship between work and motherhood. All mothers (human and otherwise) balance the job of having and tending to babies with the job of providing sustenance for themselves and their children. This is a biological reality and a strong research finding in anthropology: mothers throughout time have been both ambitious and nurturing. To care for young properly requires both. It also requires help, and mothers have seldom raised their infants alone. Sometimes the demands of nurturing have required that others help them forage for food. Sometimes others looked after their young while they did the foraging. Mothers have generally had the help of a mate or of other females related to them or in their group.

To imply that women choose between ambition (meaning they are pursuing careers) and nurturance (meaning they are staying home) is a socially constructed dichotomy that pits mothers who work outside the home against mothers who do not. We want the world to be simple—good or bad; it helps with our own decision making. Yet simplifying the world in such a way reduces the richness of understanding and embracing the variety of human experience. It also limits how we think about offering ourselves as communities of faith to people whose lives are different from ours. How mothers balance those two demands varies with culture and time, as do norms defining which choices good mothers make and which ones bad mothers make. Always mothers make tradeoffs. Only in a few, relatively brief time periods and generally for the upper classes could a mother choose to do all the nurturing, leaving the subsistence work to others.

Communities of faith can build on what we know. For example, we know that mothers and infants who spend a lot of time in close proximity are more likely to develop a strong mutual attachment. Historically, mothers did subsistence work that allowed strong attachments to their young. When they did so, they ended up with healthier, better-adjusted offspring than those who did not develop strong attachments.[19]

We also know that all day care is not equal. Developmental psychologists emphasize the need for young children to have a consistent caregiver; children respond and develop better when they can securely attach to a couple of consistent care providers. Some families manage this challenge using extended family members; some use live-in nannies; others find ways to work out of their homes; still others trade off child care and work time with spouses, and a few switch roles so that Dad stays home while Mom works.

Indeed, fathers and infants who spend a lot of time in close proximity are also more likely to develop a strong mutual attachment. Balancing subsistence with reproductive tasks has always been a challenge, and the challenge has always involved tradeoffs, but communities of faith can become active participants in crafting creative ways to meet relational needs in changing cultural landscapes.

In summary, embodied aspects of motherhood cannot be separated from embedded experience. What a woman experiences physically is interpreted and given meaning through culture. Women and men can give new meaning or, more appropriately, rediscover a meaning that childbearing once had—one that honors the amazing miracle of reproduction, a partnering with God to create and sustain human bonds and human community. Being made for relationship means we need each other and are blessed when we help others and are helped by others. Women were not meant to go through pregnancy, birth, or motherhood alone. Mothers and fathers were not meant to raise children in isolation. Being created as sexual beings drawn to others authenticates our desire to be nurtured, assisted, loved, and received and to nurture, assist, love, and welcome.

Shattered Dreams

October 22, 2001

Emma,

Eleven years ago today I lost you, and every year on this day I have remembered. Most years I spend some time grieving again, perhaps this year a bit more because I shared my/your story with a friend who is writing about miscarriages. I was surprised I hadn't written more in your journal—especially on all those "October 22nds" that I thought of you.

Life moves forward, only Megan is still at home, and she is in her senior year of high school. Rae graduates from college this year, and Sarah is a sophomore at Calvin College. And you would only be ten! I wonder what would have been different, had you been born. Missing you still.

Always, Mama

As I wrote this chapter, I was keenly aware that some birth stories are fulfilled dreams and hopes, with unexpected surprises and outcomes that surpass the imagination. Other stories are about shattered dreams. I cannot do these shattered-dream stories justice, but in naming them I want to honor them as part of the story of suffering and grace.

Some men and women long for children, yet never marry. My good friend Jana is forty-five, single, and childless. The college students she has spent the last fifteen years teaching and mentoring are now the age her children could have been. She is wisely taking time to grieve for the children she never had. Her longings for children will go unfulfilled.

Conclusion

Mourning our incompleteness is appropriate. Our losses are also embedded and embodied; one in every seven or eight couples will struggle with infertility. Some, like Allison, will eventually have children; others will not. Some will adopt children and find rich satisfaction in parenting and family life. Others will remain childless. In either case, dreams are altered and longings go unfilled.

Some women who have abortions spend time grieving that choice. Women who miscarry grieve the loss of a baby for whom they had already developed hopes and dreams. Women give birth to babies who die moments after they are born; others give birth to children with severe defects. In some parts of the world, women give birth to babies they cannot feed and watch them slowly die. Young girls without husbands and unable to support themselves get pregnant, and all three choices (abortion, adoption, raising the child as a single parent) are difficult and have life-changing implications.

Women whose lives are broken by their parents, their own or their spouse's drug and alcohol addictions, past sexual or physical abuse, mental disorders, or by a life run amok with disappointment, isolation, or detachment may find mothering difficult. These women have been wounded—their perceptions distorted and shaped by the realities that affect their everyday life.

The world is shattered by sin and brokenness. It is not supposed to be full of sorrow and suffering, but this side of heaven we will always be longing for wholeness, for completion. Mourning is appropriate.

Every day people die and babies are born. The world is shattered by sorrow but infused with hope. The Church, working with God, crafts communities of faith that support, love, and embrace people as they make decisions about contraceptives, family size, childbearing, and parenting in a changing cultural landscape.

QUERIES FOR FURTHER REFLECTION AND CONVERSATION

- What are your general perspectives and thoughts about pregnancy and childbearing? From where did these ideas come?

- On a scale of 1 to 5 (1 being Not At All, 5 being Very Much), do you think pregnant women are sensuous? Why do you think you answered as you did?

- How important is it to you to have biological children? To have a particular number of children? What keeps you from or propels you toward adoption? How have these ideas been shaped by values embedded in your culture?

- What do you think about stay-at-home dads? What are advantages to having Dad stay home as opposed to, say, using day care?

- Can you imagine having your church sponsor childbirth classes? What about having training for women who want to assist other women through their pregnancies and births? Why does this aspect of childbearing tend to be outside the Church when so many aspects of marriage and family (premarital and marital counseling, parenting classes, family-building activities) are supported inside the Church?

- If you are pro-choice, what are the concerns of pro-life you should be addressing as a Christian? If you are pro-life, what are the concerns of pro-choice you should be addressing as a Christian?

- What are the ethical questions you think are most relevant regarding contraceptives and treatment for infertility?

MYSTERIES OF MARRIAGE

BONE OF MY BONE, FLESH OF MY FLESH

Marriage, which has been the bourne of so many narratives, is still a great beginning, as it was to Adam and Eve, who kept their honeymoon in Eden, but had their first little one among the thorns and thistles of the wilderness. It is still the beginning of the home epic—the gradual conquest or irremediable loss of that complete union which makes the advancing years a climax, and age the harvest of sweet memories in common.

—George Elliot, *Middlemarch*

I MET MARK IN NINTH GRADE, a strawberry-blond-haired youth with a boyish smile that invited friendship, a clear heart, and a big mind that I found irresistible. Thirty years later, his hair is a distinguished lighter hue; the smile, his heart, and mind have grown deeper and wider. His big hands have enveloped mine in marriage for twenty-five years now. I am as familiar with them as if they were my own. The creases in his palm, the raised vein on the back of his hand that I sometimes trace with my finger, the permanently damaged fingernail from a high school football injury—I know them all, a familiarity etched into my senses along with the comfort of his smell, the tenderness of his touch, the warmth of his voice. Eden's fragrance lingers, even as we make our way through the thistles of our broken world. The pairing of people as husbands and wives is a practice as old as the Garden of Eden. Marriage provides a temporary home, one that will never satisfy completely our deepest longings for home but, nevertheless, is a place for sexual expression and celebration, a place for forgiveness and grace, a place to belong and to be loved.

We savor the taste of fulfillment while keeping our hearts resting in the hope of complete fulfillment to come. As fallible humans, we do not love perfectly; we disappoint our spouses and they disappoint us. But those who marry can yet discover a fragrance of Eden in marriage so long as they do not presume that marriage will fill completely the aloneness of their souls and their longing to be loved and known, and to belong.

Faith communities have long been involved in the process of forming, instructing, influencing, and supporting married couples. Keeping families intact and healthy strengthened both civic and religious communities. The role of religion in married life has changed throughout history. Sometimes societies granted much power to the Church to exert influence and shape married life; other times, the Church had no legitimate power but continued to influence and shape values and beliefs about marriage.

In ancient times (and still sometimes in contemporary cultures), marriages were often arranged, creating and strengthening alliances between families. The goal was to move the family into the next generation, ensuring the security and stability of the family line. Personal consent by the would-be bride may have been sought but was not required. Arranged marriages occurred frequently in biblical stories, such as the marriage of Rebekah to Isaac in Genesis 24 and of Leah and Rachel to Jacob in Genesis 29.

By the Middle Ages, the Church had taken on a more powerful role throughout Europe. The Roman Catholic church declared consent necessary for the basis of marriage, thus preventing people from being married against their will. Though the Church did not intend it to work this way, any two people who said they loved each other could consummate their marriage in the privacy of a grassy field and then declare themselves husband and wife. This created distressing confusion, particularly for women who, thinking they had just entered marriage with a man who had wooed them to bed, were deserted as he later denied any intention of marriage. The Church responded in the sixteenth century by requiring marriages to have a public dimension. In the same century, the Council of Trent required both parental consent and state registration. The State took on an increasingly important role, and marriage lost its status as a sacrament primarily under the umbrella of the Church, becoming instead a contract monitored by the State.[1] Yet we still tend to look to faith communities to uphold and support married couples.

In either case, whether under the guidance and authority of the Church or the State, marriage provided a sexual script that added stability to families, providing for the sexual and intimacy needs of adults and the physical and emotional needs of children. The script changes over time. Before the Enlightenment, marriage focused almost exclusively on the needs of the extended family, overlooking the intention for marriage to also provide companionship, love, and deep satisfaction to husbands and wives. The post-Enlightenment attitude grants greater equality between husbands and wives, greater flexibility in roles taken on by husbands and wives, and more freedom to craft marital relationships according to personal preferences. We also focus now on personal fulfillment and satisfaction, and a near-50 percent divorce rate suggests we no longer see marriage as an unfolding drama—a place of stability, familiarity, and commitment where growth comes through negotiating challenges, working hard, being long-suffering, and meeting obligations to near and distant kin.

Men and women search for each other, seeking community, communion, and consummation. God's design in creating humans as males and females drawn to each other made possible a delicate balance between meeting the needs of family and community and satisfying the desires of individuals. At its best, marriage takes our longing as sexual people and draws us toward one other. In that union, we find safety, the comfort of belonging, and the reassurance of being loved. We open ourselves fully to the sexual and emotional intimacy of being bonded to another in a life-long relationship of giving and receiving. Typically, part of marriage involves wives and husbands birthing, growing, and sending off children. Husbands and wives doctor each other through illness and laugh and cry at bodies that change as they age. In the security of a permanent marital relationship, people find freedom to change, to fail, and to grow. Marriage provides a temporal home, a place to put down roots to stay the unease of being alone in a universe, separated, for a time, from the Creator from whom we came.

Hope keeps us all, married or single, working on our relationships, seeking the life-giving blessings intended in them. Those who are single can recognize a longing that will go unfilled; they can fill their lives by loving others deeply and well. Marriage provides a foretaste of heaven for people made to be in relationship and created to desire sexual union with another. In marriage, we have the potential to share a consummate life with another that livens our passions, enriches our soul, and accompanies us as we write through the pages and chapters of our story.

Mammals and Sexuality

Humans and other mammals are remarkably different regarding their sex lives. Most female mammals will only have intercourse during days when they are fertile. Once they are past the age of bearing offspring, they stop having intercourse altogether.[2] Women, however, can and do enjoy and pursue sex, whether or not they are fertile and long after they cease bearing children. The research is a bit inconclusive on the next point, but women are apparently the only female mammal to have orgasms, though some female primates appear to have a kind of orgasm.[3] Finally, unlike other animals, a universal cultural norm for humans is a sense of modesty. Humans wear clothes, covering their reproductive organs (to varying degrees), and have sex in privacy, away from the watchful gaze of others, though some cultures seek more privacy than others.

These differences reinforce a Christian sexual script that says humans are intended to experience and attach deeper meaning to sex than other animals do. God, it would seem, intended humans to surround their sexuality with a sense of propriety and modesty, to find sex pleasurable, and to engage in it throughout life for purposes other than the making of babies.

Throughout Church history, theologians have offered defining statements on the purposes of sex in marriage. Christianity has long taught that sex is sacred, belonging only in the context of marriage. One purpose of marriage was to channel the drive humans have for intercourse into a relationship between one man and one woman. In this context, wives and husbands freely express and experience sexual fulfillment and the security of belonging and being loved. They learn to give their bodies to each other, enjoying the pleasures of sex without embarrassment or restraint.

Sex is the visual expression of a marital commitment to give and receive, to be transparent, and to offer unconditional acceptance of another. In marriage, sex represents an openness to others who will come into the marital bond—children, in-laws, grandchildren—all expanded expressions of their mutual love.[4] Marriage is a training ground of sorts, where humans learn to welcome another into their innermost being. The intimate bond of sex in marriage eases the existential loneliness and longing for consummation and connection.

This beauty and hope is distorted by sin. Myths about sex confuse and exaggerate, and create self-fulfilling prophesies that lead to disappointment when we conclude that marriage (our marriage anyway) is not living up to its promise. Some settle for disappointment; others look elsewhere for fulfillment. When people presume marriage to be the fulfillment of their longings rather than a means of pointing them toward the hope of heaven, they do find marriage disappointing. A task for communities of faith is to help people see marriage for what it is—a hope of fulfillment, a place of safety, a temporal home. Marriage is neither our ultimate fulfillment nor our final home. Exposing and correcting myths about marital sex is a step toward channeling disappointments back toward hope.

Myths About Marital Sex

Disillusionment and disappointment in marriage follow in the wake of myths about sex. Our inability to love well and be loved well means we are not always faithful, and we pursue other loves we think will satisfy. We expect marriage to be beautiful, and when the beauty is tarnished our faithfulness wavers. Debunking myths can strengthen marriages by realigning expectations.

Myth 1: Marital Sex Is Boring

Disappointment emerges out of expectation. Hollywood builds unrealistic expectations of sex that usually unfold something like this: two people meet and fall madly in love, he says amazingly creative and romantic things, and she is flawlessly gorgeous. After spending a day or an evening together, they end up in one of their apartments (or some Eden-like spot in nature) and rip off each other's clothes (or slowly disrobe) and have incredible sex that is equally pleasurable to both. Neither is self-conscious about their bodies; he never has problems with premature ejaculation or impotency, and she has a spontaneous orgasm, timed perfectly with his. Real-life couples do not report their first sexual experience with a new partner to be as satisfying as Hollywood would have us believe nor subsequent ones to be so effortless, sanitized, airbrushed and, well, perfect.

Such displays of ease and grandeur seldom accompany Hollywood depictions of marital sex. Married sex, when made visible at all, is depicted as either boring or as laughable and awkward. One gets the impression that the best sex is the sex one gets before one is constrained by the commitment of marriage. Fortunately, this impression is a debunkable myth. In a national survey of three thousand people, married people more often said they were extremely or very satisfied with sex than cohabiting or single people.[5] They had sex more frequently and found it more pleasurable. Intimacy, commitment, and time build the framework for good sex. As couples come to know each other and learn to love each other, the meaning and expressions of sex broaden and deepen. Sex becomes a lived-out metaphor of being separate people yet sharing life as one. Sex restates a commitment to the comfort and pleasure of the familiar in an unfolding story.

Although it is a myth that marital sex is universally boring, married couples do not always find sex satisfying. Sometimes sex that sounded like a great idea early in the evening loses all appeal by the time one is actually slipping beneath the covers at bedtime. Couples who eagerly and frequently sought each other out during their first year of marriage now rarely seek each other out at all.

Unsatisfying and disappointing marital sex emerges for several reasons. For some, the belief that marital sex is supposed to become boring becomes a self-fulfilling expectation. Others have unrealistic expectations for sex based on what they have read, watched, or seen in books, movies, or magazines. Expectation creates disappointment. Some struggle with fatigue and depression; some feel unattractive or harbor negative feelings toward the other. Any of these can negatively affect sexual desire. The most common sexual problem couples bring into sex therapy and marital therapy for sexual issues is low sexual desire.[6] Treating low sexual desire requires peeling away and examining the assumptions, beliefs, and patterns that couples have adopted and integrated into their marriage. Doing the work to treat low sexual desire is a wise investment in a marriage intended to bless and nurture for a long time.

Sex is not boring for most married couples, and neither does it become unimportant after the first year or two of marriage. Although newly married couples tend to have sex more frequently than they do later in life, a poll of one thousand married Americans showed sex to be most important to couples in midlife.[7] The relative importance of sex changes for couples over the course of their marriage, but sex continues to be important throughout life, woven into a tapestry of companionship and intimacy that expresses sexuality through the partnership of living, sleeping, touching, working, weeping, and laughing together.

Male and female bodies change, and the changes require adjustments. Men take longer to become erect but are also able to prolong sexual pleasure. A woman's body may also take longer to become aroused, but her sexual interest often peaks in midlife. And the meaning of sex changes and deepens. Sex after forty, says Douglas Rosenau, a sex therapist, helps heal losses, reaffirms a sense of self and attractiveness, encourages playfulness, and expresses love. With age comes greater knowledge about what is sexually pleasing, greater ability to prolong sexual pleasure, and greater flexibility.[8]

Myth 2: Marriage Is All About Sex

Juxtaposed to the "marital sex is boring" myth is an equally debunkable myth that marriage is *all* about sex. Couples that assume sex should always be fully gratifying and ecstatic can make pursuing one's sexual potential the justification for reneging on a commitment to another person and to a marriage. When marriage is all about sex, sex can become the only bond holding a couple together. Like an analgesic, sex numbs the pain of chronic relational problems. Kathleen said, "We had no emotional intimacy; we fought almost all the time. Our marriage was dead. But we still had great sex—and our sex life kept us going another year, until we finally gave up and divorced." An overemphasis on sex thwarts other purposes of marriage. Couples miss the opportunity to become skilled at developing and expressing intimacy apart from sex, through written and spoken words, touch, tender and knowing looks, time spent together, shared humor, acts of service. We stunt our potential for growth as individuals and as couples if we organize our lives around the pursuit of sexual ecstasy.

Sex is one purpose for marriage that is recognized historically by the Church; marriage is viewed as the place for sexual fulfillment. A second purpose is companionship, or having a sojourner for the trek through life. God intended people to go through life with other sojourners, and for most that includes the opportunity to be in a long-term marital relationship with another. Husbands and wives learn to trust, to be authentic as they explore and come to know each other. They learn to love sacrificially, to hold on to each other through the storms of life, to lift up, support, and cherish each other. An outcome of sex is children, and having and rearing families is a third purpose of marriage that is emphasized by the Church. The blessing of children as God gives them is a significant part of marriage, and the Catholic church's reluctance to give in to pressure to endorse contraceptives reflects this belief that marriage and sex cannot and should not be separated from the possibility of conceiving children. Through parenting children, men and women learn to give sacrificially and catch a glimpse of the unconditional love of God. Parents remember and relearn simple truths held in the innocence of childhood. Children experience love and belonging, and gain an identity that ties them to a community of others from whom they receive and to whom they will give.

Marriage includes sex but is not all about sex. Couples who, because of illness or accident, no longer share gratifying sex can still experience intimacy and a life together that nurtures, sustains, and richly blesses them.

Myth 3: Good Women Do Not Enjoy Sex

A friend, knowing I was writing about sexuality, told me the following story.

> After God made Adam and placed him in the Garden of Eden, God said, "Adam, you can choose one of two gifts—the other gift will go to Eve. I will either make you so you can pee standing up . . ."

"I want that!" Adam interrupted enthusiastically. So God made Adam so he could pee standing up and Adam went about the Garden peeing here and there. Eventually, he came back and said, "By the way, God, what was the second gift anyway?"

God looked at Adam, smiled, and said, "Multiple orgasms."

However gifted with the capacity for multiple orgasms, some women still embrace a belief that enjoying sex too much means they are perverted. Though the sexual revolution attempted to change that, "good" women rejected the revolution and anything associated with feminism. Orgasms and everything else "down there" were dirty and held suspect. The upright woman had as little to do with it all as possible.

Negative views of sex come and go throughout history. During the Victorian era, having too much sex would diminish the "male essence," and good women only wanted sex for the purpose of procreation. The Puritans appeared to enjoy marital sex. Historical accounts show Jewish women to have enjoyed sex. Redeeming the sexual pleasure found in the Old Testament's Song of Solomon has been a challenge taken on by many contemporary Christians seeking to free women, as well as men, to enjoy orgasmic sex.

Women who say they are extremely or very happy with their sex lives have orgasms. Sixty-eight percent of women say they usually or always have orgasms; 22 percent say they do sometimes, and 10 percent report rarely or never having orgasms.[9] The good news is that most women who do not have orgasms can. Sometimes knowledge and practice are all that are required; others may need to pursue medical help or counseling to overcome physical and mental barriers to good sex. Books such as Douglas Rosenau's *A Celebration of Sex: A Christian Couple's Manual* offer instruction and exercises to help couples increase their sexual satisfaction. Pursuing more satisfying sex affirms the importance of a woman's sexuality and a desire to develop a gift God intended for her.

Some husbands feel personally responsible for seeing that their wives are satisfied, believing they have failed if their wives do not achieve an orgasm every time they have sex. But sex is about more than orgasms; it is about union and connection, about giving and receiving pleasure. When orgasm becomes the goal of sex, her orgasm becomes the focus rather than a mutually pleasurable experience that says something of who they are as a married couple, not just what they are capable of experiencing. Sex is a beautiful experience of ecstasy but is also about connection beyond sexual ecstasy. Intercourse reminds couples of the union that binds them—a union that staves off aloneness and gives a foretaste of a consummation to come that will wrap them in the full and perfect embrace of God.

Husbands and wives celebrate this gift when they allow sex to have multiple dimensions—sometimes playful, other times desired for comfort, sometimes pursued purely for pleasure, other times orchestrated around romance. Husbands and wives who plumb the possibilities of sex in their marriage open themselves up to be surprised. They are humble learners, willing teachers, and adventurous partners. In the context of safety and unconditional acceptance, marriage allows the transparency, playfulness, and connection that comes from a lifetime of learning and practicing at lovemaking.

Myth 4: Men Are Always Ready, Interested, and Capable of Sex

A corollary myth to the one suggesting that women do not like sex is a myth that men always want sex and can call forth an erection and sustain sex as long as they want. Biologically, men are incapable of repeated sex without a respite between each orgasm-inducing ejaculation (remember, Adam chose the stand-up-to-pee option). And contrary to popular belief, men do *not* think about sex all the time, nor are they always interested in sex.[10] A declining interest in sex does not mean a husband is having an affair or no longer finds his wife sexually appealing.

Not only are men more limited in their sexual libido than urban legends suggest, they are also unable to feign interest in sex as easily as women can. Men cannot *will* their penises to become erect. Not that it's a good thing, but a woman can fake an orgasm; a man cannot. If a man is depressed or angry, or feels guilty, anxious, or disinterested, he may not be able to bring about an erection no matter how much he wants one. The more anxious he becomes over his failure to "achieve" an erection, the less likely it is he will be able to experience one.

Most men struggle with erectile problems (premature ejaculation or difficulty achieving and maintaining an erection) periodically throughout their lives. A man's interest in sex vacillates with anxiety, work-related stress, and general physical and emotional wellness. The public attention given to Viagra has taken some of the sting of embarrassment out of erectile dysfunction. Men who struggle know there are many other men out there struggling silently alongside them, thus making it easier to turn to psychological and medical help to overcome sexually challenging difficulties.

Men, like women, are created to enjoy sex. But however much gonad humor suggests otherwise, they are not sex-machines. Labeling men as sex-machines justifies their shutting off relational characteristics. Vulnerability and sensitivity move sex beyond the realm of physical pleasure to become a place for deep connection and openness, a place to know and be known. Although sex for men can be physically satisfying outside marriage, married men are more likely to find sex emotionally satisfying with their wives.[11] The safety of vulnerability frees people, not only in their manhood or womanhood but in their personhood. Safety offers the assurance of love and commitment, even if and when one does not measure up to culturally crafted expectations and hopes.

Myth 5: Good Spouses Are Not Attracted to Others Once They Get Married

Many Christians naively assume that neither they nor their spouses will be sexually attracted to someone else after marriage. Overconfident, they are caught off-guard and unprepared when one of them confronts unexpected attraction and desire.

As sexual beings, we continue to be energized and aroused by those to whom we are drawn. We are made to be in relationship, though married people have committed themselves to an exclusive relationship that limits their freedom to pursue sexual interest elsewhere. Married people want to honor their promises yet find themselves perplexed by their own wandering eyes and hearts.

Some social realities make fears of spousal unfaithfulness worse, creating a cycle that grace and humility help to negotiate. One social reality is that men generally gain social attractiveness in middle age, and likely well beyond if they are successful and attractive. In contrast, women lose social attractiveness with age, regardless of their level of physical attraction or success. A complicating social reality is that female beauty today is defined as being young and thin.

Eating disorders, which used to be found primarily in teens and college students, are emerging among women in their forties and fifties. Physician Katherine Halmi, a coauthor of a Cornell study exploring this trend said,

> I think what happens in middle-class and upper-class societies is that women, when they get older, naturally gain weight, and at the same time their husbands go through their own crises. Some women, in response to their husband having an affair or merely the fear that he will, become obsessed with their weight. These wives fear that they are competing with women in their twenties for their husbands' attention.[12]

The older women get, the more aware they become of losing social desirability as their husbands maintain or increase theirs. A potential negative cycle begins.

A woman can err in responding in one of two ways. One error is to give up trying to stay fit, healthy, and attractive, which she figures is a losing battle anyway. She knows there will always be younger, more beautiful women vying for, or at least catching, her husband's attention. She hangs her hope on the belief that he will be faithful because he promised to be—to love for better or for worse, regardless of her appearance. The other error is to obsess about her looks and spend much energy, time, and money (if she has it) trying to compete by staying young-looking. If she is to be the wife of a man looking around, she would like to also be a woman who catches the eye of another man. Being able to attract a man's attention validates her desirability. She may also believe that her husband's faithfulness depends on her staying attractive.

Men and women seldom have affairs simply because their spouse becomes unattractive. Yet the fear of losing attractiveness contributes to negative cycles of jealously, insecurity, and competition that erode rather than build and is expressed in suspicion rather than grace. Women will indeed age and may be less attractive than others with whom their spouses work and interact. This nagging fear affects women more than men, as they lose social attractiveness with age while he gains it. Extending grace as we age affirms commitment and the beauty of a shared life being etched on our aging bodies.

Taking care of one's body offers a gift and a blessing to one's spouse, not because of fear but in the acknowledgment of a human desire and appreciation for beauty. Maintaining a healthy and strong body that allows activity and encourages well-being affirms the desire to keep adding chapters to a joint life story—one full of energy and adventure, of hope for further adventures yet to be added to the accumulating store of memories. While husbands and wives promise faithfulness to each other regardless of changes to their physical health or well-being, making a consistent effort to do what we reasonably can to take care of our bodies and stay attractive validates that we are drawn to what is beautiful.

Husbands and wives who find beauty in their aging partners affirm the personhood of their spouse. The depth of this beauty emerges from the weaving of two lives that have come to know and love each other well, bearing joys and sorrows, children, moves, acclaim, disappointments, and deaths. Memory is etched in the creases at the corners of eyes and around the mouth, literal reminders of years of laughter, concentration, thoughtfulness, and tears. Reminders of motherhood are reflected in stretch marks and softening; a looser body becomes part of her story and his and reflects the wholeness of who they are—a woman and man who draw together, warm each other, and remind each other that they share a story marked by the changes reflected in aging bodies.

The fear of extramarital affairs is present because we believe so few couples make it faithfully to the end. The picture is not so dismal as we would believe, though; national surveys show that 75 to 80 percent of husbands and 85 to 90 percent of wives have been sexually faithful to their spouses throughout the duration of their marriages.[13] Learning to love another deeply and well over the course of a lifetime and to reflect the sacrificial, pursuing love of God brings a freedom unique to marriage. People are capable of having sex with multiple partners, yet belief in faithfulness to an exclusive sexual relationship provides mutual safety and authenticity. Faithfulness brings freedom to be accepted, loved, and embraced and to accept, love, and embrace another, in spite of our imperfections.

Exclusivity and Abundance in Marriage

God's love is one of abundance, not scarcity. Unfortunately, we often live out of a grudging acceptance of a scarcity-of-love perspective rather than an abundance-of-love perspective, focusing on what we are not allowed to have rather than on what we do have. Singles reflect the abundance of God's love in the inclusive open way they can relate to everyone. To live with a view of scarcity is to focus on a moral restraint or need to sublimate the desire for genital sexual fulfillment rather than finding abundance in the freedom to love intimately and inclusively, recognizing they can give and receive more because of singleness. Married couples reflect God's faithful covenantal love that puts down roots and grows deeply into multiple dimensions of abundant love with one person. To live in abundance rather than scarcity is to explore and embrace the depth of love possible in an exclusive relationship rather than to focus on the moral restraint that limits that kind of love to one other. Married people have the opportunity to live in the abundance of an exclusive relationship yet not become so focused on each other that they neglect caring for and being in relationship with others in their community; neither are they so open to caring for and being in relationship with others that they seek abundance through other relationships that lead to scarcity in their marriage.[14]

Sexual fidelity becomes a gift of abundant love rather than a taxation on love resulting in scarcity. Fidelity also recognizes that the bond between a husband and wife creates a community that is real and bigger than the two individuals alone. Stanley Grenz says, "To practice fidelity is to declare that community, not the solitary ego, is the ultimate dimension of humankind, that is, that community is more primary than the solitary individual."[15]

Infidelity is seldom part of the future plan for newlyweds. Given the desire people have to be faithful, one wonders why some fail. Researchers exploring reasons for extramarital sex have identified key factors predicting the likelihood of an affair.[16] Those most likely to stay faithful are highly committed to their faith, have equal power and voice within their marriage, hold to conservative attitudes, were virgins when they got married, and are generally satisfied with their marriage.

These factors reflect choices and attitudes that reinforce a value of fidelity. But committed Christians continue to have affairs, increasingly so as the prevalence and acceptance of personal and professional friendships has drawn people in good marriages into affairs.[17] Having an affair is a gradual process of self-deception that convinces people their thoughts or behaviors toward another either do not constitute a breach in their marital commitment or they are justified in doing so. Married people who have affairs may or may not be in a marriage that is growing increasingly distant and difficult. Shirley Glass, a psychotherapist, says that affairs for males used to be primarily about sex. These brief and situational affairs occurred without advanced planning and often without their wives' knowledge. Increasingly, affairs about sex are being replaced by affairs that develop out of deep, intimate emotional bonds. Glass sees these "passionate love affairs" as more threatening to marriages because of the greater emotional depth and bonding that occurs in them.

Developing close cross-sex relationships outside marriage is largely avoided in cultures that maintain sex-segregated societies in which men and women do not interact significantly outside their family relations. Most often, these are classic patriarchies such as Iran, Afghanistan, and Saudi Arabia, but sex segregation is also found among Hasidic Jews and the Amish. Those in mainstream cultures generally believe that day-to-day interaction with the other sex adds perspective, balance, and energy that enrich life and work. Sex-integrated societies provide greater opportunities for social interaction between men and women. Negotiating cross-sex friendships so that friendships and marriages benefit from the richness of relationship without compromising the integrity of marriage becomes a challenge for married and unmarried people alike.

Cross-Sex Friendship

Counselors offer reflections and advice; researchers study the phenomena, and married couples wrestle with the challenge. We are made for relationship, yet marriage is neither primarily about the fulfillment of all our longings nor intended to meet all our relational needs. Our longings are also met through friendships and through extended family relationships in our churches and communities, as well as through the work we do.

Couples have various degrees of comfort with cross-sex friendship and ascribe different meanings to cross-sex friendship behaviors. Jonathan, a man deeply committed to his marriage, also has an intimate friendship with a female coworker with whom he shares a variety of interests and activities outside work. They have shared meaningfully in each other's pains and struggles and use touch and verbal expressions of care in their friendship. Although Jonathan's wife, Haley, struggled significantly in the early years of his friendship, she wanted to give Jonathan freedom to explore friendship with women and to define his own boundaries around them. The two couples do things together to add accountability and balance to Jonathan and his friend's relationship. Haley knows that Jonathan is committed to their marriage. Jonathan would say the exclusive commitment he has to his marriage is to reserve genital sex for Haley and to cherish their life-story; she is his life partner, the mother of his children, the one he walks with daily through life.

Pete and Alicia see cross-sex friendship apart from couple friendship as potentially dangerous and not worth the risk to their marriage. They avoid risk by developing intimate friendships only with members of their own sex. While they know and dearly love people of the other sex, they are loved in the context of a couple-friendship or primarily through the friendship of their spouse. They guard their marriage carefully and would not go to lunch or coffee, or in other ways socialize alone with a member of the other sex.

Other couples negotiate the challenge somewhere between the positions taken by Jonathan and Haley, and Pete and Alicia. Mark and I want to free each other to be enriched by relationships with both men and women, but we take care to nurture the "best-friends" quality that first drew us toward each other. We invest our best energy, time, and creativity in our friendship with each other. Mostly, we do so because our friendship is deeply satisfying and still, twenty-five years later, we enjoy the richness of discovering deeper layers of each other's souls that unfold over the course of life.

But this has not always been true. We have not always invested well in our marriage nor guarded our hearts well. A number of years ago, we acknowledged the ease with which we could become emotionally entangled in a cross-sex friendship. Mark and I negotiated the challenge of cross-sex friendship by actively protecting and holding on to each other as the one we each chose as our primary life partner. We now choose to invest the most in our friendship with each other; our second tier of intimate friends consists of people of our own sex. These friends are our primary sources for emotional and spiritual encouragement outside each other; they are our playmates and social partners for various activities. Mark is thankful for Jana, my friend and backpacking partner, as it keeps him from feeling guilty about not sharing this interest of mine. In other ways, she enriches my life as an intimate woman friend. She holds me accountable to be honest with myself; she knows me as only a woman can know me.

I am likewise thankful for Clark, Scott, and Jeff—friends of Mark who know him as only a man can know him. He grunted away with Jeff on a "Bombs-Away" bathroom remodeling project. When Clark and Mark are in town together, they try to get away to watch a movie with lots of explosions. These friends also meet Mark in a tender and vulnerable place, and his life is touched by them in places I cannot reach.

A third tier of friends, less intimate than our second tier, includes those of the other sex. We share our lives with these friends, along with the joys and struggles that come from work and parenthood, but we do not discuss struggles in our marriage. We laugh, talk about ideas, and socialize with these friends. We welcome the energizing joy and warmth that comes from being in the presence of a cross-sex friend but are watchful, mindful of our need to guard our hearts.

Couples negotiate cross-sex friendship differently, coming to conclusions that reflect characteristics unique to their marriages and their personalities. Like Jonathan and Haley and Pete and Alicia, couples are wise to agree together to determine what certain behaviors mean and do not mean and what exclusivity and honor of the marital covenant looks like.

Singleness and marriage reflect different aspects of the nature of God. Corresponding to these aspects are different levels of freedom and constraint that call for definition and clarity. The Balswicks offer four guidelines for those wanting to strengthen their marriage in the face of relational challenges.

The first guideline is for people to be aware of and honest about feelings of attraction. People often see their friendship as different—as exceptional, unlike the kinds of relationships that lead to an affair. People need humility and honesty in their cross-sex friendships.

The second guideline is to refuse to keep secrets. Keeping a friendship or behaviors and activities that occur within a friendship a secret is a red flag. Refusing to keep secrets keeps spouses accountable to each other, bringing the spouse into the relationship and holding the integrity of the marriage at the forefront.

A third guideline is to pay attention to the current state of one's marriage and give it priority over other friendships. In the excitement of a new friendship, it is easy to put marriage on autopilot without realizing it.

The fourth guideline is to maintain marriage as the top priority; friendships are secondary. Invest time, energy, money, and passion into the relationship intended to bless and grow throughout a lifetime. When other friendships support and strengthen the marriage, they are a blessing; when they undermine marriage they wound.

The Case of Adultery

"Except for my infidelity we had a pretty good marriage," recently divorced, fifty-four-year-old Eilene said. She and her husband had been married thirty years. She thought their love of each other was enough and wishes that her husband could have been more tolerant of her occasional fall into indiscretion. "It was bad for me to be unfaithful; I'm not saying it wasn't. It's just that we had a pretty good life together apart from that." One wonders how her husband would have responded.

Adultery matters. It breaks a covenant and undermines the secure love found in an exclusive sexual relationship. Adultery does not have to lead to divorce, but people understand when it does.

Some kinds of unfaithfulness are fuzzier. Jill met a man in a chat room on the Internet. Over the course of several months, they went from sharing stories to talking intimately about themselves and their budding friendship. She thought about him constantly and wrote to him several times a day. They sent each other pictures of themselves and talked about the possibility of meeting somewhere. Most recently, they had begun describing fantasies with each other. She felt sick and ashamed. She loved her husband and didn't know why she was doing this. Had she been unfaithful? Did that constitute an affair?

George used the Internet to satisfy his desire for pornography. What began as an inquisitive foray into pornographic Internet sites led to sitting mesmerized at his computer screen for several hours at a time, usually late at night or in the privacy of his office at work, four or five days a week. His compulsion to view pornography interfered with his work and his relationship with his wife and children. Was he being unfaithful? Did his pornography constitute an affair? Was George guilty of a lesser offense if he only viewed pornography a couple of times a month?

Infidelity and adultery are not the same. Lists of infidelities sometimes used by Christian speakers include a workaholic spouse, a golf or sports fanatic, or one who views pornography. Spouses who find themselves thus "betrayed" are often unsure what their response should be. Is a man who works too many hours unfaithful to a marriage in the same way a spouse is who has a sexual affair?

Infidelity is breaking trust, being unfaithful to a promise to protect a covenant entered. And we can be unfaithful in many ways; for example, knowingly overspending on credit breaks a trust that money will be used wisely. Becoming consumed in another friendship or a sport, hobby, career, or ministry so that it undermines attention and investment in one's marriage are forms of infidelity. Our thoughts can be unfaithful as well. When we speak about a spouse to another in ways that betray them, or when we justify our behavior by blaming our spouse, or when we give up pursuing the good of our spouse and the good of our marriage, or when we wound each other with our words, we are betraying each other and our commitment to love well.

Adultery is a specific form of infidelity. The offended spouse has been betrayed, often feeling he or she is lacking something and struggling to know how best to respond and to whom to turn. Adultery negates marriage as a covenantal reflection of God's faithful, exclusive love. A marriage covenant says, "I chose you exclusively, and I choose you every day. I open myself up to you completely, to be vulnerable, naked, and transparent. I want to give freely and fully to you, to partner with you." Adultery takes away the freedom to trust, the safe place of belonging and acceptance found in marriage.

The impact of adultery on the betrayed spouse and the marriage depends on how power is distributed in the relationship. Historically, when women were the property of their husbands, a man's affairs were not perceived to breach any contract with his wife. In marriages in which the woman has little or no power within the marriage and few or no social or economic resources, she has few alternatives besides tolerating his infidelity. As women gained status as equal partners in marriage, betrayal was no longer tolerated or accepted by either husbands or wives.

The nature of the affair also affects the impact of the adultery. During my graduate school days, one of my professors, perhaps in defense of his own behavior, said that sex with a stranger was a much lesser offense to a marriage than a nonsexual emotional affair. For him, betraying a spouse by falling in love with another was a worse breach of marital vows than having impersonal sex. In terms of consequences, he may be right. In an "emotional affair," a spouse feels un-chosen and undesirable and questions the exclusive love commitment as a foundation of their marriage. Sexual affairs that begin as friendships strike at the core of a marital covenant in which intercourse is understood as the consummation of a love where one gives oneself fully and freely to another. These affairs, according to Glass, are the most difficult for spouses to overcome.

Our human inability to get beyond the pain of betrayal sometimes clouds our ability to extend forgiveness. Although we know that those we love are imperfect and that we are imperfect, the labor of extending forgiveness and grace can be overwhelming. Although an affair is never the fault of the offended spouse, those able to forgive are usually those able to see their own failings. They see they have loved selfishly and have been critical and controlling. A strong finding among psychologists studying forgiveness is that those with moral humility (the ability to see their own capacity for evil, even if not the same evil committed against them) are those most able to forgive.

In some cases, adultery has gone on for years; in other cases, it is a one-time sexual encounter. The level of betrayal feels different if a secret has been covered up for years, thus exposing the reality that a relationship thought to be authentic and open never was. Identities as individuals and as a married couple are redefined after an affair is exposed. Sometimes they crumble apart. But sometimes, through repentance that involves a humble change of heart and a committed change in action, through forgiveness that requires the ability to see one's own sinfulness and grace that believes God desires our best and is always working, marriages are sculpted anew; sometimes they emerge as strong, redemptive relationships.

Learning to Love Well

True freedom is the ability to choose right, always. Because the choice to sin has not yet been irrefutably eradicated, this freedom evades us and will until we go to heaven. But marriage reflects a glimpse of heaven as a safe and glorious haven. In marriage, people can experience the freedom that comes from unconditional acceptance, a place to grow old in the comfort of sustained and sacrificial loving. The reflection is limited because we cannot love as purely as God loves; we do not always choose rightly. We live in a time marked by the constraints of sin that weigh us down, wounding us and those we love. We pursue personal rights and self-fulfillment and reject a call to submission. We fail to understand the paradoxical freedom gained by living and loving well. Fortunately for us, God gave humans a great capacity for learning and, in marriage, an opportunity for lifelong learning about sacrificial loving.

Sacrificial living and loving empowers and gives voice to the dreams of a spouse, even if they are not one's own dreams. Mark encouraged my backpacking ventures, giving me gear for various birthdays and sending me graciously on my way, never begrudging the time or money my love of backpacking required. Smiling at and even finding endearing the nuances and habits of one's spouse that could otherwise be regarded as annoying or irritating is to live graciously. In doing so, marriage is lived in the freedom of grace where husbands and wives are honest about who they are and can be known and embraced in spite of imperfections. Coming home at the end of the day is returning to a place of refuge, where two people embrace, listen to, and share the events of the day, both bad and good. They nurture and accept, and are nurtured and accepted. Human sexuality, which draws us into consummate communion with another, is expressed in sacrificial loving and living.

The alternative is to live without freedom—fearful of what compromise or giving up control, or even giving too much affirmation, might cost. Instead of living in grace, couples engage in subtle battles for power, protecting themselves from being taken advantage of. Fear and habit drive much of our broken ways of relating. The models we have around us show men and women constantly taking advantage of each other, using each other, leaving each other for someone new. We are accustomed to seeing couples criticize and work to "fix" each other. To hang on to what we have; we scrutinize and criticize and control each other, fearful that if we lose control, we will lose some right or something that rightly belongs to us, including our spouse. We criticize each other for foolish words spoken in public, critique our partner's driving route from the passenger seat, or nag each other about a shuffling walk or the habit of jingling pocket change. Coming home means bracing oneself for criticism, for the next report on how one has added to an accumulating list of disappointments. There is little freedom to relax, to be securely loved for who one is. Sexuality is distorted and, instead of seeking closeness, couples move apart. A typical response to living in an unwelcoming or unsafe place is to withdraw, to distance oneself emotionally or physically from the other.

Jeanne felt her husband's aloof indifference when he came home. He seldom initiated conversation, activities, or even sex. She began to fear emotional or physical abandonment and brought up the subject of their relationship most evenings, wanting to talk through their problems. She called him during the day to say hi, dropped off gifts or notes at his office, and planned a weekend getaway. Paul felt suffocated. First criticized for being unavailable to her, for working too hard, for not being present to the children, for not being enthusiastic about a family vacation—and now suffocated by her efforts to draw close to him. He did not trust it, wondered what motivated it, and felt like she was constantly watching and monitoring him. The more she pursued, the more he distanced himself.

This distancer-pursuer dance plays itself out in conversations over breakfast, in decisions made throughout the day, and in the bedroom at night. A pursuing husband wrote Dear Abby for advice. He had been married eleven years, and he and his wife were the parents of four children. His wife wanted to move closer to family so they could help her with the care of their children. He agreed to move if she promised to have sex with him three times a week. That's all he wanted, and he could not understand his wife's refusal to promise a certain number of times she would be intimate with him every week given his willingness to move closer to her family. He wondered if he was expecting too much by asking her to commit to sex three times a week, especially given his own concession to the move. He saw it as a win-win situation and couldn't understand her inability to see it this way as well.

The more this man demands from his wife, the more she will resist him. If he can learn to empathize with what it has been like for her to have four children in eleven years and to be overwhelmed by their care, he will be on a road toward loving her better. If she can understand how left out of her love and affection he feels during this time when she is consumed with the caretaking of children, she will begin to love him better. Learning to love well means looking with humility at the patterns we adopt unthinkingly that are self-focused and unloving. It requires us to believe that eleven, twenty-two, even forty-four years into marriage we still have much to learn about how to love each other well, to adapt our hopes and expectations to the changing nature of life's demands, and to live in the freedom of extended grace.

Confession and Redemption

Women and men go into marriage hoping to find it deeply satisfying for themselves and their spouses. They hope marriage will take away their aloneness, filling the longing they have for consummation—to be part of something bigger than themselves. At some point, they become disillusioned, recognizing that marriage does not completely satisfy their longings.

God comes to where we are, calls us by name, and invites us back to that which is redemptive—to that which gives blessing and life. When spouses stop, hear, and respond to God's call, they can recognize their failure to be as faithful as they had hoped, to love as sacrificially as they might have. Turning back toward marriage, toward a covenant they made, allows God to work redemptively to heal and bless and grow a relationship that could reflect God's nature more clearly. Redeeming marriage is a lifelong process, born from commitment and desire by husband and wife to honestly examine ways we wound each other in an effort to satisfy the unfilled longings we still have. Presumption that marriage should completely satisfy is as devastating as despairing that we can ever be satisfied. Holding to hope for fulfillment in eternity keeps us in an embrace that is willing to hang on to each other, do reconstructive surgery on our marriage, repent, forgive, and work through the ways we hurt and wound in the process of learning to love well.

David decided to attend a men's retreat his church was hosting, where sexual struggles were going to be openly discussed. Mostly, he listened as the speaker and then other men shared stories of past sexual sins and admitted to current challenges. He observed how they were not ostracized but embraced. Others confronted these men with a need to follow confession with repentance—a turning away from their behavior. For the first time, David felt hope that he could admit to someone the mess he had gotten himself into and not be rejected out of hand for it.

David had reacquainted himself with an old girlfriend through the Internet. She had been recently divorced and found him while looking up old friends. They reminisced about college and the year they dated. She talked about her failed marriage and told him she would have been better off if she had married David. They planned to meet at a conference David attended that was close to where she lived, and after a lively and fun dinner together he invited her up to his room to continue the conversation. He did not intend to pursue anything inappropriate, but they ended up spending the night together and having sex. On the trip home, he was overcome with guilt and shame. He had a fine marriage and loved his wife, Kristen, and had never been unfaithful to her before. David ended the affair quickly and stopped e-mailing his old girlfriend.

David had confessed his affair to God but at the retreat also felt convinced that he needed to tell his wife about it. He returned from the retreat and later that evening began to tell her about reconnecting with a college girlfriend and his subsequent brief affair. He felt free, relieved to have nipped the affair so quickly in the bud. He had come clean by unloading this horrible secret. He knew Kristen would be hurt, of course, but he hoped she would appreciate his honesty and the ultimate integrity that made him stop the affair and recommit to her.

Kristen sat on the edge of the sofa, her hands clasped in her lap, biting her lower lip. She would say later this was the worst day of her life, followed by many more bad days spent reflecting on a world falling to pieces around her.

Many spouses will err along the way, catching themselves at some point—sometimes before an affair becomes sexual, sometimes after. The remarkable thing about redemption is that it can take something bad and refashion it in ways we never thought possible. We learn and grow from our mistakes. In the memoir *Telling Secrets,* Frederick Buechner says,

> I am inclined to believe that God's chief purpose in giving us memory is to enable us to go back in time so that if we didn't play those roles right the first time round, we can still have another go at it now. We cannot undo our old mistakes or their consequences any more than we can erase old wounds that we have both suffered and inflicted, but through

the power that memory gives us of thinking, feeling, imagining our way back through time we can at long last finally finish with the past in the sense of removing its power to hurt us and the other people and to stunt our growth as human beings.[18]

Out of a perceived need in our church, Mark and I joined a team developing guidelines that we hoped would help couples wanting to work through difficult marriages—to extend grace in the midst of suffering. Specifically, we considered how to help spouses wanting to confess sin and work through betrayal and to help offended spouses receive and respond to confession. Husbands and wives who want to foster a relationship that includes honesty regarding sexual struggles open themselves to growth and blessing, but getting there often involves significant pain.

Confession is a step in the process of repentance where we admit our sin to God and one another. When we confess, we are assured of God's forgiveness. Because confession is part of repentance—a demonstration of commitment to turn away from our sin—confession moves beyond disclosure and is accompanied by a clear commitment to change. Scripture calls us to confess our sins to one another (James 5:16), but this does not transfer our responsibility or end the consequences we may face as a result of our sin.

Practical Suggestions for Confessors

Those who confess to having a problem with pornography, a friendship, or an affair often feel an emotional relief after confessing, yet spouses pay a high price for that reprieve. With confession, the confessor's life will likely change for the better, and the spouse's will become both better (because of renewed authenticity in the marriage) and worse (because of the disappointment, anger, and betrayal they will feel). Following are some practical ideas for those who have something to confess.

- ○ Confess your sin to another person first so that you experience the relief that confession brings before talking with your spouse. Then when you confess to your spouse, you will be able to think about him or her rather than your own need to relieve the guilt you feel. When you talk with this other person, discuss how much detail should be shared with your spouse.

- ○ Before confessing, establish a clear and feasible accountability plan to turn you from this sin and the patterns that brought you there. A plan communicates commitment to change to your spouse.

○ Allow your spouse to feel whatever she or he feels. The reaction may be anger, sadness, depression, resentment, or any number of other feelings. Do not expect your spouse to handle this well at first. And if she or he does handle it well, do not expect it to last. Grief takes time and involves complex emotions. Give your spouse the space needed to face mixed and painful feelings.

○ Offer your willingness to get help from a pastor or counselor. You will likely have difficult days ahead. Seek marital help as needed. Even if you don't sense a need for help, let it be mostly the decision of your spouse.

○ Affirm your love and commitment to your spouse day after day, recognizing that he or she may sometimes return your kindness with criticism and anger.

Practical Suggestions for Offended Spouses

Some spouses suspect something is awry; others are caught completely off-guard. Some respond in immediate anger; others respond with gracious acceptance at first, only to have pain, anger, and feelings of betrayal gnaw at them later. Almost all spouses feel some amount of betrayal, sadness or depression, confusion, and loss. Disclosure signifies a spouse's desire to work toward an authentic and honest relationship.

Following are some suggestions for spouses willing to forgive and who desire to work toward healing and wholeness with a repentant spouse.

○ There is no excuse for your spouse's sin, and you did not cause it. But remember that we live in a sinful world and are all sinners. Sexual sin is easy to identify; other sins are harder to see. We easily deceive and minimize our own hard-to-see sins, choosing instead to focus on the obvious sins of our spouse. Spouses who are critical rather than affirming, who seek to control by correcting and telling spouses how and what to do are also sinning. We sin against each other in obvious ways and in less obvious ways.

○ There is much shame surrounding sexual sin that drives spouses into secrecy. Many Christians who believe they know their spouses well are shocked to hear a confession of sexual sin. Wives particularly assume that good Christian men do not struggle this way and wonder what it means about the faith commitment and character of their husbands when they do. Generally, women do not understand the nature of men's sexual temptations. Nor do most men understand the nature of women's fears, insecurities, and challenges surrounding sexuality.

○ All sexual sin is a betrayal, but not all sexual sin carries the same implications. Looking at pornography occasionally has fewer ramifications than having a pornography addiction. A friendship that becomes emotionally entangled has different consequences from those of a relationship that was only sexual or that became sexual. All of these are betrayals. All are sin. All are painful. But they are not all the same. Adultery does not have to lead to divorce.

○ Ask enough questions to be basically informed of the nature of the struggle and the sin, but do not attempt to learn all the details; they will hurt and haunt you later. Occasionally, ask how the struggle is going as your spouse seeks help from others, but do not attempt to be your spouse's conscience or to put yourself in the place of a parent, spiritual counselor, or accountability partner. If you seek to control your spouse and your spouse's behavior, he or she may become resentful and secretive, and you will become increasingly frustrated and wounded. Your spouse knows he or she has hurt you deeply, and is working to regain your trust and to love you faithfully.

○ Allow yourself to feel and express anger, sadness, betrayal, and resentment. Do not deny these feelings, but don't drown yourself or your spouse in them either. Remember that confession to a spouse allows authenticity and stretches you both toward growth and healing in your relationship. Even if your initial response is gracious, you will likely experience painful feelings over and over again. Grief takes time and involves complex emotions and a period of building trust and healing.

○ Talk to a trusted and wise friend who can hold your feelings without encouraging or allowing the conversation to become a spouse-trashing session. Talking with many friends is not helpful and will undermine your spouse's efforts to be honest with you. You need someone who will support you in the work of dealing with the pain of betrayal, forgiveness, and personal growth. Seek marital help as needed. The more extensive the sexual involvement, the more likely marital help will be needed.

○ If you are committed to staying with your spouse, affirm your love and commitment day after day, even as negative thoughts and feelings return to you. And they will for a while, but not forever. God is always working. God loves you and your spouse and desires your marriage to be one that blesses you, grows you, and draws you toward each other and God.

Conclusion

In *Money, Sex, and Power,* Richard Foster writes,

> There is power that destroys. There is also a power that creates. The power that creates gives life and joy and peace. It is freedom and not bondage, life and not death, transformation and not coercion. The power that creates restores relationship and gives the gift of wholeness to all. The power that creates . . . proceeds from God.[19]

Christians believe God gave us the gift of sexuality—a sexuality that draws us toward another, creating a longing for an intimate bond that allows us to immerse ourselves body and soul into the life of another. Together, two separate people find safety, belonging, and comfort in the familiarity of walking, loving, and embracing each other on the journey toward eternity.

Marriage fills us with hope for fulfillment, but we are presumptuous to assume we will be completely safe, comforted, or loved by one as broken as ourselves. Married people are writing a story together—one that will have tragic chapters as well as joyous ones. All marriages struggle. Some struggles, such as those involving abuse, addictions, or patterns of unfaithfulness represent great brokenness. Some of those for whom the fragrance of Eden has been replaced by the stench of a refuse pile keep hope alive by looking earnestly toward heaven for the fulfillment of their longings.

In marriages that retain a scent of Eden, husbands and wives stretch toward authenticity, toward knowing and being known. Out of richness and blessing, they open their arms to welcome and serve others, finding joy in the midst of disappointment and extending grace in the midst of suffering. The fragrance of Eden sends blessing throughout the community, along with a glimpse and hope of heaven.

○

QUERIES FOR FURTHER REFLECTION AND CONVERSATION

○ If you are married, what in your marriage sustains, warms, comforts, and encourages you? What characteristics of your spouse are "etched into your very senses"?

○ If you are married, what would you say has been the primary purpose of your marriage thus far? Are these purposes satisfying to you? Do they reflect purposes identified historically by the Church (sexual fulfillment, companionship, parenting)?

○ How does your faith community attempt to strengthen marriages? What would be helpful for a married couple that is currently not available in your church? What avenues do you have to communicate such ideas to leaders?

○ In what ways do the beliefs that personal fulfillment and an obligation to meet your potential interfere with your ability to love your spouse or others well?

○ If you are married, on a scale of 1 to 5 (1 being Not At All, 5 being Very Much) how satisfied are you with your sex life? How satisfied do you think your spouse would say he or she is? What would be a next step in moving you to a greater level of satisfaction, or if you are very satisfied, what is it that allows you to be?

○ If married, have you and your spouse negotiated shared principles about cross-sex friendships? If single, how has this issue affected your friendships with cross-sex, married friends? How can cross-sex friendships be maintained so that they bless and do not compromise either friendship or marriage?

○ Sometimes marriage is only about thorns and thistles and wounds so deep that time only numbs the sharpness of the pain but does not take it away. What kind of hope can bring some measure of healing to broken, wounded people? Hope in what?

○

SEXUALITY AND CULTURE

BODIES AND SCRIPTS

---

*People's greatness comes from knowing they are wretched: a tree
does not know it is wretched. Thus it is wretched to know
that one is wretched, but there is greatness in knowing one is
wretched. . . . They have a secret instinct driving them to seek
external diversion and occupation, and this is the result of their
constant sense of wretchedness. . . . What else does this craving,
and this helplessness, proclaim, but that there was once in people
a true happiness, of which all that now remains is the empty
print and trace? This they try in vain to fill with everything
around them* [language changed to make inclusive].

—Blaise Pascal, *Pensees*

MARK AND I SPENT A WEEK AT ST. THOMAS, interspersing writing
with snorkeling, kayaking, hiking, and eating. One night we ate dinner
on the beach, with windows open to the ocean breeze, background music
for the small band playing Caribbean-style music. A table of older women
ate beside us. At one point, a woman in her sixties, dressed in an elegant
evening gown, got up and graced us with her dancing. She sashayed
around the dance floor all by herself, moving her hips and arms with sensuous grace. After I got over the initial wonder of it, I started rooting for
her in silent praise. Here was a woman comfortable in her aging body, a
woman who loved to dance and knew she danced well. She gave us all a

gift. We clapped when the song ended, and Mark and I thanked her heartily as she passed our table on her way back to her own. I wished I could dance, and I longed for the kind of comfort she had with her body. Her ease and way of being present in her body encouraged me, comforted me.

Mark identifies less with the woman on the dance floor than with the framers pounding nails on the new house next door. We go over almost daily to watch their progress. The day they rearranged the earth to accommodate the house, our neighbor Jeff brought his three-year-old son over to watch the backhoe move dirt, shrubs, and debris. We smelled the lumber the day before framing began—a particularly sensuous experience for Mark, who sometimes wishes he worked with houses instead of ideas. We watched a team of men build walls, coordinating the raising of those walls and securing them in place. "They don't have to lift weights to look like that and to be able to do that so easily," Mark sighed. These strong men use their bodies well, gracefully coordinating their strength in a cooperative effort to build.

Part of God's image is expressed in sensuous beauty that calls forth a response and a desire to draw near. Another aspect of God's image is reflected in strength, in a cooperative effort to create. The presence, voice, and perspectives of women and men reflect aspects of God's character somewhat differently, bringing different abilities and skills to the task of caring for the earth. Certainly, women are strong and creative and men are graceful and beautiful, but women's beauty and men's strength and drive are often identified as central to sexuality. Culturally derived ways of being male and female often overemphasize female beauty and male strength and sex drive. These "ways of being" are passed down to us in the form of cultural scripts.

Cultural scripts are taken-for-granted, learned ways of being that reinforce behaviors and roles for men and women that are considered important in a society. They become almost sacred beliefs that are represented in traditions, expectations, and laws that dictate maleness and femaleness. We learn norms from Ian Fleming's British spy character James Bond, on the latest reality television show, from song lyrics, in magazine ads, from our friends, in our churches, and in our homes.

One woman relayed the following story from her husband's work as dean of students at a public middle school.

> He was going to send a seventh-grade girl home because she was wearing a pair of tight pants with "bootylicious" in sparkles on the behind. When he called her mother, she questioned why the pants she had

bought for her daughter were a problem. When the mother came to school to pick up her daughter, she was wearing a pair of tight pants and a low-cut top. The apple did not fall far from the tree.

Cultural scripts are pervasive and inescapable. Girls and boys grow up with scripts instructing them how to integrate their bodies with appropriately gendered activities that will make them acceptable and lovable. Early on, we learn how to behave to ensure that we will find someone to love us, to fill the emptiness and longing we have for connection.

Cultural scripts for men and women vary from era to era and from place to place. Scripts throughout much of the world have broadened in the last century for both men and women, bringing new opportunities for people in their communities of faith, civic communities, work, and residential communities. Some churches embrace this time in history, channeling the energy and enthusiasm of greater opportunities to better use the gifts and capacities of women and men. Others are unsure how changing cultural trends reflect what they understand as doctrines of the Church for male and female roles. The debate about what kinds of opportunities should or should not be available for men and women centers in part on the question of whether or not it is legitimate for definitions of maleness and femaleness to be flexible. What is embodied and unchanging about being male and female? And what is embedded in culture, reflecting the potential for flexibility and change? Communities of faith wanting confidence in their stance on changing roles for men and women recognize this question as a foundation for understanding how much to embrace or resist cultural change.

Explaining Femaleness and Maleness

Humans are characterized by strength, passion, compassion, motivation, nurture, vision, and creativity—all qualities that we inherit from God and that create stable and progressing societies. One popular way of telling history is that men have always been in charge as the active doers providing subsistence, while women have functioned as caregivers and nurturers. Christians endorsing this history say that the pattern is God-ordained and that God created men and women to have different roles. However, research in archeology and anthropology suggests that this interpretation of history is flawed. Although there are general patterns of male dominance throughout history, both men and women have actively provided subsistence and participated in caregiving roles.

This perspective of maleness and femaleness was passed on to me in the flannel-graph stories of heroes in Sunday School classes and at Vacation

Bible School. We learned about David who killed Goliath, about Samson who killed lots of Philistines, and about Gideon who, with a small army, wiped out thousands. Although we were taught to respect Peter as the cornerstone of the Church, we did not talk about him as though he was a hero. Our teachers talked about Jonah and Aaron as men who ran away from both adventure and battle. The unspoken message: they were an embarrassment to real manhood, but God found ways to use them anyway. Women were hardly talked about at all except for Bathsheba, who led David into adultery, and Delilah, who seduced and ruined Samson (the physically strongest prophet of God), or Esther or Mary, who submitted and did what they were told or asked to do. Societies have always used their folklore and histories to reinforce particular values that society holds. The Church has similarly used biblical stories to reinforce ideas of masculinity and femininity that reflect dominant ideas in our culture.

Explanations for male and female differences that deviate from a rooted-in-biology-thus-God-ordained explanation have been held in suspicion—a slippery slope sending us down the road toward relativism. Especially suspect is an explanation suggesting that culture rather than biology shapes and defines masculinity and femininity.

The way a culture treats babies born with ambiguous sex organs demonstrates how much culture plays a role in sculpting maleness or femaleness; biology is not allowed to have the final say. Parents and doctors quickly assess and then determine whether or not to assign intersex babies the status of girl or boy, depending on the size and presence or absence of certain genitalia. The underlying assumption is that biology is only a piece of what makes one male or female, and culture needs to manipulate biology and resolve any ambiguity by filling in necessary gaps, usually with medical interventions. So a boy born with a penis that is too small (less than half an inch) has his penis surgically removed, along with his testes. A clitoris (which may or may not produce sexual pleasure) and vagina are built in their place. Boys are given hormones to help them develop breasts and are subsequently raised as girls.[1] There are numerous ways that babies end up being neither fully male nor female in terms of their sex organs, so frequency is difficult to determine. However, in North America, one or two in one thousand babies are surgically altered to "normalize" their genital appearance.[2] Most parents in this situation are not willing to let biology have the final say about their child's sexual identity or to postpone medical intervention until the child can decide what to do; they feel the need to intervene, overriding biology, as it were. Nurture rather than nature, this explanation says, holds the ultimate power to shape femaleness and maleness in our culture.

Other explanations integrate the embedded and embodied dimensions, asserting that maleness and femaleness is an interaction between biological realities that are reinforced, focused, and exaggerated by cultural influences. The two cannot be separated; both powerfully shape how girls and boys, men and women come to understand what it means to be male and female. For instance, men have a predictable arousal response—an erection that they cannot always control, though they can control what they do with it. Culture interprets that reality and assigns meaning to it (men cannot help that they are naturally inclined to have sex with lots of different women), as well as meaning to women (since the biological goal of his desire is to have sex with her, she, as the object of his arousal, exists primarily to help propagate the species). Such an interpretation, while rarely vocalized, subconsciously contributes to a justification of male dominance over females.

How one explains broken sexuality (and Christians would see this scenario as broken) influences how one goes about redeeming it. Two explanations are particularly interesting for Christians looking at sexuality. The first explanation, from *sociobiology,* says men and women are biologically hard-wired to behave in certain ways, regardless of cultural influences. The second, from *social learning theory,* says the power and influence of culture shapes male and female behavior more than biology.

Sociobiological Explanations

A sociobiological explanation says men and women are hard-wired physically to want to reproduce themselves. Males are predisposed to desire multiple sexual partners, especially young, fertile ones, because having sex with these women provides a better chance of producing lots of healthy offspring. Men do not want other men having sex with their women because then they cannot be sure their own genes are making it into the gene pool of the future. Men band together to protect what is theirs, including their women, and they will be aggressive in their pursuit of acquiring things that do not belong to them because they want a promising future for their offspring. Males who survived and reproduced themselves abundantly were men with this high drive for sexual conquest and aggression. Gentle males died out; they were either killed or withdrew, choosing not to fight. That meant gentle males had less reproductive influence on future male generations.

Males, according to sociobiology, are more likely to be driven to create, subdue, build, and protect than to nurture relationships. For the most part, honor and achievement matter more to males than to females. Men are more likely to support dying for a cause than are women; they tend to sacrifice relationships for achievement and have been the primary force (though women have contributed significantly) in moving civilizations from their hunting and gathering beginnings into an agricultural era, followed by an industrial and then a postindustrial era. Cultures reinforce and support this creating, subduing, building, protecting tendency that seems hard-wired in males.

Females are hard-wired to reproduce themselves, too, but because they make a great physical investment with every pregnancy and can only have a limited number of children, they are more particular in their choice of sexual partner. They want good genes and someone who is likely to stick around to help protect and provide for their offspring to ensure their young make it to adulthood. Biologically, females adapt and accommodate their lives and bodies to receive and nurture others, which is evident in sexual intercourse when females are penetrated and semen is deposited in their bodies. When they become pregnant, females accommodate and adapt to fetuses that grow and are nourished in their wombs and at their breasts.

Sociobiology suggests that females generally have more of a relational driving force than males and subsequently work harder than men to protect and enhance family and community cohesiveness. As adaptable beings, they accommodate, submit, and meet obligations to others to protect relationships and those they love. Mothers are less likely to abandon their children than fathers; generally, women are less supportive of war and capital punishment and more supportive of gun control laws than men. Sanctity of life and relationships are valued more by most women than are honor and achievement. As the primary bearers and nurturers of life, it makes sense that women would value these things. It follows that cultures will find ways for this positive aspect of femaleness to be safeguarded and encouraged.

The negative aspects of biological drives can be controlled, and religious communities have been active throughout history assisting in this task. The world is not overrun with men fighting to build and keep harems because religious values prescribing a moral code along with social norms—laws and traditions like marriage licensure and monogamy—encourage men and women to control and manage biological drives. The family unit is the basic building block for religious and civic communities, and historically the Church and State have encouraged stable families.

Although aspects of sociobiology are insightful, two major criticisms give pause to Christians wanting to embrace this explanation as the final word on origins of maleness and femaleness. First, just because something occurs rather predictably in a culture (we see a consistent male desire for promiscuity, therefore it must be "natural") does not mean its roots are biological and therefore natural. Even if a behavior is rooted in biology, it does not mean the behavior is necessarily good. Our biology is also tainted by sin, and many of our desires are sinful. Second, the explanation justifies a sexual standard that legitimizes male promiscuity and aggressiveness while expecting female nurturance and monogamy.

Some Christian social scientists, such as psychologist Stanton Jones, also argue that sociobiology reduces human behavior to that of other animals and does not recognize the image-of-God element that sets humans apart from other animals, thus giving us greater responsibility and choice for our decisions.[3]

Social Learning Theory

Social learning theory suggests that boys and girls learn how to be boys and girls and what to think about sex and themselves as sexual beings through their interactions with others. This process occurs unconsciously so that in preschool Shanita knows she is to play make-believe, dress-up, and house, and Samuel knows he is to rumble around on the floor with other boys, play with balls, make swords out of sticks, and stay away from girls. Not all boys and girls fit these patterns, but boys usually learn how to be boys because they are punished when they act like girls and rewarded when they act like boys. When Samuel tries to join the girls in playing dress-up, the girls laugh at him, the boys call him a girl, and the teacher tries to smooth it over by involving him in "boy" activities.

What girls and boys are supposed to want and how they are supposed to act, feel, relate to the other sex, and relate to the same sex are all feelings and actions constructed and created by societies and various subgroups within them; they are then passed on through traditions and norms as though they contain the final absolute truth about male and female behaviors and desires.

A few years down the road, if Samuel cries and doesn't like sports he will be called a "sissy" or "fag"—both anathema to male sexuality, as one refers to females and the other to homosexuality. Social learning theory suggests that Samuel will probably learn to brag about the size of his penis, put Shanita down or treat her as a sexual object, and brag about sexual exploits. He will then be called a "stud" or "one of the guys" and affirmed for his masculinity.

Boys learn how to be boys by observing slightly older boys, who are learning how to be boys from other slightly older boys. They are taught the code: "sticks and stones can break my bones but words can never hurt me," which teaches them to be tough and invulnerable and to "suck it up" and be a man. Boys also learn how to be boys by learning how *not* to be girls. Although they may adore the mothers who care for them, they know that to be male means to not be like Mom. Boys internalize an antifemale bias in their attempts to figure out how they are supposed to be by determining what they are not. Girls are sissies, and crying is a sissy thing to do, and so is being cooperative and nurturing. Ultimately, boys want girls to like them, but boys do not want to be girly.

Media figures such as Jackie Chan or Vin Diesel often demonstrate a hypermasculinity that is aggressive, violent, and highly sexualized. The warrior, the womanizer, and the wild man emerge as icons of maleness, reflecting a set definition of masculinity that has been idealized throughout Western history. Yet this limits maleness. A much broader definition is captured in the character of Jesus, who was neither a warrior nor an adventurer. Jesus had work to do and embraced his work with integrity (he could not be tempted by fame or power), creativity (he taught using parables and miracles), and compassion (he nurtured those he worked with and ministered to); he spoke out against evil among religious leaders, submitted to authority, and ultimately died in the hands of Romans at the will of Jewish leaders. Jesus was relational and fully aware of the ache of human loneliness. He pursued time with God and developed intimate relationships with his companions. In contrast, the warrior, adventurer, and hero icon reflects a denial of anything vulnerable, cooperative, and nurturing in maleness in favor of what is strong, powerful, and successful.

The goal of being a real man and getting a woman to like you is reinforced by girls, who are taught to like boys who are tough, aggressive, and bold. Because our deepest longings are relational, the goal embedded in all of us is to belong, to be loved. A male student in a course I teach on gender roles illustrated these goals with this observation:

> At bottom, my concept of masculinity is rooted in my sexuality. Since I can remember, I have always been aware that I am different from females. I have always desired to be in a special kind of relationship with a female; I remember "falling in love" with girls in *kindergarten!* As a result of this underlying desire, many of my ideas about gender roles have been formed by their utility in reaching this relational goal. If I want to be "brave" and "aggressive," it is often because that is what I have been told that women want. If there were no females in the world, I have a feeling I would see little intrinsic value in many things masculine.

Social learning theory suggests that the "powerful force" shaping behavior is actually what we learn through relationships with others. By itself, this theory does not explain why we act as we do, but it contributes to the growing explanation, and it offers hope. If behavior is learned, then good, healthy patterns can be taught; and broken, unhealthy patterns can be unlearned. As Christians, we are to model Jesus—God incarnate—as we learn how to be women and men in communities shaped by culture. Faith communities and parents can be intentional about modeling and mentoring holistic and healthy ways of being in relationships if much of the taken-for-granted assumptions about male and female roles are arbitrary and crafted by particular cultures.

Composite Pictures of Manhood and Womanhood

Males and females act differently because of our biology and culture. The difference between the sexes creates a graceful dance that takes our good yearnings and moves us toward relationship with each other. Because men are attracted to beauty and desire sex (biological realities that get reinforced and exaggerated in culture), they will pursue relationships rather than live estranged from others. Sex is often referred to as the glue that keeps people bonded together. Men's initiation of and desire for sex keeps them drawn toward and invested in relationship. That women are accommodating and relational means they are inclined to seek out relationships and work to protect them, drawing men into relational intimacy that strengthens their bond. However, because of the fall, these good inclinations and yearnings also lead to various kinds of brokenness in exaggerated and flawed expressions of maleness and femaleness.

Prior to the sexual revolution, and still in many cultures throughout the world, the female as recipient, adaptor, accommodator, and nurturer made women easy to dominate. Men developed religious beliefs and legal sanctions to justify and support the superior status of the male embodied state. At best, women's bodies were deemed spiritually, intellectually, and physically inferior, as suggested by early Church leaders; Augustine, for example, described his godly mother as one who had a woman's body but a man's faith;[4] Aquinas held similar views. At worst, females were considered a distortion of the perfect male body, as Aristotle suggested. Yet women were good for sexual pleasure and essential for reproductive purposes, and the young, healthy, and beautiful were the most desirable. In the brokenness of sin, women, like slaves and children, became objects—commodities men owned and exchanged.

The Enlightenment era brought an end to many traditions and laws that allowed the inhumane treatment of other humans, so that most human societies touched by the Enlightenment now see the ownership or absolute control of one person by another as evil. However, women's primary contribution is still largely seen as birthing babies and raising children.

Throughout history, women have found covert ways to exert power, particularly in their relationships with men. Sometimes this averted evil and brought about good, as with Abigail, who stepped outside her husband, Nabal's, authority in a culture that gave women no voice. She went to meet David, who was on his way to kill Nabal and his household because of Nabal's refusal to offer provisions that David felt he had a right to request for himself and his men. Abigail gave David the provisions, told him what a wonderful man he was (fighting the Lord's battles and all), who has not done wrong throughout his entire life and wouldn't want the blood of all these innocent people on his hands just because of Nabal's foolishness. She succeeded in averting David from his vengeance and then married him shortly after, as God struck Nabal dead (see I Samuel 25).

Sometimes this manipulation for power brought about evil, as in the biblical account of Delilah in Judges 16; Delilah betrayed Samson into the hands of his enemies for money. And Herod's wife, Herodias, manipulated an opportunity to get John the Baptist beheaded. Herod was grieved when he realized he had been cornered, but because he did not want to look bad in front of his guests, he had John beheaded (Matthew 14:1–9). Women's use of manipulation to exert power is as old a practice as the patriarchal systems that deny them voice and power.

We still see women manipulating men in efforts to catch, keep, and control them. I was asked to talk about healthy cross-sex relationships in a Wheaton College chapel open only to women. I decided to hit the high and low points and named the longing we have for intimacy "good" and encouraged women to embrace this longing as evidence of a God who made them for relationship. Then I discussed some of the negative ways women manipulate the system to obtain the intimacy they desire but do not have, challenging a sacredly held assumption that men have to be the initiators for relationships to be good, or even godly. I described "acceptable flirting behaviors," as detailed by two Christian authors in a book about relationships. These coy, flirtatious ways of being included painting fingernails red (because fingernail beds turn red when one is sexually stimulated), tossing the hair to expose the neck, and standing with one hip higher than the other.

Behaviors like these distort female sexuality. Words that could express interest are substituted for behaviors intended to catch a male's attention. Honest communication is supplanted with manipulative ploys. Flirting isn't necessarily wrong, but when flirtatious behaviors are the only legitimate means by which a woman can attempt to gain the attention of someone she is interested in, then flirting becomes a distortion of female sexuality.

In Chapter Two of this book, I discussed the fact that women whose voices are silenced are at a higher risk for experiencing unwanted sexual experiences.[5] When women are taught to be coy and flirtatious and let men do the talking and leading and deciding, it is difficult for them to assert their voice in sexually and emotionally charged moments. In a national survey, 22 percent of women said their first sex was unwanted.[6]

Some women use the freedom to dress however they want to as a way to assert themselves, knowing they can have an effect on men, thus exerting power over male sexuality. In Wendy Shalit's best-selling book *A Return to Modesty,* she argues that women have lost much in their effort to be as openly and freely sexual as they want. Shalit says women dress provocatively and engage in casual sexual relationships, and then wonder why, in this enlightened era, women continue to feel like sexual objects who do not have the respect of many men and find some men willing to settle for sex and forgo intimacy. Whatever power women think they gain only puts them at greater risk of becoming a sexual object.

Anyone can post opinions on the Forum Wall in our Student Center at Wheaton College. Once or twice a year, males write a letter to females, imploring them to attend to how they dress for the sake of their Christian brothers. Some laugh these letters off; some are insulted and offended by them, and some assert their right as women in a free country to dress however they want. To an extent they are all right. The problem does not reside wholly with how the females are dressing or wholly with the males who are troubled by it. Nevertheless, I am disturbed when I hear women laughing, taking offense, or asserting their rights when the question is raised. Where is the obligation to serve others in such a perspective? Where is the dialogue about balancing a desire to be attractive and sensual with the tendency to use one's body in a manipulative way to compete with other women or get attention from men? Where is grace being extended in understanding and responding to the sexual struggles of others? Female sexuality is distorted when a woman's voice is asserted in ways that put her interests and desires first, at the expense of others, and often at some expense to herself. How might our daughters be different if communities of faith led the way in granting women legitimate voice and power? I imagine they would be less inclined to get power and attention through manipulative means that encourage boys to treat them as sex objects.

The composition of maleness constructed from both sociobiology and social learning theory is a picture that is antifeminine, achievement-oriented, inexpressive, and aggressive. Men are not to feel emotional pain, joy, or fear, nor are they supposed to long for closeness with another in which they could be intimately known. Boys are socialized toward a sexuality that does not require relational intimacy or emotional attachment with sex and assumes that men are automatically aroused by female anatomy and that they naturally sexualize social situations, whether or not the situation warrants it. This picture shows men as chronically concerned with their sexual performance and interested in multiple partners for the sake of variety.[7] Women become objectified and pursued to bring the release of sexual tension and an affirming sense of men's sexuality.

I have summarized some very negative views of sexuality for both males and females. Examples of distorted sexuality flow from these composite pictures and two are particularly relevant for communities of faith. These distortions usually run beneath the surface, moving through our faith communities along a current of unspoken shame, fear, guilt, and confusion: (1) female sexuality easily becomes an obsession with body image and the use of body and beauty to manipulate, control, and compete, and (2) the male use of pornography reflects a distortion in expectation and desire for relationship and intimacy. Both distortions reflect the interconnection of the sexual lives of men and women.

Beauty Is the Beast[8]

We are not sinning when we enjoy and appreciate beauty, be it in a landscape or a human body. Beauty is one means by which men and women are drawn to each other and able to enjoy the creative way God crafted males and females to desire and enjoy the beauty of the other. Our body is an intrinsically good creation. We acknowledge the beauty of body when we recognize the good gift of our embodied existence, celebrate the body's various capacities, and treat our bodies well so that they work well.

However, we have deviated from this understanding of beauty, and a woman's desirability and worth throughout history have been determined on the basis of superficial, external standards of beauty envisioned by particular cultures. For a thousand years, from the tenth to early in the twentieth century, Chinese women kept the feet of their female children small by bending and binding the toes under the arch, thus rendering them "beautiful." Critics point out that the practice also controlled women's sexuality by ensuring a subjugation of sorts, in that foot-binding crippled women and made running (or running away) impossible.[9]

In some parts of Mali, Somalia, Uganda, and Sudan, gaining desirability and social worth means undergoing a "circumcision" which, while now illegal in most African countries, continues to be broadly practiced in the name of tradition; the practice is done to honor and appease ancestors. Africans and non-Africans fighting against the circumcision ritual call it female genital mutilation (FGM). The most common form is to remove the clitoris, though some tribes also scrape off or cut the labia and sometimes stitch the labia majora together, covering most of the vagina but leaving a small hole for the release of menstrual blood and urine. Most people in the industrialized world see FGM as a barbaric and horrible distortion of what is right. Christians are concerned because FGM distorts what God intended for pleasure in an effort to control women's sexuality.

Islamic fundamentalists approach beauty and the control of women's sexuality differently. Rather than try to sculpt it physically out of female bodies or encourage women to flaunt it, they "manage" it, believing women to be oversexed and prone to entice men into sexual sins. In countries such as Iran, women are required by law to wear the *hijab*, Arabic for "curtain," which literally falls over their body covering heads, faces, arms, and legs.

Though women in politically free countries are much freer to move around, to act independently, to pursue economic gain, and to engage the world than women in the less-developed world, women are constrained and controlled by cultural beauty standards. Psychologist Judith Rodin labeled the relationship that women in the United States have with their bodies as a "normative obsession," because our obsession with food and fat and the size and shape of our bodies is so accepted and ingrained in females that it is considered normal. What cannot be corrected by dieting is altered with surgery for women wealthy enough to afford it. Beauty, as it is envisioned and practiced by a culture, becomes a commodity at best, available to those wealthy enough to add silicon to their breasts or collagen to their lips, "tuck" their tummies, suction their thighs, and stretch or burn away their wrinkles. At its worst, beauty is a beast that pursues and terrorizes women, convincing them they are not lovable or worthy of love if they are not "beautiful." Whether as a commodity or a beast, beauty creates a cold competition as women critique and criticize each other for their beauty or lack thereof. The more engaged women are in the competition, the more marketers of beauty benefit. Women who cannot afford surgery can still be convinced beauty can be bought with anti-aging creams, over-the-counter teeth-whitening products, diet pills, clothes, accessories, and cosmetics.

I do not want to compare too directly the practices of women undergoing female genital mutilation with women choosing liposuction. As philosopher Martha Nussbaum notes, those pursuing liposuction have far more choice in whether or not they conform to beauty expectations than those undergoing FGM.[10] Some females undergo FGM as infants; others are faced with ostracism by their communities and doomed to a single life of poverty for refusing to comply with these practices during puberty rites. In all cases, these cultural practices are taken-for-granted norms so embedded in the particular culture that most women do not see their own practices as odd or barbaric. Women think, "Only the practices of women in other cultures are backwards or wrongheaded; our own are reasonable." Mothers in Africa say they continue to circumcise their daughters to honor their ancestors and uphold the wisdom of tradition. Women in the United States say they get their breasts done because they want to feel good about themselves. They think, "If this vision of beauty can be obtained through surgery, and if I can afford it, why shouldn't I have the surgery?"

The pressure to conform to a culture's beauty standards is further distorted when the standard reflects one dominant ideal for beauty. In the United States, that ideal is characterized by light skin, blond hair, a thin body, and Caucasian features. Narrow definitions of beauty further separate diverse people trying to live in unity. Some Asian women "caucasianize" their eyelids; some African Americans straighten their hair.

The ability to choose is empowering, and supporters of women's right to pursue cosmetic surgery say women make choices as rational decision makers and ought to be free to do so. Others suggest that women seek cosmetic surgery because they have been persuaded by the "male gaze"— a hypothetical or real perception of beauty as defined by males. A study by Gagne and McGaughey brings these two perspectives together, suggesting both are true.[11] Women do achieve power and control over their bodies when they choose to conform or reject cultural ideals of beauty. Yet the cosmetic surgery that gives power to individual women reinforces and perpetuates beauty standards that oppress women as a group.

Following are several ethical questions to stimulate thinking about conformity to beauty norms.

○ *Will this procedure contribute to overall health or detract from it, and does this practice represent a focus on appearance that is obsessive or one that is reasonable?* Certainly, plastic surgery can bring women greater health, as when deformities are corrected or when performed after accidents or for reconstructive purposes after mastectomies. Determining the reasonableness of the attention given to appearance may require stepping back from the issue to see the bigger cultural picture.

○ *To what degree is conformity chosen or coercive?* Female infants undergoing FGM and pubescent girls brought together for a communitywide circumcision ritual experience a coercive behavior. A second criterion for determining the harmfulness of norms intended to increase women's social worth or make them more attractive to potential mates is the degree to which they are freely chosen or coercive.

○ *To what degree will a woman's sexual experience and identity be controlled or altered?* Some groups that perform FGM believe that women with clitorises will be unfaithful, wanting too much sex. FGM then, is a way to control female sexuality by removing the organ associated with sexual pleasure. A third criterion for evaluating beauty standards considers the degree to which women's sexual experience and identity are altered through physical changes to the female body.

○ *What impact will this have on narrowing definitions of beauty for other women?* If women in the United States grow old-looking or have breasts that are too small, too saggy, or too large, or if they have "fat" thighs or bellies, they fear being considered ugly or even disgusting. Because improvements can be purchased, the market encourages women to invest in surgical enhancements. Thus the wealthy define acceptable female beauty for the masses, creating a beauty gap between the haves (those who can purchase beauty) and the have-nots. Although an individual choosing to have her breasts enhanced may not be sinning against her body or her principles, she does contribute to the narrowing definition of a normal sensuous breast. Thus a fourth criterion for evaluating beauty standards considers the impact the practice has on narrowing a definition of beauty that is primarily available to those with a fair amount of discretionary income.

Another example of this principle is teeth whitening. At my last visit to the dental hygienist, I was offered the increasingly popular procedure. "Not that you really need it," she assured me, noting my less-than-enthusiastic response, "but more patients are choosing to whiten their teeth, so we offer it to everyone." I left feeling self-conscious about my teeth. "Maybe they really are yellow; maybe I should spend the $600 (or was it $800?) and get them bleached," I thought. Before bleaching procedures became popular, a wide range of tooth coloration fell within a definition of "beautiful white teeth." Teeth whitening narrowed the color spectrum and made us aware of a deficiency that did not exist a few years ago. Those who can afford the procedure can purchase "beauty"; those in the middle class can at least purchase over-the-counter products with some hope for beauty enhancement. Meanwhile, many others will grow increasingly uncomfortable with their teeth that only five years ago might have been considered beautiful. According to the U.S.

Department of Commerce, our expenditures on personal care products and services have gone up 40 percent from 1995 to 2000.[12]
The two fastest-growing areas were teeth-whitening products and
breath-fresheners.

○ *Does this practice or procedure consider one's social responsibilities?* Although beauty practices may not be harmful to people in
our culture, some aspects of our cosmetic and apparel industry
exploit women and child laborers in the less-developed world.
Animal rights activists would have us consider our exploitation
of animals in the fur trade and those used in product testing as well.

Choosing to bleach one's teeth or to have breast implants or liposuction
are valid choices for women in modern societies, but they raise questions
worth discussing. The pursuit of a healthy body is good; it celebrates the gift
of being embodied creatures capable of much work and pleasure because of
our amazing bodies. Healthy bodies are often beautiful. Striving for or maintaining a reasonable weight, good muscle tone, and health is an affirmation
of beauty. Wearing various clothing and hairstyles and jewelry, as well as
enhancing one's face through make-up in a way that the culture defines
as beautiful, are generally harmless ways of conforming to beauty standards.

However, when these standards control women, when through them
we exploit others, when women are consumed by what they look like, and
when the definition of self and value depends on one's appearance, then
conformity to beauty standards and the pursuit of beauty reflects distortion, brokenness, and sin. Liposuction, breast implants, face-lifts, and
teeth bleaching are done in the name of achieving perfection and driven
by a market economy that flourishes when it convinces us we must be
flawless to be truly worthy of love.

Another piece of the distortion surrounding women's views of their
own beauty are men's views of women and women's bodies that lead to
objectification.

Case Study: Pornography

Broken sexuality affects relationships indirectly as well as directly. For the
most part, pornography indirectly affects relationships. Pornography was
not born with the sexual revolution, though it has blossomed with the
Internet. According to *U.S. News and World Report,* the pornography
industry grossed $8 billion in 1997. The Internet porn industry alone
brings in $3 billion a year,[13] and cybersex Web sites were viewed by as
many as 20 million adults in the United States every month in 2000, 90
percent of whom are male.[14] In a *Christianity Today* survey in 2000,

about one-third of clergy and laity said they had visited a pornographic site, and almost 20 percent of clergy said they did so from a couple times a month to more than once a week.[15]

Images and descriptions of nudity and people engaged in sexual activities date far back in ancient history—from paintings on walls and ceramics, to the poetry of the Song of Solomon, to sculpture, to Chinese sex manuals. Humans have always found the body and the sexual interplay between people interesting, beautiful, and a worthwhile subject of art, entertainment, and education.

In the absence of an open environment in which questions about sex can be asked without embarrassment, pornography can become a sex education teacher. Boys ranging in age from twelve to seventeen are a primary group of pornography consumers. Boys, either alone or with peers, pore over *Playboy* and *Penthouse* and discover the mysterious power of viewing a female body without clothes. They learn what sex looks like and what they can expect from it all.

Boys' sexual curiosity is healthy. Their desire to understand the mysteries of the female body and sex come from the yearnings of a body made to be in relationship—with God, with other boys, and ultimately with a woman. Appreciating beauty in the human body is good. God gave us the capacity to respond to beauty, to be drawn to that which is lovely, beautiful. But in our sinful state, we cannot respond to our longings perfectly, and our consumer-driven culture encourages us to long for what we do not have instead of finding contentment and joy with the good we possess.

As is true with most controversial issues, researchers do not agree about how to interpret findings in studies about pornography. The topic is value-laden and closely connected to issues of individual choice and the right of free speech and a free press. The most consistently reported findings link viewing sexually violent pornography with becoming increasingly accepting of sexually violent behaviors. One study looked at men who viewed pornographic scenes depicting rape and found that they increasingly accepted the belief that the victim becomes aroused during rape and subsequently reported an increase in their own openness to and likelihood of raping someone.[16]

Pornography that depicts only nudity or nonviolent and nondegrading sexuality still raises concerns for social scientists, feminists, and religious groups. One concern about pornography is its addictive nature. Approximately 200,000 Americans, most of them males, have lost or jeopardized their jobs and family relationships because of obsessive preoccupation with Internet pornography.[17] Pornography acts as a powerful sexual stimulant that is usually followed by a sexual release. Over time, users often desire more explicit and deviant material, so their pornography escalates from erotic soft porn to hard-core pornography, as users become desensitized to what once was perceived as repulsive or immoral. Some studies suggest that there is an increased tendency to act out in sexually inappropriate or aggressive ways.

A second concern is that the message of pornography makes it acceptable and normal to treat women as sexual objects, perpetuating a sense of power that males have over females. Robert Jensen, one of the authors of *Pornography: The Production and Consumption of Inequality*, illustrates with his story. He concludes that his own use of pornography centered on issues of control over women and their sexuality. Pornography is not simply an appreciation of female beauty, Jensen says, but an act of male supremacy. Women in pornography are treated as objects, affecting the way men treat women in real life. To mentally undress and fantasize about a woman whom a man passes on the street, performing some act he has seen in pornography, objectifies her. Pressuring a partner to perform sexual acts seen in pornography that focus only on male pleasure is also objectifying and controlling. Although no particular user may intend to control women with his use of pornography, nevertheless pornography creates, maintains, and reinforces a culture in which males are perceived to have control over women. Pornography becomes a consumable item, packaged with ideas about how men are to relate to women.

A male student in my Sociology of Sexuality course summarized the issue:

> I'm concerned that our consumer orientation leaves us open to objectifying sex as a consumable product, and it seems that both erotica and pornography are designed to provide consumable sexuality. Thus, erotica and pornography objectify and dehumanize sex, the people performing it, and the people watching it.

A third concern is that pornography hurts relationships. Women in relationships with those who use pornography express feeling betrayed, question their sex appeal to their spouse, or feel inadequate. Males who use pornography find the sexual curiosity of their mates lacking, their mate's performance less gratifying, and their sex life boring, compared to what they see in pornography.[18] Some males use pornography as an excuse to avoid engaging real women in relationships, finding it easier to objectify and control females through pornography. Other males use pornography to escape unsatisfying relationships with women who attempt to control and cajole them into forced intimacy.

Although some males use pornography proudly, others use it with a profound sense of shame that causes them to hide their struggle, distancing themselves from real relationships with either males or females. In an attempt to be helpful, Michael and Debi Pearl take on this issue in a bimonthly publication they post on the Web that is dedicated to child training and family. They do so in a way that contributes to males disappearing in secrecy and shame. Following are excerpts from their article, "Pornography—Road to Hell":

> If you isolate yourself in a room and indulge in pornography, you are not sick, you are evil. . . . You are not over sexed. You are not even sexed. You are alone. At best you are copulating with yourself. . . . You are a pervert. A real man is bigger than his member. . . . God created us with sexual drive, but he also gave us a steering wheel and a brake to direct and control our drives. If you can't control yours, it is not a statement of the strength of your drive, but of the weakness of your soul. You are plunging your soul into eternal destruction. You do not deserve sympathy or understanding; you deserve condemnation and scorn.[19]

If faith communities are to be holistic in their care of souls, one challenge is to encourage men to strive toward sexual lives that enrich and sustain them. Pornography itself is a problem in the Church, but more significant is the underlying attitude toward sex and sexuality that fuels the desire for pornography. Christian men who do not use pornography may still have a "pornographic mind-set" that encourages relating to and seeing women primarily as sexual objects, preventing men from engaging in authentic relationships with other men or women.

Over the last couple of years, Blanchard Road Alliance Church in Wheaton, Illinois, has worked actively to help men and women move toward greater sexual health. John Casey, the senior pastor at Blanchard, said the church was seeing men struggle with sexual purity and decided to take positive steps. Two task forces, one for men and one for women, worked to define sexual health and to develop biblical principles relevant to sexual health. They focused primarily on casting a positive vision for healthy sexuality rather than stipulating rules with the goal of affair-proofing marriages. Men were encouraged to fill their lives with good things, particularly relationships. Subsequently, Blanchard planned breakfasts for men, where they talked about issues of sexuality, legitimizing the Church as a place where honest conversation occurs. Blanchard held a retreat where a safe community was crafted that allowed men to be honest about their struggles and to find companions to walk with them. Following the retreat, men were encouraged to join groups or establish one-on-one relationships that would continue to meet and hold each other accountable for pursuing healthy sexuality. The emphasis is always on relationship.

"Accountability might be why they began to meet," Casey said, "but what they are getting, whether or not they recognize it, is relationship." In addition to emphasizing the importance of relationship and talking openly about sexuality rather than ignoring it, men are encouraged to look at the practices of spiritual disciplines as a way to nurture their relationship with God, further filling their lives with good things.

Men experience greater sexual health when they pursue relationships with other males based on vulnerability and authenticity. It is no surprise that the pull of pornography or the temptation to pursue inappropriate sexual encounters diminishes through authentic relationships with others. Casey said, "This experience has awakened me to see what men are in trouble. They are the loners, the high achievers, the ones who aren't making time for relationships."

Male students have said that the more meaningfully connected they felt to others, the less compelled they were to use pornography. God made us for relationship, not just for a marital relationship one day but for deep connections with God and a community of others—all intended to fill us with good things. Pornography, affairs, and casual sex are ultimately painful substitutes for relationships intended to bring fullness and blessing.

These theories and examples present maleness, femaleness, and sexuality negatively. They induce shame or defensiveness rather than bring inspiration and celebration. The propensity to sin has a negative impact on men and women's own sex, as well as on the other sex. Women's obsession with beauty is a problem because of women's sinful tendency to compete for affection and to desire control and power over others. Women's obsession with beauty is also problematic because our culture reinforces beauty as the standard of worth and lovability. Men's pornography is a problem because of men's sinful propensity to be drawn to sex and beauty in indiscriminate ways. Men's pornography is also problematic because of a culture that constructs a masculinity that leads men to nonrelational sexuality, a substitution of real relationships for a self-involved way of experiencing sexuality.[20] And some women attempt to control and force men into intimacy, thus driving them away. We wound ourselves. We wound each other.

Perhaps one reason John Eldredge's best-selling book *Wild at Heart* is so well liked is that he gives men a picture of masculinity they can embrace proudly and enthusiastically. He calls men to live impassioned lives rather than unfulfilled lives characterized by boredom. Eldredge affirms how many males are drawn to adventures and challenges that exploit no one and allow them to test their skill, strength, and creative problem solving. Passion, perseverance, courage, protectiveness, intelligence—all these have been used to partner with God to create beautiful and amazing artifacts that speak of human values of exploration, discovery, and development. If we define male sexuality as only exploitative, aggressive, and oppressive, we perpetuate and exaggerate what is broken, allowing the good desire men have to co-create, to be drawn into relationship, to invest in other people, and to build sustainable, moral communities to atrophy.

Although Eldredge's celebration of a good masculinity is refreshing, his approach is flawed. Not all men are drawn to the kind of adventurous living Eldredge describes, nor are they seeking a battle to fight (even if the battle is being distinctively masculine), nor do all believe the way to pursue a woman is to woo and then whisk her into an adventure. To suggest that these men are not experiencing maleness fully takes one's own embedded definition of manhood and says it must apply to all males. Eldredge powerfully affirms maleness as good, though his approach does not take into account that many men legitimately affirm the goodness of maleness in ways that are quite different from his.

At the core of our sexuality is our desire for relationship. Men and women fundamentally want the same things, though for biological and cultural reasons they go about obtaining those things somewhat differently. Much can be redeemed.

Redemptive Perspectives on Femaleness and Maleness

Thomas Merton says,

> We do not exist for ourselves alone, and it is only when we are fully convinced of this fact that we begin to love ourselves properly and thus also love others. What do I mean by loving ourselves properly? I mean, first of all, desiring to live, accepting life as a very great gift and a great good, not because of what it gives us, but because of what it enables us to give to others.[21]

Freely choosing to love others well is at the core of our redemption—a mutual submission that encourages men and women to look beyond their own desires for control and power to want what is truly good for another.

Mutual submission is a form of love, of living in grace with others. True submission is freely given, but subjugation is submission demanded. Mutual submission is relinquishing the need to be in control and letting obligation to others and the needs of others take precedence over one's own desires and needs. People who take care of elderly parents and young children are submitting to the needs of those with whom they have an obligation due to the intimacy of family relationships. We maintain and grow intimate relationships when we live out the truth that life is, as Merton says, "a very great gift and a great good, not because of what it gives us, but because of what it enables us to give to others." When we freely love others sacrificially and our love is received and reciprocated, we move toward redemptive sexuality. Redemption of broken sexuality begins with submission to God and to others. Submission and sacrificial love has an active role in the redemption of many aspects of male and female sexuality, such as issues of body image for women, and in definitions of masculinity.

Redeeming Beauty and Body

We are drawn toward beauty; men and women are created to appreciate and respond to beauty. Women comfortable and at peace in their bodies are able to enjoy beauty in other women without envy. Faith communities uphold women when they name and sit with the suffering that comes from a distorted sexuality where beauty has been objectified, controlled, and exploited. Many American women exposed to the media's rendition of beauty fear they are not beautiful enough to be lovable or to keep love once they get it. Women feel constant pressure to be beautiful, and aging dooms them to failure.

Wanting to look attractive is not sinful; it reflects our appreciation of both beauty and body. Being attractive and sensuous is a gift wives and husbands give each other, and efforts made to stay attractive acknowledge that we delight in beauty and the sensuality that comes from feeling good and comfortable in one's body.

The challenge for women is to balance embracing the freedom to determine how they dress with loving others well by dressing in ways that contribute to others' comfort and to the building of community. Of course, someone will always be uncomfortable with something. The goal is not to attempt to please everyone but to bring blessing and good to others in how we choose to live. Wearing sexually provocative clothing perpetuates both the treatment of women as sexual objects and a competition with other women for the male gaze. Choosing to dress in ways that reflect mutual submission extends grace to other women by refusing to participate in a competition for attention and to men who are sometimes uncomfortable and confused as they strive to treat women as people and not sexual objects.

Men extend grace to women when they find in them a beauty that goes beyond narrowly defined cultural definitions. When Mark tells me (his wife of twenty-five years who thinks she needs to lose ten pounds) that I am beautiful and sensuous and that he loves my body, he extends grace to me. We extend grace to the men in our lives when we allow them to notice or engage in conversation with a beautiful woman without fear that we are diminished because of someone else's sensuous appeal. Imagine a husband and wife walking down the street when a beautiful woman walks by. If she says to her husband, "That is a beautiful woman," he is freed from guilt lest she criticize him without words for noticing a beautiful woman. If she says, "That woman sure wants attention!" then her husband feels judged for noticing the woman's beauty and thus granting her the attention she apparently seeks. The first response extends grace, the second judgment.

Redeeming Definitions of Masculinity

That men are drawn to beauty so that they want sex and seek relationships is a good that keeps men in relationship. One could argue that men's sex drive is healthy for community life. But this sex drive is overemphasized in our culture. A unique approach to addressing this overemphasis and so redeeming masculinity is reflected in the work of James Nelson, a professor of Christian ethics at United Theological Seminary.[22] Nelson explores how the erect penis has been used metaphorically to justify notions of masculinity. The erect penis is strong, hard, penetrating, upward, large—physical characteristics that reflect a cultural and psychological metaphor for masculinity. Some of this identification is good, representing the energy that builds, creates, brings fulfillment to dreams, hopes, and desires. Some of this is dark, controlled and controlling, proving worth by accomplishment, dominating females and males who do not measure up—the antithesis of submission.

Nelson uses the metaphor to expand the experience of maleness. The erect penis tells only half the story—much less than half, actually. When the penis is flaccid (which is its state far more often than not), it is flexible, soft, small—characteristics that have been defined as feminine. And always, whether flaccid or erect, male genitalia are vulnerable. Nelson affirms using metaphors of the body to derive and legitimate ideas of masculinity, but he encourages a full accounting—one that considers both the flaccid and erect penis so that one gains a rich, complete understanding of masculinity that allows men to be both motivated by sex and affected in relationships.

Within the male body there is a good drive and desire for strength, action, and power, along with a corresponding desire for flexibility, vulnerability, and submissiveness. Males are not only biologically engineered to effect change but they are affected in relationship, as illustrated by the transformation of the erect penis to flaccid after intercourse. True power—authentic and whole masculinity—is embracing both aspects of the penis and, with it, the concept of mutual submission in relationships.

Redeeming masculinity involves redeeming what has been devalued in the male body; it means recognizing that the fullness of maleness includes strength, drive, and initiation but receptivity, softness, and vulnerability as well. It means learning to express a range of emotion that includes anger but is not primarily defined by anger. Redeeming masculinity also means becoming teachable, even at the hands of a woman, whose abilities to affect, to know, and to love create the possibility of touching that part of embodied aloneness that longs to be affected, known, and loved. As men drawn to relationship do so in relationships characterized by mutual submission that is nonexploitive, neither subjugating nor objectifying the one who is the focus of attention, they reclaim the fullness of being male. When men can be friends with men and women without fearing that sex will destroy the relationship because they know intimacy does not mean sex and friendship compromises only self-reliance and isolation but not masculinity, then males are moving toward authentic healthy relationships.

Traditional masculinity puts men in a precariously lonely place. Because experiencing emotional closeness without sex is not understood or legitimated, men's ability to develop close friendships with either women or other men is hindered. The Church's goal of moving men toward sexually healthy and authentic lives is met when men can relate to women as partners rather than sexual objects and when men's relationships with other men are characterized by vulnerability and intimacy rather than practicality or competition or a latent fear of homosexuality.

Men and women's willingness to give up control, to serve and nurture, to create, to give sacrificially for the sake of others, to invest in authentic relationships with others reflects a God who graciously serves, nurtures, creates, sacrifices, and invests in those whom God loves. These are acts of redemptive sexuality that maintain relationships and communities that are strong and vibrant.

Conclusion

We are made to be in relationship, to seek unity, to find completion in others. Male and female sexuality are Good Things. Sexuality brings life-giving passion, energy, and enthusiasm to relationships. Sexuality connects men and women to the world outside themselves and draws them toward new challenges, possibilities, and relationships. The aloneness of being embodied sexual creatures creates a longing we satisfy by forming relationships with others. The redemption of sexuality starts with seeing the sexual drives and desires of women and men as fundamentally good. From that vantage point, men and women can explore what is broken and work toward refocusing sexuality on that which is life-giving and affirming rather than life-destroying.

From its radical beginning, Christianity has called followers to challenge status quo assumptions about human nature and social structures.

Men and women can refuse to accept ideas that reduce us to our biology, put us at the mercy of our hormones and chromosomes, and leave us hard-wired to play out particular gender roles based on sex. Humans are created for relationship and community, with God and others. We reflect a God who is deeply relational, faithful, loving, protective—a God who feels and shows emotion and desires what is good and right and holy.

When men enter relationships that draw them into authentic communion with others, they diminish the temptation to be isolated or exploitative in their sexuality. Redemption comes from granting males permission to pursue intimate relationships with other men that allow for mutual vulnerability and a full range of expression of emotions.

Women who accept the beauty of body and encourage other women to find comfort and beauty move them toward redemption. When we emphasize what our bodies are capable of experiencing rather than how our bodies are capable of looking, we extend grace to others and to ourselves.

Women, men, and communities of faith play an important role in encouraging healthy sexuality in each other. Women generally want to believe their husbands and boyfriends have never or would never view pornography, would never be dissatisfied with her body or their sex life, would never look at another woman and wonder what she looked like naked or want to sleep with her, would never say or do or think anything inappropriate in his relationships with other women. In effect, she wants him to be safe, by either being asexual, except when it comes to her, or by managing his sexuality perfectly. Her fears can deepen her insecurities about her own self-image and increase any tendency he has toward hiding his sexuality.

It takes bold communities of faith to tackle issues of sexuality publicly. But faith communities that can encourage men and women to talk about their particular struggles with sexuality and to attempt to understand the kinds of struggles experienced by the other sex are creating the possibility for the Church to be a safe place for healing and for growing relationships characterized by grace.

Embracing a love that gives rather than takes grants permission for others to be confused sometimes about what it means to be male or female and to be vulnerable, needy, and sometimes imperfect in their responses to the challenges of being male or female. Our sexuality is about who we are, not just what we do. As sinful people, we are utterly broken, and sin is wrapped into all aspects of our sexuality. Our hearts will not always be faithful, our longings will not always be pure, and attempts to satisfy sexual desires will sometimes exploit others. Part of redeeming our sexuality is accepting our brokenness, as well as the brokenness of those with whom we live. We are on a journey toward wholeness. Extending and receiving grace as we live with our unfulfilled longings and the consequences of sin is part of the redemptive journey home.

But we are also made in the image of God, with a longing to be connected to God and others and a desire to live well, to pursue virtue. Part of our journey is striving toward greater maturity and holiness. Our longings for connection allow us to enter relationships in which we can know others and be known, to build bonds with others that help us as we partner with God to do the work of God. We move closer to wholeness when we recognize that our deepest longings can only be satisfied by God while embracing the gift of relationships and community that give us a foretaste of heaven.

――――――― ○ ―――――――

QUERIES FOR FURTHER REFLECTION AND CONVERSATION

○ How were you socialized to think about masculinity and femininity growing up? Have your ideas changed? If so, in what ways, and what made you think differently? Changes in your environment? Exposure to different ideas?

○ "Men are in a precariously lonely place." Do you agree? If so, how can the Church help remedy that?

○ What is lacking in a sociobiological explanation of gender differences? What is lacking in a social learning explanation? What is helpful in each theory?

○ What did you think about the section on women and dress?

○ Apart from the stark discomfort of reading about James Nelson's discussion of the erect and flaccid penis, what did you think of his argument?

○ *For women:* On a scale of 1 to 10 (with 1 being Very Unsatisfied and 10 being Very Satisfied), how satisfied are you with your body? To what expectations or standards of beauty do you find yourself most vulnerable? What would it look like for the Church to help women move toward healthy perspectives about their bodies?

○ *For men:* On a scale of 1 to 10 (1 being Not At All, and 10 being Very Well), how well are you known by the person who knows you best? Do you wish for someone who knew you and your private struggles? Would you attend a men's retreat that focused on male sexuality? What would it take to make it happen at your church?

○ Does mutual submission seem like a reasonable part of redeeming sexuality? Why or why not? What makes mutual submission so difficult?

――――――― ○ ―――――――

EPILOGUE: BEAUTY FROM ASHES

He has sent me to comfort the brokenhearted . . . to tell those
who mourn that the time of the Lord's favor has come. . . . He
will give beauty for ashes, joy instead of mourning, praise
instead of despair. For the Lord has planted them like strong and
graceful oaks for his own glory.

—Isaiah 61:1–3

BEAUTY INFUSES AND SUSTAINS HUMAN SEXUALITY. Much of that
beauty has been destroyed, reduced to ashes by a sexuality distorted by sin—
our own sin, the sins of others, and the sins of societies. We wound and hurt
those we are created to love. Yet God is always working—redeeming what
has been broken, finding what has been lost, exchanging beauty for ashes.

Beauty

That humans are drawn to each other and capable of relating in ways that
bring deep satisfaction and connection is poignantly beautiful. A fundamental aspect of our sexuality is our relational nature—our sexuality
draws us toward others. A student in Sociology of Sexuality wrote this:
"I think being sexual may have something to do with the ideas of communion, relationship, belonging, sacrificing, and focusing. It has to do
with balancing physical, spiritual, and personal factors together to more
fully experience relationships with other people."

People are sexual whether married or single, stretching toward others
for completion that cannot be found within themselves. We desire friendship and need community—a place to belong where we find identity,
safety, and comfort. Males and females were also created to find each
other irresistibly interesting, attractive, and beautiful. Most people hope
to find one with whom they can make a lifelong commitment to delve the
depths of a secure, authentic, mutually sacrificial love.

We are created for relationship, and in our relationships we have the capacity to reflect the glory and image of God. Much about our sexuality is beautiful.

Ashes

Being sexual is also about ashes. We are *imago Dei* but are broken by sin. Some have been profoundly wounded by the sins of others and live in a dark sadness, in ashes. Some husbands who have promised to love their wives abuse them. Abused women live in oppressive darkness, sometimes fearing for their lives or the lives of their children. Children are sexually molested and raped by family members they should have been able to trust. They grow up unloved or poorly loved and become despondent and feel unlovable, unable to believe beauty exists for them. They live among ashes. Women and men become the victims of others' sexual violence. Expectations and hopes of a life of beauty crumble, as many learn that intimate relationships are unsafe and that the only way to survive is to escape or live in passive silence. What was intended for beauty is turned to ashes. Lives are crippled, and the capacity to reflect God's life-breathing, life-giving character through sexuality is lost.

Ashes are strewn throughout whole social systems. In countries like Thailand, over 800,000 children under the age of eighteen are victims in the global sex-trade.[1] Most are sold, bribed, or kidnapped into prostitution as early as six years of age. Their experience of sexuality will not provide them a glimpse of heaven, a place of safety where they will be loved and cherished. Their ability to see God in their sexuality is utterly broken.

We all sin and inflict pain on those near us with our words, our wandering hearts, our selfish love. Although some wounds cut more deeply than others, we all wound. God pursues the wounders, no matter how significantly they wound, even as God pursues the wounded, desiring that all would turn away from brokenness toward redemption.

In my husband's book *Why Sin Matters: The Surprising Relationship Between Our Sin and God's Grace,* Mark tells the stories of Jeff and Carl, two Christian men involved in their churches who worked with youth. Both were accused of sexually molesting high school girls, and the evidence in both cases was compelling. Attorneys in both cases recommended they plead "not guilty" and refrain from talking about their case with others.

Carl followed his attorney's advice and did not talk about the circumstances surrounding his situation and the charges against him with friends and family. He pled "not guilty" and fought the fight. Jeff felt convicted of his sin and convinced of his guilt. He refused the advice of his attorney and changed his plea to "no contest." At the recommendation of his pastor, Jeff confessed his guilt to his church. Both men were convicted, both spent time in prison, both lost their careers. But one has been restored. Jeff, who admitted his guilt and vulnerably put himself in the center of community, found people willing to embrace, love, and forgive him, including his wife. Mark writes, "Perhaps Jeff was willing to admit his guilt because he had a loving community that would catch him. Or maybe it is the other way around: he found love and support in others because he was willing to speak the language of sin."[2] Meanwhile, Carl now lives alone in a trailer park, divorced and estranged from family and friends. One lives again in beauty, the other among ashes.

God is always working to heal those wounded by the sins of others and is pursuing wounders, wanting men and women to use their sexuality for the good intended. God does not measure us according to our successes and failures, but for our own good God pushes us, as individuals and communities, toward empathy, virtue, and perfection. In *Mere Christianity*, C. S. Lewis says this:

> God knows our situation; He will not judge us as if we had no difficulties to overcome. . . . Very often what God first helps us towards is not the virtue itself but just this power of always trying again. For however important chastity . . . may be, this process [of trying again] trains us in habits of the soul which are more important still. It cures our illusions about ourselves and teaches us to depend on God. We learn, on the one hand, that we cannot trust ourselves even in our best moments, and, on the other, that we need not despair even in our worst, for our failures are forgiven. The only fatal thing is to sit down content with anything less than perfection.[3]

Beauty from Ashes

Always God is working to bring beauty from ashes—to wrap our sexuality in grace ideally found in communities of faith. Thomas Merton reminds us that our successes and failures are part of our existence in larger communities. Merton says,

> Only when we see ourselves in our true human context, as members of a race which is intended to be one organism and "one body," will we begin to understand the positive importance not only of the successes but of the failures and accidents in our lives. My successes are not my own. The way to them was prepared by others. The fruit of

my labors is not my own: for I am preparing the way for the achievements of another. Nor are my failures my own. They may spring from
the failure of another, but they are also compensated for by another's
achievement. Therefore the meaning of my life is not to be looked for
merely in the sum total of my own achievements. It is seen only in the
complete integration of my achievements and failures with the achievements and failures of my own generation, and society, and time.[4]

So it is that healing is bigger than the healing in our own lives; God
uses communities of faith to bring healing to individuals, and God builds
on the generational redemption of individuals over time to bring healing
to faith communities.

As we stretch toward healthy sexuality, we stretch through broken and
diseased hearts, bodies, and relationships to get to the place that reflects
God's inclusive and faithful love. Embracing our sexuality with grace is
accepting our wounds and yearning as part of our fallenness. Henri
Nouwen said, "The great challenge is *living* your wounds through instead
of *thinking* them through. It is better to cry than to worry, better to feel
your wounds deeply than to understand them, better to let them enter into
your silence than to talk about them. . . . You need to let your wounds go
down to your heart. Then you can live through them and discover that
they will not destroy you. Your heart is greater than your wounds."[5]

A final aspect of embracing our sexuality with grace is recognizing the
abundance found in the life of faith. The New Testament writer of
Hebrews summarizes Jewish history, highlighting examples of those who
lived faithfully. The author then writes, "Therefore, since we are surrounded by such a huge crowd of witnesses to the life of faith, let us strip
off every weight that slows us down, especially the sin that so easily hin-
ders our progress. And let us run with endurance the race that God has
set before us. We do this by keeping our eyes on Jesus, on whom our faith
depends from start to finish" (Hebrews 12:1–2a). Living a virtuous life
brings us closest to experiencing on earth the fulfillment that awaits us in
heaven. Being authentic and vulnerable, turning toward virtue, and staying connected in community is our best hope for finding abundance and
contentment in our sexuality. Grace bestows forgiveness when appropriate, speaks out for those without voice, enables us to sit with those who
suffer and to celebrate with those whose lives are blessed—in essence, to
support and live in community with others. God made us incomplete so
that we would be drawn toward life-affirming relationships. We can
embrace our sexuality, for our yearning is a holy longing that draws us
ultimately toward God, offering a glimpse and fragrance of heaven that
keeps us hoping for a fulfillment yet to come.

NOTES

INTRODUCTION

1. DeWight Middleton offers an anthropological, cross-cultural discussion of embedded and embodied aspects of human sexuality in *Exotics and Erotics: Human Cultural and Sexual Diversity.* Prospect Heights, Ill.: Waveland Press, 2002.

2. Occasionally, babies are born with ambiguous sex organs. The treatment of intersex babies raises significant questions about the interaction between biology and socialization in coming to understand and accept one's sexual identity.

3. Meadows, S. "Memoirs of a Bare Naked Lady." *Newsweek,* May 27, 2002, p. 70.

4. Postema, D. *Space for God: Study and Practice of Spirituality and Prayer.* Grand Rapids, Mich.: CRC Publications, 1983, p. 34.

5. Nelson, J., and Longfellow, S. *Sexuality and the Sacred: Sources for Theological Reflection.* Louisville, Ky.: Westminster John Knox, 1994, p. xiv.

6. Grenz, S. "Is God Sexual? Human Embodiment and the Christian Conception of God." *Christian Scholars Review,* Fall 1998, pp. 24–41.

7. Rolheiser, R. *The Holy Longing: The Search for a Christian Spirituality.* New York: Doubleday, 1999.

8. Plantinga, C., Jr. *Not the Way It's Supposed to Be: A Breviary of Sin.* Grand Rapids, Mich.: Eerdmans, 1995.

9. May, G. *Addiction and Grace.* San Francisco: HarperSanFrancisco, 1988.

10. Nouwen, H., McNeill, D., and Morrison, D. *Compassion: A Reflection on the Christian Life.* New York: Doubleday, 1982.

CHAPTER ONE: RITES OF PASSAGE

1. Grimes, R. L. *Deeply into the Bone: Re-inventing Rites of Passage.* Berkeley: University of California Press, 2000, p. 344.

2. Ward, M. C. *A World Full of Women*. (3rd ed.) New York: Allyn & Bacon, 2003.

3. Grahn, J. *Blood, Bread and Roses: How Menstruation Created the World*. Boston: Beacon Press, 1993. Offers an interesting alternative cultural history that includes much anthropological history regarding menstrual taboos and rituals.

4. Pheromones, chemical substances unconsciously given off by the body, are attributed to the phenomenon of "menstrual synchrony," the tendency for the menstrual cycles of women who live together to become synchronized.

5. "Women: A True Story: Body Politics." Films for the Humanities and Sciences. Princeton, N.J., 1997.

6. Firestone, S. *The Dialectic of Sex: The Case for Feminist Revolution*. New York: Morrow, 1970.

7. Elson-Poznik, J. "Castration, Hysterectomy and the Construction of 'Woman': Medical Discourse & Women's Voices." Paper presented at the conference of the *Society for the Study of Social Problems*, 1996.

8. "Incidence of Hysterectomy." *Disease-A-Month*, 1998, 44(9), 520–522.

9. Coutinho, E., and Segal, S. *Is Menstruation Obsolete?* New York: Oxford University Press, 1999.

10. Rueben, D. *Everything You Always Wanted to Know About Sex*. New York: D. McKay, 1969, p. 287.

11. Matthews, K. A., Wing, R. R., Kuller, L. H., Meilahn, E. N., Kelsey, S. F., Costello, E. J., and Caggiula, A. W. "Influences of Natural Menopause on Psychological Characteristics and Symptoms of Middle-Aged Healthy Women." *Journal of Consulting and Clinical Psychology*, 1990, 58(3), 345–351.

12. Zamecki, K. J. "Resisting Disease and Constructing Experience: Menopausal Women's Resistance to Medical Hegemony." *Menopause and Beyond*. [www.geocites.com/menobeyond/beyond.html]. 2001.

13. Ward, 2003.

14. Wolf, N. *The Beauty Myth*. New York: Doubleday, 1991, p. 231.

15. Bly, R. *Iron John*. Reading, Mass.: Addison-Wesley, 1990.

16. Pollack, W. *Real Boys*. New York: Henry Holt, 1998, p. 151.

17. Hantover, J. "The Boy Scouts and the Validation of Masculinity." In M. S. Kimmel and M. A. Messner (eds.), *Men's Lives*. (3rd ed.) Boston: Allyn & Bacon, 1995, p. 77.

18. Ibid., p. 78.

19. "A Sea of Alcohol." *20/20,* ABC News. C. Kaye (producer), Mar. 16, 1998.

20. Kilmer, S. "A Modern Girl's Quest." In L. C. Mahdi, N. G. Christopher, and M. Meade (eds.), *Crossroads: The Quest for Contemporary Rites of Passage.* Chicago: Open Court, 1996, pp. 353–354.

21. Van Gennep, A. *The Rites of Passage.* Chicago: University of Chicago Press, 1960. (Originally published 1906)

22. Oldfield, D. "The Journey: An Experiential Rite of Passage for Modern Adolescents." In Mahdi, Christopher, and Meade, 1996.

23. Grimes, 2000.

24. Eckert, R. P. "Guidelines for Creating Effective Rites of Passage." In Mahdi, Christopher, and Meade, 1996.

25. Lewis, R. *Raising a Modern-Day Knight: A Father's Role in Guiding His Son in Authentic Manhood.* Wheaton, Ill.: Tyndale House, 1997.

26. Higgins, C., Jr. "Father and Son in Egypt." In Mahdi, Christopher, and Meade, 1996, p. 337.

27. These come from Nguzo Saba, which refer to the Seven Principles of Kwanzaa plus respect. Kwanzaa is an African American cultural celebration from December 26 to January 1. The practice and observation of those principles are year round.

28. Grimes, 2000, p. 148.

CHAPTER TWO: ADOLESCENCE

1. Thompson, S. *Going All the Way: Teenage Girls' Tales of Sex, Romance, and Pregnancy.* New York: Hill and Wang, 1995, p. 156.

2. Ali, L., and Scelfo, J. "Choosing Virginity." *Newsweek,* Dec. 9, 2002, p. 62.

3. Levine, J., and Elders, J. M. *Harmful to Minors: The Perils of Protecting Children from Sex.* Minneapolis: University of Minnesota Press, 2002.

4. Pogany, S. B. *Sex Smart: 501 Reasons to Hold Off on Sex.* Minneapolis: Fairview Press, 1998.

5. Joyner, K., and Laumann, E. "Teenage Sex and the Sexual Revolution." In E. O. Laumann and R. T. Michael (eds.), *Sex, Love and Health in America: Private Choices and Public Policies.* Chicago: University of Chicago Press, 2001.

6. Wolf, N. *Promiscuities: The Secret Struggle for Womanhood.* New York: Fawcett Columbine, 1997.

7. Joyner and Laumann, 2001.

8. Stenzel, P. "Time to Wait for Sex." Grand Rapids, Mich.: Rooftop Video Productions, 2000.

9. Ventura S. J., Mathews, T. J., and Hamilton, B. E. "Births to Teenagers in the United States, 1940–2000." *National Vital Statistics Reports,* 2001, 49(10). Cited in McIlhaney, J. S. "Testimony of the President of the Medical Institute for Sexual Health before the Subcommittee on Health of the Committee on Energy and Commerce," U.S. House of Representatives, Apr. 2002.

10. Brener, N., Lowry, R., Kann, L., Kolbe, L., Lehnherr, J., Janssen, R., and Jaffe, H. "Trends in Sexual Risk Behaviors Among High School Students: United States, 1991–2001." *MMWR Weekly of the Center for Disease Control,* Sept. 2002, 51(38), 856–859.

11. Caron, S. L. *Sex Matters for College Students: FAQ's in Human Sexuality.* Upper Saddle River, N.J.: Prentice Hall, 2003, p. 25.

12. Ibid., p. 37.

13. Balswick, J. K., and Balswick, J. O. *Authentic Human Sexuality: An Integrated Christian Approach.* Downer's Grove, Ill.: InterVarsity Press, 2002.

14. Ali and Scelfo, 2002, p. 65.

15. Laumann, E. O., Gagnon, J. H., Michael, R. T., and Michaels, S. *The Social Organization of Sexuality: Sexual Practices in the United States.* Chicago: University of Chicago Press, 1994.

16. Balswick and Balswick, 2002.

17. Tiefer, L. *Sex Is Not a Natural Act.* Boulder, Colo.: Westview Press, 1995.

18. The organization referred to is Greater DuPage MYM (Meld Young Mothers) in Wheaton, Ill.

19. Michael, R. T., and Joyner, K. "Choices Leading to Teenage Births." In E. O. Laumann and R. T. Michael (eds.), *Sex, Love and Health in America: Private Choices and Public Policies.* Chicago: University of Chicago Press, 2001.

20. Stenzel, 2000.

21. Ibid.

22. Ibid.

23. Lindvall, J. *Youthful Romance: Scriptural Patterns.* Springfield, Calif.: Bold Christian Living, 1992.

24. For examples, see Judy and Jack Balswicks's *Authentic Human Sexuality* (2002) and Stanley Grenz's book *Sexual Ethics: An Evangelical Perspective* (1990).

25. Grenz, S. *Sexual Ethics: An Evangelical Perspective.* Louisville, Ky.: Westminster John Knox Press, 1990.

26. Rosenberg, D. "The Battle over Abstinence." *Newsweek,* Dec. 9, 2002, p. 70.

27. Clapp, S., Helbert, K. L., and Zizak, A. "Faith Matters: Teenagers, Sexuality and Religion." Christian Community, Inc. [www.religiousinstitute. org/matters.html]. 2003.

28. Ibid.

CHAPTER THREE: SLEEPING ALONE

1. U.S. Bureau of the Census. "Americans' Families and Living Arrangements: March 2000." *Current Population Reports,* series P20–537 (Table A1). Washington, D.C.: U.S. Government Printing Office, 2001.

2. Grenz, S. J. *Sexual Ethics: An Evangelical Perspective.* Louisville, Ky.: Westminster John Knox Press, 1990.

3. Ibid., p. 193.

4. Laumann, E. O., Gagnon, J. H., Michael, R. T., and Michaels, S. *The Social Organization of Sexuality: Sexual Practices in the United States.* Chicago: University of Chicago Press, 1994.

5. Newman, D. *Sociology of Families.* Thousand Oaks, Calif.: Pine Forge, 1999.

6. Goldstein, J. R., and Kenney, C. T. "Marriage Delayed or Marriage Forgone? New Cohort Forecasts for First Marriage for U.S. Women." *American Sociological Review,* 2001, 66, 506–519.

7. Taylor, S. E., Klein, L. C., Lewis, B. P., Gruenewald, T. L., Gurung, R.A.R., and Updegraff, J. A. "Biobehavioral Responses to Stress: Tend and Befriend, Not Fight or Flight." *Psychological Review,* 2000, 107(3), 411–429.

8. Laumann, E. O., and Youm, Y. "Sexual Expression in America." In E. O. Laumann and R. T. Michael (eds.), *Sex, Love and Health in America: Private Choices and Public Policies.* Chicago: University of Chicago Press, 2001.

9. Waite, L. J., and Joyner, K. "Emotional and Physical Satisfaction with Sex in Married, Cohabiting, and Dating Sexual Unions: Do Men and Women Differ?" In Laumann and Michael, 2001.

10. Laumann and Youm, 2001.

11. Eshleman, J. R. *The Family.* (10th ed.) Boston: Allyn & Bacon, 2003.

12. Eshleman, J. R., and Armas, G. C. "Census: More Elderly Live Together." Associated Press. [/www.soft.com.net/webnews/wed/av/Aolder-and-unmarried. ROFV_CIT.html]. July 2002.

13. U.S. Bureau of the Census. *Statistical Abstracts of the United States: 2000* (Table 58). Washington, D.C.: U.S. Government Printing Office, 2000.

14. Brown, S. L., and Longmore, M. A. "Union Type and Adult Self-Esteem." *Center for Family & Demographic Research,* Working Paper Series 02–09. Bowling Green, Ind., Bowling Green University. [/www.bgsu.edu/organizatin/cfdr/main.html]. 2002.

15. Eshleman, 2003.

16. Balswick, J. K., and Balswick, J. O. *Authentic Human Sexuality: An Integrated Approach.* Downer's Grove, Ill.: InterVarsity Press, 1999.

17. Waite and Joyner, 2001.

18. Laumann and Youm, 2001; Waite and Joyner, 2001.

19. U.S. Bureau of Census. *Marital Status and Living Arrangements* (Unpublished tables: Table A), pp. 20–514, 1998 Update. [www.census.gov/prod/99pubs/p20–514u.pdf]

20. Newman, 1999.

21. U.S. Bureau of the Census, 2001.

22. U.S. Bureau of the Census, 2000.

23. Wang, H., and Amato, P. R. "Predictors of Divorce Adjustment: Stressors, Resources, and Definition." *Journal of Marriage and Family,* 2000, *62,* 655–668, as cited in J. R. Eshleman, *The Family* (10th ed.). Boston: Allyn & Bacon, 2003.

24. Laumann and Youm, 1994.

25. See [www.coralridge.org/cmsearch.asp?qu=homosexuality] for information about Kennedy's views. Paul Cameron's views are articulated in "No Dr. Dobson, Homosexuality Is a Choice." Editorial in the *Journal of the Family Research Institute,* 2002, *17*(4). [www.familyresearchinst.org/FRR 02 07.html]. July 2002.

26. See James Dobson's book *Bringing Up Boys.* Wheaton, Ill.: Tyndale House, 2001, for his views and go to [www.falwell.com] for information about Falwell's views.

27. The General Assembly of the Presbyterian Church USA (PCUSA), United Methodists, and Episcopalians continue to debate this point within their denominations.

28. LeVay, S. *Queer Science: The Use and Abuse of Research into Homosexuality.* Cambridge, Mass.: MIT Press, 1996.

29. Jones, S. L., and Yarhouse, M. A. *Homosexuality: The Use of Scientific Research in the Church's Moral Debate.* Downer's Grove, Ill.: InterVarsity Press, 2000.

30. I had this conversation with a Christian psychologist who prefers to remain anonymous because of the stigma among evangelical Christians against taking such a position.

31. Ford, M. *Wounded Prophet: A Portrait of Henri J. M. Nouwen.* New York: Image Books, Doubleday, 1999, p. vi.

32. Ibid., p. 213.

33. Anonymous. "No Easy Victory." *Christianity Today,* Mar. 11, 2002, pp. 50–51.

34. De la Vina, M. "Speed Dating Breaks the Ice." *Mercury News.* [http// www.bayarea.com/mld/mercurynews/living/fashion/5713922.htm]. Apr. 25, 2003.

35. Pieper, J. *On Hope.* San Francisco: Ignatius Press, 1986.

36. John Paul II. *The Theology of the Body: Human Love in the Divine Plan.* Boston: Pauline Books & Media, 1997.

Chapter Four: Birthing Babies

1. Hrdy, S. B. *Mother Nature: Maternal Instincts and How They Shape the Human Species.* New York: Ballantine Books, 1999, p. xvii.

2. Sweden has the lowest infant mortality rate, with 3.47 deaths for every 1,000 births. Angola has the highest with 193.7 infant deaths for every 1,000 births. Norway, Hong Kong, Portugal, Ireland, Canada, Japan, and the United Kingdom are several of the countries with lower infant deaths than the United States. *Geography IQ* [www.geographyiq.com/ranking/ ranking_infant_mortality_rate_dall.htm], 2002.

3. Jarmel, M., and Schneider, K. "Born in USA: A Documentary About Childbirth in America." Video produced by Patchwork Productions, Boston, 2000.

4. Simkin, P., Whalley, J., and Keppler, A. *Pregnancy, Childbirth and the Newborn: The Complete Guide.* Minnetonka, Minn.: Meadowbrook Press, 2001.

5. Jarmel and Schneider, 2000.

6. Rooks, J. P., Weatherby, N. L., and Ernst, E. K. "Outcomes of Care in Birth Centers: The National Birth Center Study." *New England Journal of Medicine,* Dec. 1989, *321*(26), 1804–1811.

7. Klaus, M. H., Kennell, J. H., and Klaus, P. H. *Mothering the Mother: How a Doula Can Help You Have a Shorter, Easier, and Healthier Birth.* Reading, Mass.: Addison-Wesley, 1993.

8. Jarmel and Schneider, 2000.

9. Klaus, Kennell, and Klaus, 1993; Hrdy, 1999.

10. See Klaus, Kennell, and Klaus, 1993, for comparative studies looking at mothers' experiences in childbirth and subsequent views of self and motherhood.

11. Tyre, P., and McGinn, D. "She Works, He Doesn't." *Newsweek,* May 12, 2003, pp. 45–52.

12. Hrdy, 1999.

13. As quoted in Miall, C. E. "The Stigma of Involuntary Childlessness." In A. S. Skolnick and J. H. Skolnick (eds.), *Family in Transition.* (6th ed.) Boston: Little, Brown, 1989, p. 392.

14. Newman, D. *Sociology of Families.* Newbury Park, Calif.: Pine Forge Press, 1999.

15. Paris, J. W. *Birth Control for Christians: Making Wise Choices.* Grand Rapids, Mich.: Baker Books, 2003, p. 23.

16. Paris, 2003.

17. Kim, S. C. *Pros and Cons: Social Policy Debates of Our Time.* Boston: Allyn & Bacon, 2001.

18. For a complete discussion of these issues, see Kim, 2001, pp. 1–26.

19. Hrdy, 1999.

Chapter Five: Mysteries of Marriage

1. Whitehead, B. D. "Marriage: Just a Piece of Paper." Film produced by Boyer Production Ltd. for University of Chicago and WTTW-TV, 2002.

2. Hrdy, S. B. *Mother Nature: Maternal Instincts and How They Shape the Human Species.* New York: Ballantine Books, 1999.

3. Ibid.

4. Grenz, S. *Sexual Ethics: An Evangelical Perspective.* Louisville, Ky.: Westminster John Knox Press, 1990.

5. Laumann, E. O., Gagnon, J. H., Michael, R. T., and Michaels, S. *The Social Organization of Sexuality: Sexual Practices in the United States.* Chicago: University of Chicago Press, 1994.

6. Sytsma, M., and Taylor, D. "Current Thinking on How to Help Couples and Individuals Struggling with Low Sexual Desire." *Marriage and Family: A Christian Journal,* 2002, 5(2), 311–319.

7. DeClaire, J. "Your Marriage: Getting Better All the Time: The Surprising Truth About Sex and Lifelong Love." *Reader's Digest,* Feb. 2003, pp. 66–75.

8. Rosenau, D. *A Celebration of Sex: A Christian Couple's Manual.* Nashville: Thomas Nelson Publishers, 1994.

9. Laumann, 1994.

10. Ibid.

11. Waite, L., and Joyner, K. "Emotional and Physical Satisfaction with Sex in Married, Cohabiting, and Dating Sexual Unions: Do Men and Women Differ?" In E. O. Laumann and R. T. Michael (eds.), *Sex, Love and Health in America: Private Choices and Public Policies.* Chicago: University of Chicago Press, 2001, pp. 239–269.

12. Bellafanta, G. "When Midlife Seems Just an Empty Plate." *New York Times.* [www.NYTimes.com]. Mar. 9, 2003.

13. Laumann, 1994.

14. Parker Palmer has a wonderful discussion of abundance and scarcity in *The Active Life: A Spirituality of Work, Creativity, and Caring.* San Francisco: Jossey-Bass, 1999.

15. Grenz, 1990, p. 113.

16. Balswick, J. K., and Balswick, J. O. *Authentic Human Sexuality: An Integrated Christian Approach.* Downer's Grove, Ill.: InterVarsity Press, 1999.

17. Glass, S. Not *"Just Friends": Protect Your Relationship from Infidelity and Heal the Trauma of Betrayal.* New York: Free Press, 2002.

18. Buechner, F. *Telling Secrets.* San Francisco: HarperSanFrancisco, 1991, p. 32.

19. Foster, R. *Money, Sex, and Power.* San Francisco: HarperSanFrancisco, 1985, p. 196.

CHAPTER SIX: SEXUALITY AND CULTURE

1. Fausto-Sterling, A. "How to Build a Man." In Robert A. Nye (ed.), *Sexuality.* Oxford: Oxford University Press, 1999, p. 237.

2. Biologist Anne Fausto-Sterling has done considerable research on intersexuality. Her frequency table of various types of intersexuality can be found in "Frequency: How Common Are Intersex Conditions?" at the Intersex Society of North America. [isna.org/faq/frequency.html]. June 2003.

3. Jones, S. "Between Consenting Adults." *Christianity Today,* Apr. 24, 1995, pp. 14–18.

4. Augustine. *The Confessions of St. Augustine.* (Hal M. Helms, trans.) Brewster, Mass.: Paraclete Press, p. 160.

5. Neal, C., and Mangis, M. "Unwanted Sexual Experiences Among Christian College Women: Saying No on the Inside." *Journal of Psychology and Theology,* 1995, *23*(3), 171–179.

6. Laumann, E. *The Social Organization of Sexuality: Sexual Practices in the United States.* Chicago: University of Chicago Press, 1994.

7. VanLeeuwen, M. S. *My Brother's Keeper: What the Social Sciences Do (and Don't) Tell Us About Masculinity.* Downer's Grove, Ill.: InterVarsity Press, 2002.

8. The title comes from Saltzberg, E. A., and Chrisler, J. C. "Beauty Is the Beast: Psychological Effects of the Pursuit of the Perfect Female Body." In E. Disch (ed.), *Reconstructing Gender: A Multicultural Anthology.* Toronto: Mayfield, 1997.

9. Ibid.

10. Nussbaum, M. *Sex and Social Injustice.* New York: Oxford University Press, 1999.

11. Gagne, P., and McGaughey, D. "Designing Women: Cultural Hegemony and the Exercise of Power Among Women Who Have Undergone Elective Mammoplasty." *Gender and Society,* 2002, *16*(6), 814–838.

12. "Americans' Spending on Personal-Care Products and Services." The U.S. Commerce Department: Mediamark Research, Inc., and Procter & Gamble, as reported in *Reader's Digest,* Sept. 2002.

13. Fries, S. "Pornography: Hot and Bothered." *Newsweek,* Jan. 20, 2003, p. 13.

14. VanLeeuwen, 2002.

15. Ibid.

16. Kilmartin, C. *The Masculine Self.* (2nd ed.) New York: McGraw-Hill, 2000. Kilmartin cites a 1993 study by Linz and Malamuth, p. 253.

17. VanLeeuwen, 2002.

18. Kilmartin, 2000.

19. Pearl, M., and Pearl, D. "Pornography—Road to Hell." *No Greater Joy.* Pleasantville, Tenn.: No Greater Joy, 2000. [http://NoGreaterJoy.org]

20. Levant, R. F., and Brooks, G. R. (eds.). *Men and Sex: New Psychological Perspectives.* New York: Wiley, 1997.

21. Merton, T. *No Man Is an Island.* New York: Harcourt Brace, 1955, p. xx.

22. Nelson, J. B. "Embracing Masculinity." In J. B. Nelson and S. P. Longfellow (eds.), *Sexuality and the Sacred: Sources for Theological Reflection.* Louisville, Ky.: Westminster John Knox Press.

Epilogue

1. "Trafficking in Women, Including Thai Migrant Sex Workers, in Canada." Prepared by: The Toronto Network Against Trafficking in Women, The Multicultural History Society of Ontario, The Metro Toronto Chinese and Southeast Asian Legal Clinic. [http://citd.scar.utoronto.ca/MHSO/ trafficking_women.html]. 2000.

2. McMinn, M. *Why Sin Matters: The Surprising Relationship Between Our Sin and God's Grace.* Wheaton, Ill.: Tyndale House, 2004, p. 57.

3. Lewis, C. S. *Mere Christianity.* New York: Collier Books, 1943, pp. 92, 94.

4. Merton, T. *No Man Is an Island.* Orlando: Harcourt Brace, 1955, pp. xxi–xii.

5. Nouwen, H. *The Inner Voice of Love.* London: Darton, Longman and Todd, 1997, p. 91.

THE AUTHOR

LISA GRAHAM MCMINN, author of *Growing Strong Daughters,* is an associate professor of sociology at Wheaton College. She received her Ph.D. in sociology/systems science from Portland State University in 1995. She teaches courses, speaks, and researches in the areas of gender roles, family, sexuality, and social change. Students and friends know her as one who takes long walks, likes digging in her garden, watches fireflies in the summer and hearth fires in the winter. She and her husband, Mark, live in Winfield, Illinois, and are the parents of three daughters, Rae, Sarah, and Megan, who are now making their way out on their own.

INDEX

A

Abortion: factors affecting pregnant teen's choice about, 48–49; legalization of, 41, 119; prevalence of, 119; pro-choice argument for, 119; pro-life argument against, 120; and rights vs. obligations, 120–121

Abstinence: educating teens about, 39, 40; teens' choosing, 44–45, 52, 55–57. *See also* Celibacy

Addictions, 8

Adolescence, 37–66; abstinence in, 44–45, 52, 55–57; awakening sexuality in, 38–39, 63–65; "buddy" sex in, 47; Christian view of sexual activity in, 47, 52, 53; consequences of sexual behavior choices in, 47–52; dating in, 53–55; and faith communities, 58–60; first sexual experiences in, 45–46; masturbation during, 60–63; post-sexual-revolution morals in, 43–47; pre-sixties sexuality in, 40–41; pregnancy in, 43, 47–50; prevalence of sexual activity in, 40, 42, 43; queries about, 66; sex education in, 39–40, 57–58; and sexual revolution, 41–43; and STIs, 50–53. *See also* Adolescent females; Adolescent males

Adolescent females: with abusive boyfriends, 37–38; contemporary rites of passage for, 30–32, 33–34; markers of womanhood of, 14–22; pregnancy among, 47–50;

prevalence of sexual activity among, 40, 42, 43; virginity among, 38, 44. *See also* Adolescence

Adolescent males: contemporary rites of passage for, 32–33; double message about sexuality given to, 23–24; markers of manhood of, 22–26; prevalence of sexual activity among, 40, 42, 43. *See also* Adolescence

Adoption: as choice of pregnant teens, 49–50; cultural views of, 116–117

Adultery: confession and redemption with, 146–150; distinction between infidelity and, 142–143; emotional vs. sexual involvement in, 139; forgiveness for, 143–144, 149–150; likelihood of, 138–139

African Americans: community connection among, 29; rites of passage for young males, 32–33, 185n27; teen pregnancy among, 48

Aging: by females, 21–22, 153–154; and marriage, 136–137

AIDS: emergence of, 42; and sexually active teens, 50, 51–52

Alcohol consumption, in fraternities, 25

Allen, Claude, 57

Antinatalism, 115

Antwone Fisher, 23

Aristotle, 161

Attachment: mother-infant, 112–114; parent-child, and time spent together, 124

Other Books of Interest

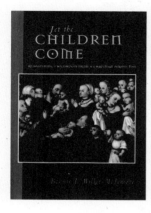

Let the Children Come:

*Reimagining Childhood from a
Christian Perspective*

Bonnie J. Miller-McLemore

Hardcover

ISBN: 0–7879–5665–1

"*Let the Children Come* is not only engagingly written and filled with common sense, it is also theologically illuminating and pastorally astute."

—From the Foreword by Lisa Sowle Cahill,
J. Donald Monan, S.J. Professor
of Theology, Boston College

"This book will help us to live with and care for children with greater understanding, compassion, and respect."

—Dorothy C. Bass, editor, *Practicing Our Faith*

"In this appealing book, Bonnie J. Miller-McLemore rescues the traditional themes of Christian theology for a positive, practical theology of children and child raising."

—Rosemary Radford Ruether, Carpenter Professor of Feminist Theology,
Graduate Theological Union, Berkeley, California

In this important and much-needed book, theologian, author, and teacher Bonnie J. Miller-McLemore writes about the struggle to raise children with integrity and faithfulness as Christians in a complex postmodern society. *Let the Children Come* shows that the care of children is in itself a religious discipline and a communal practice that places demands on both congregations and society as a whole. The author calls for clearer and more defined ways in which Christians can respond to the call to nurture all children (not just their own) as manifestations of God's presence in the world. Miller-McLemore raises and investigates questions that up until now have largely been left unasked, such as: What are the dominant cultural perceptions of children including religious perceptions with which parents must grapple? How have Christians defined children and parenting, and how should they today?

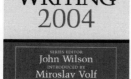

The Best Christian Writing 2004

John Wilson (Editor)

Paperback

ISBN: 0-7879-6964-8

This collection of the finest contemporary Christian writing is "a prime example of diverse beliefs among Christians."

—*Los Angeles Times*

"Chosen by *Christianity Today* editor Wilson, this eclectic treasure trove, on subjects as diverse as repentance, being an unmarried believer, and the evangelical Christian Book Association convention, contains some truly extraordinary writing. . . . Rich in whimsy, overflowing with gentle wonder, and laced with both irony and anguish, these pieces by and large live up to their rather audacious billing, as the best of the best."

—*Publishers Weekly,* **August 25, 2003**

This year's volume brings together an elegant and engaging array of essays by Christian luminaries tackling relevant issues. These writers distill the riches of belief into lucid explorations of faith and truth, reflecting the many dimensions of today's Christianity. As John Wilson puts it, "This collection of Christian writing is for anyone who acknowledges the dilemma of being human. . . . What you will find in these essays is Christianity in its natural habitat, which is the whole world with all its beauty and suffering, its simplicity and complexity, its clarity and its muddle."